Étienne Cartier, Raymond of Capua, Mother Regis Hamilton

Life of Saint Catharine of Sienna

Étienne Cartier, Raymond of Capua, Mother Regis Hamilton

Life of Saint Catharine of Sienna

ISBN/EAN: 9783337339999

Printed in Europe, USA, Canada, Australia, Japan

Cover: Foto ©Lupo / pixelio.de

More available books at **www.hansebooks.com**

LIFE

— OF —

SAINT CATHARINE

OF SIENNA

BY THE BLESSED RAYMOND OF CAPUA

HER CONFESSOR

WITH AN APPENDIX

CONTAINING THE TESTIMONIES OF HER DISCIPLES, RECOLLECTIONS IN ITALY
AND HER ICONOGRAPHY

BY E. CARTIER

Translated from the French by the Ladies of the Sacred Heart

P. J. KENEDY & SONS

44 BARCLAY STREET, NEW YORK

CONTENTS.

PREFACE TO THE AMERICAN EDITION, - - - 5
PREFACE TO THE FRENCH EDITION, - - - 11
PROLOGUE, - - - - - - 19

FIRST PART.

CHAPTER 1.—Of Catharine's parents and their worldly condition, - - - - - 22

CHAPTER 2.—Birth of Catharine—Her Infancy—Wonderful circumstances that take place, - - 25

CHAPTER 3.—Of Catharine's Vow of Virginity, and a circumstance of her early years, - - 30

CHAPTER 4.—Of a relaxation of fervor, which God permitted in order to augment her grace, and of the great patience of Catherine in supporting persecutions for the love of Jesus Christ, 33

CHAPTER 5.—Her austere penances, and the persecutions of her Mother, - - - - 43

CHAPTER 6.—Of her self-conquest at the Baths, and her clothing with the Holy Habit of St. Dominic, - - - - - - 49

CHAPTER 7.—Of the origin and establishment of the "Sisters of Penance" of St. Dominic, and of their mode of life. - - - - 54

CHAPTER 8.—Of Catharine's admirable progress in the ways of God, and of some particular graces she received, - - - - 57

CHAPTER 9.—Of the admirable doctrines taught her by our Lord, and which she adopted as her rule of life, - - - - - - 63

CHAPTER 10.—Of the admirable victories which she gained over temptations, and her extraordinary intimacy with our Lord. - - - 67

CHAPTER 11.—Of the marriage with our Lord, and of the miraculous ring that she received, - - 75

(iii)

CONTENTS.

SECOND PART.

CHAPTER 1.—Our Lord commands Catharine to employ herself for the good of her neighbor, — 78

CHAPTER 2.—Of some wonderful things that occurred at the commencement of Catharine's relations with the world, and of her exertions in supplying the necessities of the poor. — 83

CHAPTER 3—Of the wonderful things Catharine performed when serving the sick. — 93

CHAPTER 4.—Of her manner of living and of the reproaches which were made her concerning her complete abstinence, — 111

CHAPTER 5—Of Catharine's wonderful ecstasies and of the great revelations which she received from God. — 123

CHAPTER 6.—Of miracles wrought by Catharine's intercession for promoting the salvation of souls, — 155

CHAPTER 7.—Of some miracles obtained by Catharine for the life or health of the neighbor, — 175

CHAPTER 8.—Of miracles performed by Catharine for delivering such as are possessed by the Devil, — 194

CHAPTER 9.—Of Catharine's gift of Prophecy and in what manner she delivered several persons from danger which threatened their souls and bodies, — 203

CHAPTER 10.—Of the miracles our Lord produced, by means of Catharine, on things inanimate, 217

CHAPTER 11—Of Catharine's frequent communions, and of the miracles produced by Almighty God, for her, relative to the Holy Eucharist and the relics of the Saints, 229

THIRD PART.

CHAPTER 1.—Concerning the witnesses present at Catharine's death, and who related the attendant circumstances to the Author, — 244

CHAPTER 2.—Of circumstances which happened a year and a half before the death of the Blessed Catharine, and of the martyrdom that Satan caused her to undergo, — 256

PROTESTATION.

In obedience to the decrees of Urban VIII. I protest that of the miraculous deeds and gifts ascribed in this work to certain servants of God, and not already approved by the holy See, I claim no other belief than that which is ordinarily given to history resting on mere human authority, and that in giving the appellation of Saint or Blessed to any person not canonized or beatified by the Church, I only intend to do it according to the usage and opinion of men.

Preface to the American Edition.

The providence of God in the government of the world, but especially the divine economy with regard to the children of his Church, is best learned from the study of the lives of His faithful servants. The world, with its own views, and means, and end, being always antagonistic to the spirit of God, must not be taken as a standard or as a testimony of God's providence towards his people. The Apostle St. Paul warns us "not to be conformed to the world," and St. James urges the motive "that the world is the enemy of God." Profane history even, is often elucidated by this principle, whilst its light is almost always necessary to follow correctly the path which sacred or ecclesiastical history points out.

The life of St. Catharine of Sienna by the Blessed Raymond of Capua, is now, for the first time, presented to the American reader in the English language. Its perusal will, at times, be sustained with interest by remembering the time, and circumstances in which that wonderful woman lived and acted. And it is not unlikely that the reader, may perchance, become startled at some of the facts narrated by her biographer. A closer acquaintance, however, with the history of the times in which she lived, and the circumstances in which she acted, and by which, we may say, her conduct and history became a portion of the history of the Church, will, in a great degree verify her actions, by revealing the providence of God, in the government of the Church.

The commencement of the fourteenth century saw the Church surrounded by difficulties, at once the consequence and source of many evils. The wild ambition of Princes, and the lawlessness arising from habitual warfare, which then disturbed the heart of Christendom, exercised an unhappy influence on the interests and possessions of the Church. Men of worldly views, either themselves desired, or by the interests of their families were urged to seek, preferment in the Church; and the records of that period but too frequently exhibit the sad and fatal consequences. The spirit of the world had, in many instances, stained the holiness of the Sanctuary: and the virtues of ecclesiastics were diminished or destroyed by the dangerous contact with worldly interests. Amidst the conflict of such opposing elements it is not to be wondered that a wily and ambitious Prince, conceived the idea, and was enabled to carry it into execution, of transferring the venerable See of Peter from Rome to Avignon.

It was during this melancholy and eventful period of the Church, whilst the seventy years captivity of the Roman Pontiffs was being endured, that a simple daughter of a wool dyer, was practising in the retirement of her father's house, virtues of self-denial and penance that were, one day, to manifest the sublime power of prayer and enlighten even the councils of the Princes of the Church. That St. Catharine was raised up a simple and uneducated female, to confound the wisdom and direct the actions of those to whom God confided higher destinies need not, now, be doubted. Nor does the divine economy require that the guidance of the bark of Peter should not be directed by the holy and required warnings of a saintly woman. Her prudence and persevering energy in reconciling the Florentines with the Sovereign Pontiff, induced the devoted Urban VI., to seek, and in essential political arrangements, to adopt the salutary counsel of St. Catharine; and the restoration to the Holy City of the residence of the Papacy in his person, and by the continuation of his successors, may in no small degree justify the assertion, that to the inspired wisdom of the wool dyer's daughter, Rome was indebted for the return and perpetuity of the successors of St. Peter.

A word may here be said regarding her biographer, the Blessed Raymond of Capua. Ample opportunity was afforded him, for years, as her Confessor, to become acquainted not only with her actions and mode of thinking, but also of most perfectly understanding her motives, and the sincerity of her conduct. He was himself, moreover a man of sober thought, of respectable theological knowledge, and of no rash and precipitate judgment. His frequent reference to the testimony of living witnesses and his own not unfrequent difficulty of belief, sufficiently testify his appreciation of the responsibility he was assuming in narrating facts open to the doubts and startling to the faith of many. It was beside mainly from the facts mentioned by him, and by reference to the testimony which he so often, and so urgently quoted, that the act of her Canonization was produced. That he states many things of a most wonderful character upon the sole testimony or conviction of St. Catharine is true, but matters though bearing strong interior evidence of their truth, by no means constitute subjects of divine faith, and may be taken or set aside, as their evidence will appear sustainable or otherwise to the judgment of the reader. And yet, perhaps, it would savor of rashness, if not of deep presumption to reject as unfounded, facts that have been thought worthy of credit by many wise and prudent men, possessing means of forming judgment which are not now at our command

The pious reader will find in her life much to console and strengthen his conviction, that the providence of God deals wonderfully in his Church, with the actions and integrity of her children, whilst the less credulous may discover some difficulty in rejecting consequences which correctly flow from facts sustained by respectable testimony. No one however is required to give to purely historical facts a credence beyond that demanded by merely human testimony, and even the more timid will be shielded by the remark of the learned and critical De Feller, in his Historical Dictionary, speaking of St. Catharine, that "The canonization of the Saints does not ratify either their opinions or their revelations," and he quotes the remark of Gregory the Great, "That Saints the most favored by God frequently deceived themselves, by mistaking for a divine light, that which was merely the effect of the activity of the human soul." St. Jerome well remarks upon this point, "That they are nevertheless the effect of a piety to be always much respected, both in its principle and in its object."

The confidence extended, both in Italy and France, to this life of St. Catharine, should recommend it to the English reader; and the fact that the venerable author has already received from the Church the title of Blessed testifies that the pages of the volume are free from serious or obnoxious doctrines.

J. P. D.

Preface to the French Edition.

ONE of our most dearly cherished hopes, is that of beholding Science consecrated to the glory of HIM, who is its life and light,—an historical edifice of which Divine Providence has disposed the elements from the beginning, God himself having traced its plan, and immortal Truth fashioned its immoveable foundations. Every age, and every people will be represented; each exterior or interior stone will be a name or an event placed with order and with justice. Those deeply obscure beginnings, those different tongues and defined nationalities, those rapid revolutions, those elevations and those falls, so unforeseen, will appear in magnificent unity and the *Church* taking possession of that temple which Science will have prepared for her, will give within it a last and most solemn lesson to man.

The materials of that majestic edifice are already preparing throughout the world. God, like Solomon, employs on it foreign hands; the workmen of Tyre and Sidon, though far distant, carve the stones and cut the cedars. The Protestant and the unbeliever draw forth from the heart of ages past, the most precious metals and daily present to knowledge the admirable fruits of their criticism and their studious labors. Historical studies have never been so active or so complete. Every ruin is explored, all monuments are studied, traditions are interrogated, inscriptions are deciphered; Asia conceals not her doctrines, Egypt explains her mysteries, and Nineveh opens to our inspection the annals and gigantic remains of her civilization.

Man, in presence of these wrecks of ages and of empires, inquires what power produced those revolutions, and vivified that dust; he perceives that *doctrines* animated those people and fashioned those monuments, and he discovers in their relation with truth, the causes of their grandeur and their decay. Then, beyond time, appears to him Eternity in which God reigns and governs all things. Life, light and power emanate from his throne, and the Church distributes them to intelligent creatures. All those laws written and effaced, those forms of government that are modified, those dynasties which pass, are exterior phenomena which have profound causes. The inner life of humanity is in *Religion* and her saints are the true princes of the world. Providence gives them to mankind according to its necessities, and charges them with the execution of its will. Hence they occupy an important place in the field of history, and whosoever wishes to explain events, without considering their agency, will necessarily fall into grave errors.

Saint Catharine of Sienna was to the fourteenth century, what St. Bernard was to the twelfth; that is, the light and support of the Church. At the moment in which the bark of St. Peter is most strongly agitated by the tempest, God gives it for pilot a poor young girl who conceals herself in the poor shop of a Dyer. Catharine sets foot in the territory of France, to lead the Sovereign Pontiff Gregory XI. from the delights of his native land; she brings the Popes from Avignon to the tomb of the Apostles, the real centre of Christianity. Her zeal is inflamed at the view of the disorders which are preparing the great schism of the West, and she displays an extraordinary activity in order to avert it. She addresses herself to cardinals, princes and kings; she negotiates peace between the nations and the Holy See, brings back to God a multitude of souls, and communicates by her teaching and examples a new vigor to those great Religious Orders which are the living, vibrating pulse of the Church. Urban VI. claims her counsels; she hastens to Rome, sustains by her word the Sacred College, alarmed by the threatening storm; and in presence of the evils which overturn the heritage of Christ, she offers herself to God as a victim, and terminates her sacrifice, at thirty-three years of age, by a painful martyrdom.

To *write* the life of St. Catharine was a task beyond our strength; but God who watches over his own glory, has preserved all the documents that justify that great historical miracle, and we have only filled the part of translator. Instead of judging of facts through the prejudices of our time, and thus tinging them perhaps with a false and fading hue, we have been so happy as to meet with a contemporary author who describes them with incontestable fidelity. The life of St. Catharine by the Blessed Raymond of Capua, her confessor, is a work that may be compared to those churches of the middle ages, which charm us as much by their general harmony, as by the richness of their details. The soul reposes within, far from the contests of the world; she is sensible too of the presence of God which invites her to prayer, and excites her to become better. We had besides another motive for selecting this book, which we are happy to make known. The Sovereign Pontiff, Pius IX., condescended himself, to name it for our "*Dominican Library,*" and we were delighted to follow an indication so paternal and so august.

The Blessed Raymond of Capua presents the most precious qualites that could be united in a historian. He is not a simple and credulous man whose imagination can be easily seduced, but a Religious of profound knowledge and renowned sanctity, who relates to the Church what he saw and heard; and he does it with all the conditions which oblige his testimony to be accepted. A descendant of the celebrated Pierre des Vignes, Chancellor of Frederick II., he employed eminently better than his ancestor, the activity of his mind and the splendor of his talents. Entering betimes into the Order of St. Dominic, he exercised its most important offices. After directing during four years, the Monastry of Montepulciano, he became Professor of Theology at Sienna, and was the Confessor of St. Catharine, whom he accompanied in her journies to France and Italy. Urban VI., confided to him the most delicate and the most difficult affairs. In 1380, he was named General Master of his order which he governed during nineteen years. Schism and plague had enfeebled the children of St. Dominic; the Blessed Raymond restored its ancient vigor, and it was under his agency that was developed in the Order of Friar Preachers, that epoch so fruitful in virtues and talent. The blessed Jean de Dominici, Antoine Neyrot, Constant de Fabriano, Pierre Capucci, Saint Antonino, Fra Angelico, Fra Benedetto, are sons of that reform which he established in the convents of Lombardy, Tuscany, Sicily, Hungary, Germany, Spain and France. He died in the midst of his work, in 1399, at Nuremburg, and his body was transported to Naples,— where it now reposes amid the splendors of the church of St. Dominic

The fatigues of his apostolate, did not prevent him from leaving precious writings behind him. Besides the life of St. Agnes of Montepulciano and that of St. Catharine, he translated into Latin, the spiritual treatises of her of whom he was at once the Confessor and Disciple. He composed an admirable commentary on the *Magnificat*, the Office of the Festival of the Visitation, a treatise on reform, and a great number of very remarkable letters.* All his cotemporaries laud his science and his virtues; the Sovereign Pontiffs wished to raise him to the highest dignities of the Church, but his humility opposed it. Urban VI. in the briefs which he addresses to him, styles him his head, eyes, and mouth, his feet and his hands; he claims for him the veneration of the Emperor, of kings, cardinals and people.

This is the eminent man whom God promises for Confessor to Catharine, as a special favor; he becomes the witness of her life, and the depositary of all the secrets of her soul; he writes what he saw, and what he heard; ne addresses himself to those who could be capable of contradicting him and carefully discusses the facts which he relates; he confesses his constant hesitations and all the means that he adopts in order not to be deceived. He requests, through the intercession of her whom he fears to be in illusion, an extraordinary contrition for his sins; and when he has obtained that abundance of tears which the spirit of darkness can never bestow he still doubts; then he meets on the countenance o Catharine, the threatening looks of our Lord himself

---

*Echard. Scriptores ord. præd. 1 v, p. 680

The manner in which he exposes the miraculous abstinence of Catherine, her spirit of prophecy, and her frequent communions, shows that he brings to the examination of the facts all the lights of theology, and all the guarantees of prudence. In fine there is in the recital, such a simplicity of language, such an evidence of sincerity, that it seems impossible not to believe in his testimony; God will never allow falsehood thus to assume the garb of truth.

The life of St. Catharine, written by the Blessed Raymond, has been confirmed by all the depositions of his cotemporaries; it has served as the basis of the process of cononization, and the bull of Pius II. recalls its most extraordinary facts. We will not, therefore, discuss the doubts that might be conceived by a timid faith. The miracles are proved by testimony, and as soon as the Church admits them, we believe them as easily as the most simple phenomena of nature; they emanate from the same infinite power.

It may perhaps be found that the Blessed Raymond does not sufficiently bring forward the social action of St. Catharine. It is true that he scarcely speaks of it; he shows it rather in its principle than in its effects. Saints are not statesmen who draw their plans in form and combine their means. They act under the immediate direction of God, and have no other policy than his Providence. Prayer, word and example render them powerful in heaven and on earth. They triumph over justice itself and change its most vigorous decrees into treasures of mercy. It was thus that St. Catharine influenced the events of her time.

After having made known Saint Catharine in the verity of her life, we hope to cause her to be admired in the beauty of her doctrine, and in the greatness of her action. If God permit, we shall give to the public her spiritual dialogues, which contain the sublimity of her teaching, and her letters which will lead to the comprehension of her extended power.

Our translation has been taken from the text of the Bollandists. We have striven to preserve the simple and poetic form of the recital; at the risk of being prolix, we would not retrench any fact, nor any pious reflection. We have given but one of the author's prologues, the other appeared useless to us, and indeed not in harmony with the work. We have preferred adding to the narrative of the Blessed Raymond, the testimonies of other disciples of St. Catharine, who were summoned to depose before the Bishop of Venice.*

The Dominicans were accused of celebrating the feast of St. Catharine before the decision of the Holy See. They explain triumphantly the honors that they rendered to her memory, and the documents of the processes, that God permitted for the glory of his Spouse, to be used in her canonization.

In fine, desiring to render our work more complete, we resolved before terminating the impression of this volume, to see Italy again, and the localities consecrated by the presence of our beloved Saint. We have followed her footsteps to Rome, to Sienna, to Florence and to Pisa; we there venerated her relics and her memory; we sought in the ancient monuments of Christian art, the tradition

---

*We have translated by "Eveque de Venise," the title of EPISCOPUS CASTELLENSIS. *Castello is one of the quarters of Venice, of which the Bishop of the City took the title, until the extinction of the Patriarchs of Grade, their metropolitans.*

of her portrait, and we offer to those who desire to know them, the result of our studies and of our pilgrimage.

We dedicate this volume to our Brethren and Sisters of the third Order of St. Dominic, who have, in France, chosen St. Catharine for their patroness. May the examples and teachings of that great Saint, develop in our hearts the love of the Church which inflamed her burning heart! May France by her devotedness to the Holy See, ever merit to be blest among the nations!

Sienna, April 29th, 1853.

LIFE OF
St. Catharine of Sienna.

PROLOGUE.

DAVID, the prophet of Christ, son of Isai, the sweet singer of Israel, said, when speaking of the coming of the Messiah: "Let these things be written unto another generation; and the people that shall be created, shall praise the Lord." The holy man Job, desiring to announce the Resurrection, exclaimed: "Who will grant that my words may be written? Who will grant me that they may be marked down in a book? with an iron pen and in a plate of lead, or else be graven with an instrument in flint-stone?" These passages of Holy Writ prove to us that whatever can glorify God and edify men, ought not to be related in one age and in one locality, but should be written down and taught to those who live, or who will live hereafter. Solomon said, *Generatio præterit et generatio advenit,* (Eccl. i. 4,) One generation goeth, and another cometh. It is not just that one generation should alone possess what may be useful to all, and that the works of divine wisdom, which are worthy of never-ending praise, should obtain a transient eulogium. Moses also wrote of the beginning of Creation and the history of the human race until his own epoch; Samuel, Esdras and the other prophets continued his sacred recitals, and *we* religiously preserve their sacred words. The Evangelists are, by their dignity, entitled to the first rank among historians; not only did they announce the word of God, but they preserved and fixed it by committing it to writing; and a great voice said to one of them: *Quod rides, scribe in libro*, What thou seest write in a book. (Apoc. i. 11.)

I, therefore, brother Raymond of Capua, called in the world *Della Vigne*, humble master and servant of the order of *Friar Preachers*, in the justifiable astonishment, excited by the wonders I have seen and heard, am resolved to write, (after having proposed them with the living voice to the admiration of the faithful,) the deeds of a holy virgin, named Catharine, to whom Sienna, a city of Tuscany, gave birth. The present age as well as future ages, on becoming acquainted with the prodigies that Almighty God produced through this woman, must praise him in his Saints, and bless him according to the multitude of his great works, and excite themselves to loving him with all their strength and above all things, as well as to serve him interiorly and exteriorly without ceasing.

I assure all the readers of this book, in presence of the God of truth, that there is in my narrative neither fiction nor falsehood, and that the facts are as faithfully reported as my weakness would allow. In order to satisfy even the least credulous, I will cite, in the different Chapters, the witnesses of what I relate; and it will be clearly seen from what source I have drawn what I offer to refresh the soul. And as I purpose doing ALL in the name of the adorable Trinity, I have divided the book into three parts. The *first* will contain the birth, infancy and youth of Catharine, until the mystic nuptials with our blessed Lord. The *second*, her relations with the world from that period until her happy death; the *third*, the latter days of her life and the miracles which accompanied and succeeded her death. I do not pretend to tell all; it would not only make too voluminous a work, but my lifetime would not suffice for its accomplishment. May God allow me the privilege of accomplishing this task, and others that I purpose concerning her doctrine and devotions to the glory of the ever blessed Trinity, to whom be all the glory now and forever more. *Amen.*

FIRST PART.

CHAPTER I.

OF CATHARINE'S PARENTS AND THEIR WORLDLY CONDITION.

THERE lived in the city of Sienna, in Tuscany, a man named Jacomo, who was descended from the family of the *Benencasa*, a man simple, loyal, fearing God, and separated from every vice. After losing his parents he married a countrywoman called Lapa. This woman had none of the defects so common at the present day; she was industrious, prudent, well-versed in domestic affairs, and as she still lives, those who are acquainted with her may still render her this precious testimony. The good couple dwelt peaceably together, and although of the humbler class, they possessed a certain position among their fellow-citizens, and besides enjoyed a considerable fortune for their rank. God blessed them with a numerous offspring which they reared in the ways of eminent virtue.

As Jacomo has, as we have every reason to believe, gone to the abodes of the blest, I can with propriety make his eulogium here. Lapa has assured me that he was so mild and moderate in his words that he never gave way to anger, notwithstanding the numerous occasions which might have led him to do so; and whenever he saw any member of his household becoming vexed and speaking with violence, he would try to calm the person, saying cheerfully, "Now, now, do not say anything wrong, so that God may grant you his blessing." On one occasion a fellow-citizen had injured him very considerably, by claiming a sum of money from him unjustly, and employing the influence of his friends, and falsehood also to bring about the ruin of poor Jacomo. Still he would not hear his enemy spoken of in any way that could detract from him, and as Lapa thought it no fault he gently reproved her; saying, "let him alone, dear, let him alone, and God will bless you; he will show him his error, and will become our defence." This soon took place; the truth was discovered almost miraculously; the guilty man was condemned and acknowledged the injustice of his persecutions.

The testimony of Lapa is above suspicion; all who are acquainted with her will easily credit her; she is an octogenarian, and is so simple that even would she, she could not invent anything false. The friends of Jacomo can also testify to his simplicity, uprightness and virtue; he was so reserved in his speech that his family especially the female portion of it, could not support the least irregularity in conversation. One of his daughters named Bonaventura, had married a young man of Sienna, named Nicolas. This young man received at his house friends of his own age, and their conversation sometimes savoured of levity. Bonaventura became so depressed in spirits on this account, that she fell into a languishing state of health, and sensibly wasted away. Her husband inquired the cause of her illness; she replied: "I have never been accustomed to hearing in the house of my father, language such as I hear in yours; my education has been widely different, and I assure you that if these unbecoming discourses continue, my life must soon terminate."

This reply inspired the husband with a great respect for her and her family. He forbade his guests to pronounce in the presence of Bonaventura any words that could possibly displease her; they obeyed, and thus the correct government in the household of Jacomo, corrected the license of the house of Nicolas, his son-in-law.

Jacomo's occupation was the preparation of colors employed in dying wool; hence his surname of the dyer. The daughter of this virtuous artisan was destined to become the spouse of the King of Heaven.

The above account I have obtained either from Catharine herself, from her mother, or from some religious and seculars who were neighbors, friends or relatives of Jacomo.

CHAPTER II.

BIRTH OF CATHARINE—HER INFANCY—WONDERFUL CIRCUMSTANCES THAT TAKE PLACE.

Lapa became the mother of two delicate daughters at a birth; [1347] but the weakness of their bodies was not destined to impair the energy of their souls. The mother not being able to nourish both, found herself obliged to confide one of them to the care of a stranger. God willed that the infant she herself retained, should be her whom he had chosen for his spouse; and when the infants received baptism, the mother's choice was called Catharine, and the other Jane. Jane soon bore to Heaven the name and grace that she received in baptism; she lived but a few days, and Catharine remained alone to save, in after years, a multitude of souls. Lapa consoled herself on the death of her daughter, by tending more carefully the one that was left, and she frequently acknowledged that she loved her more tenderly than all the others, probably because she had been able to nurse her herself, for it was the only one out of the twenty-five children, with which God had blessed her, to whom she had been able to give this maternal attention.

Catharine was educated as a child that belonged to God. As soon as she began to walk alone, she was loved by all who saw her, and her conversation was so discreet, that it was with difficulty her mother could keep her at home; her neighbors and relatives would bring her to their houses in order to listen to her child-like reasonings, and enjoy her infantine sweetness. They found so much consolation in her company that they did not call her Catharine, but Euphrosyne, which signifies joy, satisfaction. Perhaps they were ignorant of this meaning, and did not know what I learned later, that Catharine had resolved to imitate St. Euphrosyne; and it may be, also, that in her childish phrases she uttered some words resembling Euphrosyne, and those who repeated her words gave her this name.

Her youth realized the promises of her early infancy: her words possessed a mysterious power which inclined the soul to God. As soon as one conversed with her, sadness was dispelled from the heart, vexations and troubles were forgotten and a ravishing peace took possession of the soul, so extraordinary indeed that one could only imagine it to resemble that enjoyed by the Apostles on Mt. Thabor when one exclaimed—"it is good for us to be here!" *Bonum est nos hic esse.* She was scarcely five years old when she would recite an Ave Maria, on each step of the stairs on going up and coming down, accompanying it with a genuflexion, and she has since assured me that she thus strove to raise her mind from things visible to things invisible. The mercy of God, deigned to recompense this pious being, and encouraged her by a wonderful vision, thus lavishing the dews of his heavenly grace on this tender plant which was destined to become a towering and magnificent cedar.

Catharine was six years of age, when her mother sent her, with her little brother Stephen, to the house of their sister Bonaventura, either to carry something, or obtain some information: their commission being executed, the children were returning by the valley known as the *Valle Piatta*, when Catharine, raising her eyes to heaven, saw opposite to her, on the gable end of the Church of the Friar Preachers, a splendid throne occupied by our Lord Jesus Christ clothed in pontifical ornaments, and his sacred brow adorned with a tiara. At his side were St. Peter, St. Paul and St. John the Evangelist. Catharine stood still ravished with admiration and contemplated with love Him who thus manifested himself to her in order to captivate more fully her devoted heart; the Saviour gave her a look of serene majesty, smiled upon her with benign tenderness, and then extending his hand gave her his blessing in the form of a cross, as is customary with Bishops. But whilst she was looking at our Lord, her little brother Stephen, continued descending, fancying that she followed him, while on the contrary he had left her far behind. Turning around, he perceived his sister looking up to heaven; he called her with his utmost voice, but she made no reply; until at length he went to her, and taking her by the hand, said, "Come on, why do you stay there?" Catharine appeared to awake from a profound sleep looked at him an instant and then said: "O did you but see what I see, you would never have disturbed me in such a sweet vision," and her eyes again turned towards heaven, but all had vanished, to the great grief of Catharine, who wept, and reproached herself for having lowered her eyes. From this moment Catharine seemed to be no longer a child; her virtues, her manners, and her thoughts were superior to her age, and would have done honor to *men* of mature years. The fire of divine love inflamed her heart and enlightened her understanding; her will strengthened, her memory developed, and her every action became conformed to the rules of the Gospel. She disclosed to me since, that the Holy Spirit then taught her, without any human teaching, and without any reading, the life pursued by the Fathers of the desert, and proposed to her the imitation of some saints, particularly of St. Dominick. She experienced **such an ardent desire to follow their example, that she** could not dwell upon any other thought; and to the astonishment of all, she sought retired spots in order to scourge her feeble body with a little discipline. Her meditation and prayers became continual, and to accomplish them she forsook all the ordinary amusements of her age; she became daily more silent, and diminished her food, contrary to the habits of growing children. Catharine's example attracted other little girls who wished to hear her pious discourses, and imitate as far as possible, her devout practices. They assembled in an apartment remote from the house, practiced corporal austerities with Catharine and said as many times the *Pater Noster*, and *Ave Maria*, as she prescribed to them. This was only a prelude of the future.

Our Lord deigned to encourage these acts of virtue by sensible graces. Her mother informed me, and Catharine was obliged to acknowledge it to me, that when purposing to mount the stair-case she was borne up to the top without touching the steps with her feet, and such was the rapidity of her ascent that the mother trembled lest she should fall. This favor happened to her when she shunned little assemblies, above all when persons of the other sex were present.

The knowledge of the life of the Fathers of the Desert, which Catharine had received from heaven, also determined her to withdraw into solitude; but she was ignorant how to accomplish her project; and God who destined her to another mode of life did not furnish her the means and left her to the dreams of her imagination. One morning, she set forth in search of the desert; after having prudently provided herself with a loaf of bread she directed her course towards the residence of her married sister, who lived near one of the gates of Sienna. She left the city for the first time in her life, and as soon as she perceived the valley, and the habitations a little more distant from one another she thought she was certainly approaching "the desert." Having found a kind of grotto underneath a shelving rock, she joyfully entered it, convinced that she was now in her much desired solitude. She knelt, and adored Him who had condescended to appear to her and bless her, and God who accepted the pious desires of his spouse, but who had other designs over her, would testify to her how agreeable her fervor was to him. She had scarcely begun her meditation, than she was elevated little by little to the very vault of the grotto, and remained thus to the hour of None. Catharine, presuming that this was a snare of Satan to distract her, and turn her from her holy purpose, increased the ardor of her prayers.

At length about the hour in which the Saviour completed his sufferings on the cross, she descended to the earth, and God revealed to her that the moment of sacrifice had not yet come, and that she was not to quit the house of her father. On leaving the grotto she became anxious on finding herself so far from the town, and dreaded the trouble that would arise in the hearts of her family who would imagine her to be lost; she recommended herself to God, and suddenly the holy child was transported, in the twinkling of an eye, to the gates of Sienna, whence she speedily returned home, and never disclosed this circumstance to any but her confessors, of whom I am the last and the most unworthy.*

---

* The Blessed Author, has faithfully fulfilled his promise given in the Prologue, of scrupulously naming his informants and authority, but we think it irrelevant to put them in this translation, on account of the reverence due to him, and the faith of the Catholic reader; besides it would increase the volume beyond the intention of the zealous publisher.—TRANSLATOR.

CHAPTER III.

OF CATHARINE'S VOW OF VIRGINITY, AND A CIRCUMSTANCE OF HER EARLY YEARS.

The apparition of our Lord exerted such a powerful influence over the heart of this devout child, that the germs of self-love were destroyed, and it became inflamed with the sole love of Jesus Christ and of the glorious Virgin Mary. All besides appeared to her only misery and corruption, and her supreme desire was to be united to the Saviour. The Holy Spirit gave her grace to understand that purity of soul and body is necessary for pleasing the Creator, and she sighed after the treasure of perpetual virginity. She implored the Queen of Angels, and of virgins, to be so kind as to obtain from God, the lights which were necessary for accomplishing what would prove most acceptable to his divine majesty and the most conducive to her soul's salvation, expressing to her merely the extreme desire she felt of embracing on earth an angelic mode of life. At length heavenly prudence bade her no longer stifle the holy emotions produced in her soul by the Spirit of God, and being one day retired quite solitary in prayer, she knelt down and invoked the Blessed Virgin, concluding her prayer thus—" I promise thy Son, and I promise thee, never to accept any other spouse and to preserve myself to the best of my ability pure and unspotted."

Catharine did indeed obtain her divine Spouse, and was strictly united to him by her vow of virginity: the blessed Mother of Jesus performed the nuptial ceremony which was miraculously celebrated, as we shall see in the course of our narrative.

After this perpetual vow, Catharine advanced rapidly in sanctity; in imitation of Jesus Christ, she crucified her innocent body, and she resolved to deny herself as far as possible, all nutritious aliments. When meat was served to her, she secretly gave it to her brother Stephen, or put it secretly away; she continued and augmented her disciplines, either alone or in concert with her youthful friends. She felt a burning zeal for the salvation of souls, and entertained a special devotion towards such saints as had labored most diligently in promoting it: she chiefly loved St. Dominic, whose apostolical charity God had made known to her.

The child advanced in age, but faith, hope and charity were developed far before her tender years, and her daily conduct commanded the respect of her seniors. The following instance Lapa often related. Catharine had scarcely attained the age of ten, when Lapa desirous of having a Mass said in honor of St. Anthony, sent her to the curate of the parish to acquiesce in her wishes, and to offer a certain number of candles on the altar, and present a sum of money mentioned. The pious child joyfully fulfilled her mother's commission, but would profit by adding her own prayers to what she felt was promoting God's glory. She therefore remained in the Church until the end of Mass, and did not return home until the Office had terminated. Her mother, — persuaded that she should have come home after having spoken with the priest, found her absence too much prolonged, and reproached her in a way common among *"the people"* for her slowness. *"Cursed,"* said she, *"*be the tongues that pretend that thou shouldst not have returned!"

The child listened to these words without making any reply, but a few moments after, she invited Lapa aside, and said to her with as much gravity as humility, "Dear mother, whenever I commit any fault, or execute your orders badly, punish me, beat me even if you will, to force me to do my duty better, but, I entreat you, never to curse any one on my account, for it is unbecoming your years, and gives me great pain." The mother was greatly surprised at this lesson from her child, and more edified than surprised when she discovered that she had remained to offer the Holy Sacrifice, instead of loitering by the way as she had hastily judged.

CHAPTER IV.

OF A RELAXATION OF FERVOR, WHICH GOD PERMITTED IN ORDER TO AUGMENT HER GRACE, AND OF THE GREAT PATIENCE OF CATHARINE IN SUPPORTING PERSECUTIONS FOR THE LOVE OF JESUS CHRIST.

THE increated Wisdom, which governs all things, sometimes permits the fall of his Saints, so that they may afterwards arise and serve him with much greater ardor, and tend with greater prudence towards perfection, and gain more splendid victories over the enemies of their salvation.

When Catharine, who had consecrated her virginity to God, had attained the age of twelve years, she never left the paternal roof alone, according to the usage established for all unmarried females. Her father, mother and brothers, who were ignorant of her solemn promise, thought of finding her a suitable partner. Her mother who desired for her a husband worthy of her merit, and who knew not that she had already selected a spouse far above all human alliances, took great pains in adorning her interesting daughter; she caused her to have her hair dressed, and her head covered with ornaments, while her neck, face and arms were attempted to be displayed in a manner calculated to please such as might ask her hand in marriage. Catharine entertained other thoughts, but she concealed them from her parents, fearing to afflct them; she *submitted* unwillingly to the wishes of her mother, seeking to please God rather than men. Lapa was pained at the opposition she could not help observing; she summoned to her aid her married daughter

Bonaventura, and charged her to persuade her sister to assume the ornaments suited to young persons of her age. She was well aware of Catharine's tenderness towards her sister, whose influence was able to produce the success of her projects. She was not deceived, God suffered the victory of Bonaventura's little manœuvres; sue influenced Catharine by her conversations and examples to devote herself to the occupations of her toilette, without however prevailing upon to renounce her vow. She accused herself of this fault with so many tears and sobs, that one would have supposed she had committed some great crime. And now that this lovely flower is transferred to the parterre of heaven, I may disclose the secrets that will redound to God's glory, and expose what passed between us on this subject. There was a question of it in all her general confessions, and it was always with signs of the liveliest contrition. I knew well that holy souls frequently fancy they discover faults where there is none in reality, and exaggerate much the imperfections they commit. But as Catharine appeared to believe she deserved eternal misery I thought it my duty to inquire if she had thought of renouncing her vow of virginity when acting thus. She answered me no, and that such an idea never even approached her heart. I then inquired whether, without wishing to infringe her vow of virginity, she had sought to please men in general, or any one man in particular; her reply was that nothing was more painful to her than to see men or to find herself with them. When her father's apprentices, who lived in the house, came where she was, she fled as though she had met with serpents, to the astonishment of all. Neither would she ever take her place at a door or in a window, in order to look at those who passed by But then, said I to her, how can you believe that .he care you took in your toilette can cause you to merit hell; above all if there was nothing excessive in your attire? She said that she had loved her sister too well, by prefering her pleasure to God's will, and then recommenced her tears. On my deciding that there might be imperfection, but that there was no violation of a formal precept, she exclaimed, "O dear Lord, see! my spiritual father excuses my sins. Can a creature so vile and contemptible, who has received so many graces from her Creator, without having ever merited them, have thus passed her precious time innocently in adorning her miserable body, and that to please a mere creature?"

This conversation proves how that beautiful soul was ever preserved from mortal sin, that she guarded her virginity spiritually and corporally, and never tarnished her purity either by word or action. In all her general confessions, and in all her particular ones, I have found no other faults than those which I have just related. Her whole time was consecrated to prayer, meditation and the edification of her neighbor. She granted herself but a quarter of an hour of sleep daily. During her repast, (if the little food she took could be called by that name,) she prayed and meditated on what our Lord had taught her. I know, and can attest before the Church, that during the period of my acquaintance with her, it was more painful for her to take food, than it is painful for one who is fainting with hunger to be deprived of it, and that she suffered more when she took any, than others endure in a violent fever—hence eating became to her a cruel penance. It would be difficult to imagine what fault a soul could commit which was so continually occupied with God, and yet she accused herself with so much sorrow, and succeeded in finding so many imperfections, that a Confessor who did not know her mode of life, might be deceived and fancy there was evil where none in reality existed. I have dwelt at length upon this fault of Catharine in order to show to what a high degree of perfection grace had raised her.

Bonaventura who had succeeded in occupying her with her toilette, had not inspired her with a wish to please the world, yet her fervor in prayer and meditation had abated. Our Lord would no longer permit that his chosen spouse should thus be separated from his heart, and he destroyed the obstacle that prevented this holy union. Bonaventura, who had led Catharine in the path of vanity, died in childbed, and in the flower of her age—and her death caused Catharine to comprehend more deeply the vanity of earth, and she devoted herself with new ardor to the service of her divine spouse. At this epoch she dates her devotion to St. Magdalen, of whom she asked a contrition similar to hers; this devotion always increasing, our Lord and the Blessed Virgin gave her Mary Magdalen for mistress and mother, as we shall hereafter see.

The enemy of salvation, perceiving that his snares were overthrown, and that she whom he was desirous of destroying, had sought refuge with more love than ever in the bosom of her spouse, determined to excite obstacles in her house, and bind her to the world by the violence of his persecutions; he inspired her relatives with the determination of obliging her to marry so as to fill the void created in the family by the death of Bonaventura. Catharine, enlightened from above, only increased her vocal prayers—her meditations and austerities,—avoiding the society of men, and proving in every way the inflexibility of her resolution never to give to a simple mortal the heart that had been accepted by the King of kings.

Her parents left no means untried of overcoming her resistance, and addressed themselves to a Friar Preacher, whom they besought as a friend of the family to do all that he could to procure the consent of Catharine. He promised to second their views, but when he conversed with her, and found her will so firm, his conscience obliged him to sustain her, and instead of contending with her, he said to her: "Since you have decided to consecrate yourself to God, and those who surround you oppose it, prove to them that your resolution is not to be shaken. Cut off your hair, entirely; perhaps they will then let you enjoy tranquility." Catharine received this advice as coming from heaven; she took her scissors and joyfully cut off her beautiful tresses, now become hateful to her, because she supposed them to have been the cause of her committing a fault. She then covered her head, contrary to the custom of youthful maidens, whom however the Apostle recommends never to go forth without a veil. When Lapa saw this veil, she asked her the reason of wearing it; Catharine neither dared to tell a falsehood nor avow the truth, and spoke in as low a tone as possible. Her mother then seized the veil, and in removing it discovered her head shorn of its beautiful locks. "Ah! daughter what have you done?" cried she, but Catharine quietly resumed her veil and withdrew. At the mother's shriek the whole family met, and when they learned what had been done all in unison gave way to violent anger.

This was the occasion of a new persecution for Catharine, and more terrible than the former; she triumphed over it by the aid of heaven, and the means they adopted for separating her from our Lord, served on the contrary to unite her more closely to him. They loaded her with injurious words and harsh treatment, telling her that her hair should be allowed to grow notwithstanding the revolts of her heart, and that she should enjoy no peace until she consented to be married in obedience to their determinations. It was also decided, that she should perform all the menial work of the house, and that no leisure should be left her for conversing with God. So as to humble her to the utmost, they even dismissed the kitchen-maid, and forced Catharine to fulfil her functions. Every day they loaded her with affronts such as are most sensible to a woman's heart—and at the same time proposed to her a highly honorable connexion, and took every possible means to induce or constrain her to accept it. But the devil was again vanquished; Catharine instead of yielding, became stronger with the help of grace, and gave way to no trouble in this storm; the Holy Spirit had taught her to erect a little cell in the interior of her soul, whence she resolved never to come forth, notwithstanding her pressing exterior occupations. When she was privileged with a room, she was often obliged to leave it, but, nothing could oblige her to leave this interior retreat—eternal truth has declared that the kingdom of God is within us—*Regnum dei intra nos est*, (Luke xvii 21.) and the prophet proclaims that all the glory of the King's daughter is within. *Omnis gloria filiæ regis ab intus.* (Ps. xliv. 14.)

The Holy Ghost also inspired Catharine with a means of supporting affronts and of maintaining in every crisis the joy and peace of her soul. She imagined that her father represented our divine Saviour, and that her mother took the place of the Blessed Virgin. Her brothers and and other relations were the Apostles and disciples of our

Lord to her; hence she served them with a delight and ardor that astonished every one; this means assisted her to enjoy her divine spouse whom she believed she was serving; the kitchen became a sanctuary to her, and when she seated herself at table, she nourished her soul with the presence of the Saviour. O richness of Eternal Wisdom, how numerous and admirable are the ways thou hast for delivering those who hope in thee! Thou canst draw them out of every danger and conduct them to the port through the most difficult and dangerous channels.

Catharine considered that recompense which the eternal Spirit promised her, and suffered all these trials with joy rather than patience, and her soul was inundated with the sweetest consolations, while fulfilling her duties. As she was not allowed an apartment to herself, but was ordered to share one with another, she chose that of her youthful brother Stephen, who was unmarried: because she could profit by his absence during the day, and his profound sleep at night, to devote herself to her practice of prayer; thus she continually sought the presence of her sponse, and was never weary of knocking at the door of his sacred tabernacle. She implored God to deign to protect her virginity, repeating with St. Cecilia this verse of the Psalmist *Fiat Domine cor meum et corpus meum immaculatum.* (Ps. cxviii. 80.) Her spirit of recollection and her hopes gave her such strength and energy that with her trials her spiritual joy increased; and her brothers who witnessed her constancy, said to one another; "We are vanquished!" Her father, who was better than the others, examined her conduct in silence, and comprehended daily more and more that she was doing the will of God, and not following the fancies of a capricious maiden.

One day while the servant of Jesus Christ was praying fervently in her brother's room; the door being open, because her parents had forbidden her to shut it; her father entered to take something that he needed in the absence of his son. While looking about, he saw his daughter who was kneeling in one corner of the chamber, and having a snow-white dove reposing on her head; at his approach it fled, and seemed to disappear through the window: he enquired of his daughter what dove that was that just flew away; she replied that she had not seen a dove or any other bird in her room. This occurrence filled him with astonishment, and awakened serious reflections in his mind.

Catharine felt an increasing desire to accomplish a project which she had entertained indeed from her infancy; namely to be clothed with the habit of the order founded by the illustrious St. Dominic, hoping she could thus more easily occomplish her holy vow. She prayed continually to God through the intercession of that saint, who had displayed such an impassioned zeal for the salvation of souls. Our Lord, seeing this young and generous athlete combating in the arena, encouraged her by the following vision. During her sleep, she seemed to behold all the Founders of the various orders, and among them St. Dominic, whom she recognized by a lily of dazzling brightness which he bore in his hand, and which was burning without being consumed. They each and all engaged her to select an order, so as to serve God in higher perfection; she turned towards St Dominic whom she saw advancing towards her and presenting her with a habit of the *Sisters of Penance* of St. Dominic, who are very numerous in Sienna. He addressed her in the following consoling words: "Daughter, be of **good** heart, fear no obstacle, excite your courage, for the happy day will come when you shall be clothed in the pious habit you desire." This promise filled her heart with joy, she thanked the great St. Dominic with an effusion of tears, which awakened her, and restored her to her senses.

This vision so comforted and strengthened her, that on that very day she assembled her father and mother with her brothers, and with great assurance declared to them: "During a long time you have resolved that I should marry, and have endeavored to force me to do so; you are aware that I hold this project in horror; my conduct must have convinced you of this; I have not however explained myself, on account of the respect due to my parents, but duty obliges me to be silent no longer; I must speak candidly with you, and declare to you an engagement I have assumed, which is not novel, since I contracted it in my infancy. Know therefore, that I have taken a vow of virginity, not through levity, but deliberately and with full knowledge of what I was doing; now that I have a maturer age and a more perfect acquaintance with the nature of my actions, I persist with the grace of God in my resolution, and it will be easier to dissolve a rock than to induce me to change my will; renounce therefore these projects for an earthly union; it is quite impossible for me to satisfy you on this point, because it is better to obey God than man. If you desire to retain me as a domestic in the house, I will render you cheerfully all the services in my power, but if you desire to oblige me to leave it, know that I shall remain immoveable in my resolution; my spouse has all the riches of heaven and earth, his power can protect me and provide abundantly for my every necessity."

At these words all present melted into tears; the sobs

broke forth with such vehemence that no one could respond to her words; there were no longer any means of opposing the accomplishment of her vow. The hitherto timorous and silent maiden had declared calmly and firmly her resolution; she was ready to quit the home of her infancy and all the delights of social intercourse rather than be wanting to it. When the emotion of the listeners had subsided a little, the father who loved his daughter devotedly, and who feared God more, recalling to mind the mysterious dove and other remarkable circumstances, gave her this reply. "God preserve us, dearest child, from longer opposing the resolution with which he inspires you; experience proves it, and we clearly perceive that you have not been actuated by levity, but by a movement of divine grace. Accomplish freely therefore the vow you have taken, do all that the Holy Spirit commands you; henceforth we will no longer oppose your pious exercises; only pray for us that we may become worthy of the promises of that Spouse who chose you at so tender an age." Then turning to his wife and children he added: "Let no one presume to contradict my dear child or seek to turn her from her saintly resolution; let her serve her Saviour as she will, and render him propitious to us. We can never find a more beautiful and honorable alliance; for it is not a mortal man whom we receive into our family, but a man God that never dies." After that, some still wept, especially the mother who loved her daughter too sensibly. Catharine on the contrary rejoiced in the Lord and thanked him for rendering her thus victorious; she humbly thanked her parents also, and disposed herself to profit in the best possible manner by the liberty that had been granted to her.

CHAPTER V.

HER AUSTERE PENANCES, AND THE PERSECUTIONS OF HER MOTHER.

As soon as Catharine had the liberty of serving God conformably to her desires, she set to work in an admirable manner; she procured a small apartment separate from the others, in which she could erect a solitude, and torment her body at will. It is impossible to describe the austerities that she practiced and the ardor with which she sought the presence of her Spouse.

From her infancy, Catharine seldom touched meat; she interdicted herself so completely at that time, and so habituated herself to this privation, that in the end, she could not smell the odor of it without her stomach being offended. One day as I found her in a state of extreme weakness, because she had taken nothing to sustain her strength, I caused a bit of sugar to be put into the water that she was drinking; when she perceived it, she said to me: "I see that you are anxious to extinguish the remnant of life that I yet have." As I asked her why, she replied that she had become so accustomed to taking unsavory dishes, that whatever was sweetened, sickened her; it was the same thing in reference to animal food: as to wine, she mingled it so, that at the time in which she dwelt in her cell, it had neither taste or odor, and hardly preserved the rich color of the wine of that region. At the age of fifteen she renounced it entirely and drank only pure water, and by daily retrenching some new article of diet, she terminated by taking only a little bread, and some uncooked vegetables.

Her body was weighed down with infirmities, and subject to insupportable indispositions; her stomach was incapable of performing its functions, and yet the want of nourishment did not diminish her physical strength, her existence was a miracle, for medical men assured me that it was quite inexplicable to them. During the whole time that I had the privilege of being witness of her life, she took no food, and no drink that was capable of sustaining her, and this she supported, however, joyously even when undergoing sufferings and extraordinary fatigue.

We must beware of supposing that this was the natural consequence of a certain diet and graduated abstinance; it is quite evident that her strength was maintained by the ardor of her soul, for when the spirit superabounds in the body and is satiated with heavenly food, the body easily endures the torments of hunger.

Her bed was composed of a few planks without any covering: she sat on them when meditating and knelt on them when praying, and then extended herself on them for sleeping, without laying aside any portion of her clothing which was wholly composed of wool. She wore a hair-cloth, but as she cherished exterior neatness as a figure of interior purity, she exchanged this hair-cloth for a chain of iron which she drew around her person with such force that it entered her flesh: this I learned from her companions who were obliged to change it on account of the profuse perspirations, which caused her fainting fits. When her weakness increased towards the close of her life I obliged her, in virtue of holy obedience, to quit this chain, which occasioned her great pain. At first she prolonged her vigils until the hour of Matins; afterwards she overcame sleep so entirely, that she gave a short half hour to sleep every other day, and she did not allow herself that repose, but when the feebleness of her body forced her to do it. She acknowledged to me that no victory had cost her so dearly, and that she had undergone great combats in this triumphing over sleep.

Had she found persons capable of understanding her, she would willingly have passed the days and nights in talking of God, and her discourses, instead of weakening her, on the contrary rendered her more joyous and appeared to fortify her, for while she spoke of holy things, she seemed to be redolent with the vigor of youth, and when she ceased, she became languid and without energy. Sometimes she spoke to *me* of the profound mysteries of God, and as she never wearied, and I did not possess her sublime elevation of soul, I would fall asleep. But she, absorbed in God, would not perceive it, and continue talking, and when she discovered me asleep, she would arouse me with a louder tone of voice, and recall to my mind that I was losing precious truths and considerations in thus allowing her to converse with the walls.

Peruse the lives of the fathers of the desert; run over the pages of the Sacred Writings, and in vain will you seek any similar instance. You will see that Paul the Hermit lived a long time in the wilderness, but a raven daily brought him half of a loaf. The celebrated St. Anthony practiced astonishing austerities, but he had gathered, like odorous flowers, the example of the other anchorites whom he visited; for St. Jerome relates that St. Hilarion, during his youth, had gone to find St. Anthony, and had taught him the secrets of solitude, and the means of acquiring victory. The two Saints Macarius, Arsenius, and numerous others, had masters who led them in the paths of the Lord; all these lived amid the peace of solitude, and in the protecting shade of some monastry; whilst this worthy daughter of Abraham was neither in a convent nor in the wild, but in the bosom of her family, without the help of spiritual direction, and surrounded by obstacles of every sort; and yet she attained a degree of abstinence that no Saint besides had ever attained. True, Moses fasted twice during a period of forty days; Elias did it once, and the Gospel teaches us that the Saviour deigned to give us the same example, but these are not fasts during consecutive years. When John the Baptist was conducted by the spirit of God into the wilderness, it is written, that his food was the locust and wild honey; but this was not an absolute fast; there is none but St. Magdalen of whom *history*, and not the Gospel, writes that she fasted during thirty-three years on a rock which is still pointed out, and therefore we may conclude, that the holy examples I have cited give us to understand with what magnificence, and inexhaustible bounty, God enriches his saints and bestows on them *new* perfections. They should also prove the admirable virtue of Catharine, and that the Church may say of her, without injury to her other saints: "We find none like her!" *Non est inventus similis illi.* The infinite power of Him who sanctifies souls, can give them, when it seems to him good, a particular glory.

One more fact will recapitulate all I have said of Catharine, and will give you to comprehend to what point she had weakened her body and subjected her mind. Her mother informed me that her daughter, before her penances, posssessed such physical strength, that she could easily take on her shoulders a weight sufficient for a horse, and carry it with speed up two flights of stairs, that is to the attic on top of the house. Her body was twice as strong and twice heavier than at her twenty-eight years of age, and she became so weak that a miracle was necessary to sustain her. When I was acquainted with her, the spirit had so exhausted her physical energies, that we always believed her end was approaching, and yet she was filled with an admirable ardor, especially when there was question of the salvation of souls; *then*, she forgot all her infirmities and after the example of her holy patroness St. Magdalen, she suffered in her body and prayed by her soul, which communicated to her exhausted members, the superabundance of its strength.

The old serpent whom she had vanquished, did not, however, renounce his efforts to torment her; he addressed himself to Lapa, whom he knew to be a true daughter of Eve, and succeeded, by means of the love which led her to consider Catharine's body more than her soul, in inspiring her with the thought of hindering her penance. When she found Catharine lying on simple planks, she conducted her forcibly into her room, and obliged her to share her own bed. Then Catharine, docile to the lessons of Wisdom, would fall on her knees, before her mother, soften her by words full of humility and sweetness, entreating her to calm herself, and promising to repose by her side in accordance with her wishes. She would then lie down on the extreme edge of the bed and there meditate with fervor; and when she found her mother was asleep, she would softly arise and return to her devout exercises. It would not be long; for Satan provoked by her constancy, would awaken Lapa. Then Catherine sought a means of satisfying her love of austerities, and of leaving her mother in tranquility; she managed to slide one or two planks under the sheets in the place she was to occupy; but after some days her mother perceiving it said: "I see that all my endeavors prove futile; at least do not try to conceal it from me, and sleep now as you wish." She yielded to such perseverance, and permitted her to follow the divine inspiration.

CHAPTER VI.

OF HER SELF-CONQUEST AT THE BATHS, AND HER CLOTHING WITH THE HOLY HABIT OF ST. DOMINIC.

Catharine resumed her pious exercises, and was continually speaking to her parents of her desire to give herself more fully to her divine Spouse. She also solicited the "Sisters of Penance, of St. Dominic," who are denominated *Mantelees*, to condescend to receive her among them, and allow her to wear their costume. Her mother afflicted at these requests, dared not, however, refuse her, and so as to try to distract her from her austerities she, without precisely knowing it, became the accomplice of Satan, by proposing to go to the Baths and to take Catharine with her. The spouse of our Lord, combatted with invincible arms, and all the attacks of the devil turned to her advantage. She found a method of torturing her body; for, under pretext of bathing herself better, she approached the canals by which the sulphurous waters enter the Baths, and she endured the burning heat, on her uncovered and delicate flesh, to such a degree, that she suffered more than when scourging herself with iron chains. When her mother told me this fact, Catharine told me that she had asked to bathe after the departure of the others, because she was well assured that she would not be suffered to do this; and when I inquired how she could support such atrocious torture without dying, she answered me with dovelike simplicity: "When *there*, I thought much on the pains of Hell, and of Purgatory: I besought my Creator, whom I had so often offended, to deign to accept for the torments I had merited, those that I then voluntarily underwent; and the thought that his mercy consented to it, filled my soul with such heavenly consolation that I was happy in the midst of my pain."

On their return Lapa tried in vain to obtain from Catherine a relaxation in her austere practices; her daughter turned a deaf ear, and only implored her, day by day, to go and press the "Sisters of Penance," to no longer refuse her the holy habit for which she languished. Lapa, overcome by her importunities consented to it. The sisters replied that it was not their custom to give their habits to young maidens, but to widows of mature age, who had consecrated themselves to God; that they kept no enclosure (or cloister,) but that each sister must be capable of governing herself at home. Lapa returned with this answer, which was, we may presume, less painful to her, than to her pious daughter.

The Spouse of Jesus Christ was not however troubled; she trusted in the promise she had received from heaven, and solicited anew its accomplishment. She told her mother that she was not discouraged, and that she must insist with the sisters, and Lapa yielded at length to her earnestness, but returned home without any better success.

In the mean time Catherine was seized with a malady common to young persons in her country. Providence had his designs. Lapa loved all her children with tenderness, but this one in particular. The poor mother sat by her bedside, giving her every imaginable remedy and seeking to console her; but Catharine, amidst her sufferings, only pursued with new ardor the object of her desires and strove to profit by a moment in which her anxious and loving mother was ready to accord her any thing she requested. She said to her sweetly: "Dearest mother, if you wish me to recover my health and strength, try to obtain for me the habit of the 'Sisters of Penance.' I am convinced that God and St. Dominic who call me, will take me from you, if I wear any other religious dress."

Lapa gave way to sadness on hearing these words, but as she feared losing her daughter, she once more addressed herself to the Sisters, and was so importunately persuasive that they were shaken in their resolutions. They answered: "If she be not handsome, nor of a beauty too remarkable, we will receive her, on her account and yours, but if she be too pretty, we are bound to avoid the inconveniences that might spring from the malice of men of the present period." Lapa invited them to come and judge for themselves. Then, three or four of the sisters, selected among the most enlightened and prudent, accompanied her to see Catharine and examine her vocation. They could not judge of her personal appearance, for her whole body was covered with a kind of eruption consequent on her malady, which quite disfigured her, besides her beauty was not excessive; but they heard her express herself with so much fervor, and remarked in her such a profound wisdom that they were quite enchanted; they comprehended that the maturity of her mind redeemed the fewness of her years, and that there were not very many aged persons who were as rich in virtues before God

They retired filled with pious joy and edification, and rendered an account of their visit to their associates. These after having taken the opinion of the monks of the Order, assembled and received Catharine unanimously.

They announced to her mother that, as soon as she would be recovered from her illness, she might repair to the church of the Friar Preachers, to take the habit of St. Dominic, in presence of the Brethren and Sisters, with the customary ceremonies. At this happy news, Catharine shed tears of joy, and gave thanks to her heavenly Spouse and to Saint Dominic, who realized at last his promise. She implored her restoration to health, not in order to be released from sufferings, but so as to accomplish more promptly the first and strongest wish of her heart. She was heard, and became quite well in a few days, for how could our Lord refuse her when she asked him to remove an obstacle in the way of his greater glory, and the service of one who loved him so devotedly.

The mother now sought to retard the happy day of her reception, but in vain; she was obliged to yield to the pressing solicitations of Catharine, and repair to the Church, where in the presence of many Sisters of the Order who rejoiced at it, and the Friar Preachers who directed them, Catharine was clothed with their habit which by its black and white draperies represented humility and innocence. It seems to me that the habit of no other Order would have been so suitable for her; had it been wholly white or wholly black, the signification would have been incomplete: gray which results from their mixture, could indeed have represented her mortification, but not her triumph over poisonous natural pride, nor the bright purity of her virginal innocence. Catharine was the first Virgin that was ever received, in Sienna, among the *Sisters of Penance*, but many followed her, and the words of David may appropriately be applied to her: *Adducentur regi, virgines post eam.* (Ps. ivl. 15.) In her train virgins were presented to the Lord. Had the Sister reflected more seriously I presume they would not have refused her request, for she was more worthy than they to wear a habit given to the Church to symbolize innocence, and the innocence of virginity is assuredly superior to the chastity of widowhood.

CHAPTER VII.

OF THE ORIGIN AND ESTABLISHMENT OF THE "SISTERS OF PENANCE" OF ST. DOMINIC, AND OF THEIR MODE OF LIFE.

THE following particulars I have drawn from manuscripts which I consulted in Italy, from informations taken from the seniors of the Order, and the members of it most worthy of trust, and the history of our blessed Founder St. Dominic. That glorious defender of the Catholic Faith, that valiant soldier of Jesus Christ, combatted so victoriously the heresies that arose in Toulouse and in Italy, that by himself and his disciples, it was proved at his canonization that his doctrine and his miracles had converted, in Lombardy alone, more than a hundred thousand heretics.

However the poison of error had corrupted minds to such a degree, that all the benefices of the Church were usurped by laymen, who transmitted them in regular inheritance. The Bishops, obliged to beg for their own subsistence, had no means of reforming these abuses, and could not, in accordance with their charge, provide for the wants of regulars nor of the poor. St. Dominic who had chosen poverty for his own portion, did not wish however to see it in such a degree in the Church, and he resolved to strive to restore to her, her wealth. He collected some laymen, whom he knew to be filled with the fear of God, and organized from amongst them a pious soldiery, for recovering the riches of the Church, defending them, and resisting the injustice of the heretics; this plan succeeded Those who enrolled themselves, swore to do all in their power for the attainment of their ends proposed, and to sacrifice if necessary, their fortunes and their persons; but as their wives might sometimes offer obstacles, St. Dominic induced them to promise never to hinder their husbands, but on the contrary to assist them as far as possible. These Associates took the title of *Brethren of the Militia of Jesus Christ*. The holy founder desired to distinguish them among other laymen by an exterior badge and assign them some particular obligations. He prescribed to them the color of the habit of his Order; the garments of the men and women, whatever might be their shape, were to be black and white, as emblematic of innocence and humility. He imposed on them the recitation of a prescribed number of *Pater* and *Ave*, which were to supply the canonical hours, when they could not assist at the Divine Office.

Later, when our blessed Father St. Dominic had quitted the earth and soared away to Heaven, and his numerous miracles had decided the Church to inscribe his name in the catalogue of her Saints, the Brothers and Sisters of the *Militia of Jesus Christ* wished to honor their glorious founder, by taking the title of *Brothers of Penance of St. Dominic*; besides, the merits of St. Dominic and the apostolical labors of his Order had almost banished heresy; exterior combats were no longer necessary, but it remained yet to overcome by penance, the interior enemy of the soul, and hence the new appellation was more becoming than the old one. When the number of the Friar Preachers had augmented, and Peter, (virgin and martyr,) had shone among them as a radiant star, in triumphing over his enemies, still more by his death than by his life, the troop of foxes that wished to ravage the vineyard of the Lord, was completely destroyed, and

God restored peace to his Church. The reasons which led to the institution of the *Militia of Jesus Christ* no longer existed, the association therefore lost its military characteristic. When the men who were members of it died, their widows accustomed to the religious life which they had observed, renounced marriage, and persevered in their holy practices until death. Other widows who had not contracted the same engagements, but who would not marry again imitated the *Sisters of Penance* and adopted their rule in order to purify themselves from past faults. By degrees their number increased in the different cities of Italy, and the Friar Preachers directed them according to the Spirit of St. Dominic. But as there was nothing settled in this direction, a Spanish Friar, called Brother Munie, a Religious of saintly memory, who had governed the whole Order, committed the Rule to writing, and it still exists. This Rule is not absolutely a religious Rule, because it does not require the three Vows, which are the foundation of every Religious Order.

The *Sisters of Penance* continually increasing in numbers and sanctity, the sovereign Pontiff Honorius IV., in consideration of their merit, granted them by a bull, the permision to hear the Offices in the Churches of the Friar Preachers, even during the period of the interdict; John XXII, after having promulgated the bull *Clementina* against the Béguines and the Bégards, declared formally that his prohibitions did not extend to "St. Dominic's *Sisters of Penance*, which existed in Italy and in whose Rule there was nothing that needed change.

CHAPTER VIII.

OF CATHARINE'S ADMIRABLE PROGRESS IN THE WAYS OF GOD, AND OF SOME PARTICULAR GRACES SHE RECEIVED.

CATHERINE did not pronounce the three Vows of Religion on taking the habit of Saint Dominic, but she took the resolution of observing them perfectly: there could be no deliberation concerning that of chastity, because she had already taken the Vow of Virginity. She promised to obey all that the father Master of the *Sisters of Penance* prescribed her, and also the orders of their Prioress. During her whole life she was so faithful to this engagement, that she was able to declare to her Confessor on her death-bed: that she could not remember having failed even once in obedience.

Catharine also observed the Vow of Poverty perfectly. When she lived in her father's house and plenty reigned in it, she took nothing for herself; only she bestowed alms on the poor, for her father had given her full latitude on this point. She loved poverty so much, that she acknowledged, that nothing could console her for not finding it in her family. She asked God ardently to deign to render her parents poor: "Lord," said she, "is it not better that I ask for my parents and brothers, the goods of eternity: I know that those of earth are accompanied with ills and dangers, and I wish that they may not be exposed to them." God heard her prayer: extraordinary circumstances reduced her parents to extreme poverty, without any fault on their part, as can be easily proved by those who know them. After laying such foundations, Catherine began to raise the edifice of her perfection, like an industrious bee she profited by every occasion of advancing and took every means possible of living a more retired life and one more closely united to her divine Spouse. She proposed, in order to preserve herself unsullied by the world, to observe the most rigorous silence, and never to speak except when she went to confess her sins. Her Confessor who preceded me, declared and wrote that she observed this resolution during three years. She remained in her cell continually except when she went to Church; not even leaving it to take her food, which was, as we have already said, the veriest trifle; again, she bedewed her repasts with her tears, and never commenced one without offering to God the tribute of her grief. Who can recount her vigils, her prayers, her meditations and her sighs, in the solitude which she had found in her own house and amid the noise of the city. She had arranged her time so as to watch while the Dominicans whom she called her Brothers were sleeping, and when she heard the second toll for Matins, she said to her divine Spouse: "Lord, my brethren who serve you, have slept until now, and I have watched for them in thy presence, praying thee to preserve them from evil and the wiles of the enemy. Now that they are rising to offer thee their praises, protect them and suffer me to take a short repose"—and then she would lie down on her planks using, a piece of wood for her pillow.

He whom she loved, smiled upon her ardor and encouraged it by new graces, he was unwilling that so faithful a lamb should be destitute of a pastor, and a pupil so desirous of improvement without a good master; but he gave her neither an angel nor a man, but appeared to her himself in her little cell and taught her whatever might prove useful to her soul. "Be sure, father," said she to me, "that naught that I know concerning the ways of salvation was taught by mere man; it was my Lord and Master, the cherished Spouse of my soul, our Lord Jesus Christ, who revealed it to me by his inspirations and by his apparitions. He spoke to me, as I now speak to you." She owned to me that, in the beginning of her visions, when she perceived them by her exterior senses, she dreaded being deceived by Satan; our Lord far from being offended extolled her prudence. The traveller, said he to her, should be ever on his gaurd, for 't is written: Blessed is the man that liveth in fear. (Prov. xxviii. 14.) "If thou wilt I will teach thee, how thou canst discern my visions, from the visions of the enemy." And as Catherine begged him earnestly, our Lord continued: "It would be easy to enlighten thy soul directly and show thee how to distinguish at once, the origin of thy visions; but for thy utility and the benefit of others, I will tell thee what the doctors teach, to whom I have made known my truth: *my* visions commence by terror and continue in peace; their arrival or presentation is attended with a certain bitterness which little by little changes into sweetness. The contrary happens in the visions of the bad spirit;—they begin with a certain joy, but always terminate by plunging the soul into trouble; and this is just, for our ways are widely different. The way of penance and my commandments at first appears rude and painful; but as the soul advances, it becomes easy and delightful; in the way of evil on the contrary, the first moments are agreeable; but trouble and danger soon show themselves. I will give thee one more, and an infallible sign. **My visions** render the soul humble, by giving it the grace of comprehending the truth of its unworthiness. But as the demon is the father of falsehood and the prince of pride, he can only give of what he possesses: his visions always engender in the soul a certain self-esteem which excites it to vanity. Examine thyself therefore, with care, and see whether thy visions proceed from the truth, or the opposite; truth excites humility, falsehood creates pride."

From this moment, her heavenly visions and communications multiplied to such a degree, that the most active conversation between two friends, would not suffice to illustrate the exchange of thoughts between Catharine and her divine Spouse. Her prayers, meditation and spiritual reading, her vigils and her short repose, all were blessed with the same divine presence. These supernatural relations are the origin and cause of her abstinence, her admirable doctrine and her miracles, of which God rendered us witnesses during her life.

In the beginning of my acquaintance with her, I had heard so many marvellous things concerning her, that I hesitated in believing them; God permitted it for greater good. I sought in all possible ways to discover some means of assuring myself, whether these phenomena came from God or from some other source—whether they were true or false. I have found many deluded souls, especially among females, whose heads are easily turned, and who are more exposed to the seductions of Satan. Certain remarks troubled me, and I desired to be satisfied by him, who can neither deceive nor be deceived, when suddenly the thought came to my mind, that if I were to obtain from God by Catharine's prayers, a contrition for my sins superior to that which I felt habitually, it would be an evident sign, that all that occurred came from the Holy Spirit, for no one can have a true contrition except by the Holy Spirit, and although we are ignorant, whether we are worthy of love or of hatred, contrition of heart is a proof that we are in the grace of God. I did not say a word of these thoughts which occupied me; but went to Catharine, and earnestly asked of her to please to obtain from God the remission of my sins. She answered me with a joy replete with charity, that she would most willingly comply, and I then added, that to satisfy my desire I must have a satisfactory evidence, namely, an extraordinary contrition for my sins. She assured me that she would obtain it, and on the morrow she was conversing with me, when her discourse insensibly turned on God and on the ingratitude with which we offend his goodness. Whilst she spoke, I had a sudden vision of my sins, of surprising accuracy and distinctness: I saw myself, divested of all things, in the presence of my Judge, and I felt that I merited death, as do malefactors when stricken by the justice of men; I saw also the bounty of my Judge, who by his grace took me into his service and replaced death by life, fear by hope, sorrow by joy, and shame by glory. These mental visions so triumphed over my hardness and obduracy of heart, that I began to shed torrents of tears over my sins: and my grief became so profound that I thought I should die of it.

Catharine, whose end was accomplished, kept silence, and left me to my tears and sobs. Some moments after in the midst of my surprise at these interior dispositions, I remembered my request and the promise she had made me on the eve: I turned towards her, and said, "Is not this the gift I asked for yesterday?" "The same," answered she, and added "Remember the graces of God." My companion and myself were filled with gladness and edification—and I exclaimed with the incredulous Thomas—"my Lord and my God"—*Dominus meus et Deus meus*. (St. John xx. 28.)

I received another proof of Catharine's sanctity which I relate to her honor and my own confusion. She was detained by sufferings in her bed, and she sent me notice that she desired to speak with me concerning some revelations. I went and approached her couch; she began then, notwithstanding the fever which burned in her veins, to discourse to me of God, and to explain to me all that had been revealed to her during the day; the things were so extraordinary, that I forgot what had just happened to me, and I asked myself, "must I believe what she says?" Whilst I hesitated and looked at her, her countenance suddenly changed into that of a stern man who was regarding me fixedly, and who filled me with terror: her oval face indicated the plentitude of life; her scanty beard was the color of wheat, and her whole countenance bore the impress of that majesty which revealed the holy presence of God. It was impossible for me to perceive any other countenance than hers. I was thoroughly terrified, and exclaimed, with lifted hands: "Oh! who looks at me thus.?" Catharine answered, "*He that is.!*" The vision disappeared, and I again saw the face of Catharine, which I could not distinguish before. My understanding was enlightened with such an abundant light, chiefly upon the subject of our discourse, that I then comprehended that word of our Lord, when promising the coming of the Holy Ghost: "*Et quæ ventura sunt annuntiabit vobis*. (St. John. xvi. 13.)

CHAPTER IX.

OF THE ADMIRABLE DOCTRINE TAUGHT HER BY OUR LORD, AND WHICH SHE ADOPTED AS HER RULE OF LIFE.

LET us now examine the spiritual edifice of Catharine's perfection, with the grace of Him who is its corner-stone and foundation; and as faithful souls find their life and their strength in the word of God, let us first dwell upon the lessons that she received directly from the beloved Master. In the beginning of her visions, Catharine related to her Confessors, that our Lord appeared to her, whilst she was meditating and said to her: "Know, my daughter, what thou art and what I am; if thou learnest these two things, thou shalt be truly blest: thou art what is not, and I am the great I AM; if thy soul is deeply penetrated with this truth, the enemy cannot deceive thee and thou wilt avoid all his snares; thou wilt never consent to do any thing against my commandments, and thou wilt acquire without difficulty, grace, truth and peace." In this short and simple doctrine, do we not find the "length, breadth, and height" of which St. Paul speaks to the Christians of Ephesus? Our Lord also said to her in another apparition: "Daughter think of me and I will think continually on thee." Catharine comprehended this saying to mean, that God commanded her by this, to banish all her own thoughts from her heart, and keep no thoughts but his, without being anxious about herself and her salvation, so that no distraction could enter into it—for God knows all, and can do all, and he will watch and provide for the necessities of such as meditate on him and find in it supreme happiness. Hence when we entertained any fear concerning ourselves or our Brethren, she would often say—"What do you wish to do with yourselves; let Providence act: amid your greatest dangers the divine eye watches over you; and it will ever protect you." This virtue of hope her divine Spouse had infused into her soul, when he said to her I will think on thee.

I remember that, being on board of a ship with her and many other persons, the wind lowered into a dead calm towards midnight, and the pilot became extremely anxious. We were in a dangerous channel; if the wind had taken us sideways, we might have been thrown on some neighboring islands or floated into the open sea. I gave notice to Catharine of our danger. She answered in her ordinary tone: "Why do you annoy yourself with that, or suffer yourself to be distracted?" I remained silent and became re-assured; but soon the wind veered in the direction dreaded by the pilot; I mentioned it to Catharine: "Let him change the helm, in the name of God," said she, "and let him sail in the direction of the wind that Heaven will send him." The pilot obeyed and we returned backward, but *she* prayed with her head bent forward, and we had not advanced farther than a bow shot, when the favorable wind that had forsaken us blew freshly, and we arrived at the hour of *Matins*, at the desired port, while singing the *Te Deum*. This narrative should not be placed here, in the order of time, but I relate it because it serves and explains my subject. Yes, whoever reflects, must see that the second verity follows as a consequence from the first, if a soul recognizes that she is nothing in herself, and that she exists solely by God, she will not confide in herself in any action, but in the agency of God alone. She will put all her trust in the Lord, and "*place all her thoughts in him,*" according to the words of the Psalmist. This does not hinder her from doing all that is possible to her, because this holy confidence proceeds from love—love produces in the soul a desire of the object beloved; that desire provokes to the performance of all acts that are capable of satisfying it. Activity is in relation with love, but that does not hinder her giving her confidence to God, and rejecting all self-reliance, as she is taught by the knowledge that she has acquired of her own nothingness and of the perfection of her Creator.

She frequently spoke to me of the state of a soul which loves her Creator, and she told me that, "*that soul finished by no longer perceiving herself, and forgetting herself together with all creatures.*" As I requested an explanation, she told me: "The soul that comprehends its nothingness, and is convinced that all its good comes from the Creator, resigns itself so perfectly and plunges itself so totally in God, that all its activity is directed towards him, and exercised in him. She is unwilling to come forth from the centre in which she has found the perfection, of happiness: and that union of love which daily augments in her, transforms her, so to speak, into God so that she is incapable of entertaining other thoughts, or other desires, or other love than love of him, indeed the remembrance of all things else forsakes her. This is the lawful love of ourselves and of creatures, a love that cannot err, because the soul of necessity follows the divine will, and does nothing, and desires nothing out of God."

In this union of the soul with God, Catharine found another verity, which she taught continually to those whom she directed: "The soul united to God," said she, "loves him as much as she detests the sensual part of her being. The love of God, naturally engenders a hatred of sin, and when the soul discovers that the germ of sin is in her senses, and that in them it takes its root, she cannot avoid hating her senses, and endeavoring, not indeed to destroy them, but to annihilate the vice that is in them, and she cannot attain to this but by great and continued efforts: the root of faults will indeed always exist; for according to St. John. 'if we say that we have no sin we deceive ourselves, and the truth is not in us." (St. John 1 Ep. i. 8.)

"O eternal bounty of God!" exclaimed Catharine, "what hast thou done? From faults spring virtue, from offence pardon, and in contempt love puts forth its blossoms. O then, my children, endeavor to possess that holy hatred of self, it renders you humble, it will give you patience in tribulations, moderation in prosperity, restraint in your deportment, and you will become agreeable to God and man." And she added: "Woe, woe to the soul which has not this holy hatred, for where it does not exist, self-love must reign, and self-love is the cause of all sin, and the root of all vices."

The same doctrine is found in the words that the Apostle heard in Heaven, when he prayed for deliverance from temptation: "Strength is perfected in weakness;" and he added, "I glory in my weaknesses, in order that the power of Christ may dwell in me." We may, therefore, conclude that the doctrine of Catharine had for its foundation the firm rock of virtue which is Jesus Christ.

CHAPTER X.

OF THE ADMIRABLE VICTORIES WHICH SHE GAINED OVER TEMPTATIONS, AND HER EXTRAORDINARY INTIMACY WITH OUR LORD.

THE pacific King had erected the fortress of Libanus, for protecting Jerusalem against Damascus. The haughty prince of Babylon, the enemy of peace, was enraged; he collected his armies against it, and wished to overthrow it. But he who gives and preserves peace, surrounded his fortress by magnificent and impregnable ramparts. Not only the darts of the enemy were powerless, but they returned against those who launched them and gave them death. So, when the old serpent saw Catharine, so young, mounting to such a high degree of perfection, he feared lest, with *her* salvation, that of many others would be secured; and that she might assist the Church by her virtues and her teaching. He therefore sought in his infernal malice, every means of seducing her; but the God of mercy, who permitted these attacks, in order to augment the glory of his spouse, gave her such excellent weapons wherewith to combat, that the war proved more profitable to her than peace. He first inspired her with the thought of asking God for the gift of fortitude: she did so continually during several days; and God to recompense her prayer, gave her the following instructions:

"Daughter, if thou wilt acquire fortitude, thou must imitate me. I could have, by my divine power, arrested the efforts of Satan, and have taken other means of overcoming them, but I was desirous of instructing thee by my examples, and teaching thee to overcome by means of the Cross. If thou wishest to become powerful against thy enemies, take the Cross for thy safeguard. Hath not my Apostle told thee that I ran with joy to the cruel and ignominious death of Mt. Calvary. (Heb. XII., 2.) Choose, therefore, to have trials and afflictions; endure them not only with patience, but embrace them with delight; they are lasting treasures, for the more thou wilt suffer for me, the more thou wilt be like me, and according to the doctrine of the Apostle, the more thou wilt resemble me in sufferings, the more, also, thou shalt be like unto me in grace and glory. Regard, therefore, my beloved child, on my account, sweet things as bitter, and bitter things as sweet, and be certain thou shalt always be strong." Catharine profited so well by this lesson, and after it received trials with so much joy, that she acknowledged to me, that nothing exterior consoled her so much as pains and afflictions; she suffered when she was deprived of them, because she felt that they were the gems which would enrich her heavenly crown.

When the King of heaven and earth, had thus armed her who was destined to defend his cause, he permitted the enemy to advance and assail her. The devils attacked her on every side, and made unheard of efforts to overthrow her: they commenced by the most humiliating temptations and presented them to her imagination, not only during sleep, but in exciting phantoms which might have defiled her eyes and ears, and they tormented her in a thousand ways. These combats are horrible to relate, but the victory which followed them ought to be a source of joy to pure souls. Catharine combatted courageously against herself, by mortifying her flesh with a chain of iron and shedding an abundance of blood. She augmented her vigils so far as to deprive herself of all sleep.

Her enemies refused to retire,—they assumed the appearance of persons who came to pity and advise her: "Why poor little one, will you thus torture yourself and so uselessly ? Why use all these mortifications—do you suppose you can be able to continue them—will you not thus destroy your body and become guilty of suicide? It is better to renounce these follies ere you become their victim, you can yet enjoy the world, you are young and your body would speedily recover its strength. You desire to please God, but there are many among the Saints who were married, as Sarah, Rebecca, Leah and Rachel, why be so imprudent as to select a mode of life in which you cannot persevere." To all these discourses Catharine only opposed prayer, and as to perseverance she simply replied, "I trust in the arm of the Lord, and not in mine." The devils could never obtain more. She gave as a general rule against such temptations, never to dispute with the enemy, for he relies very much on vanquishing us by the subtilty of his reason.

Then Satan laid aside his reasonings and adopted a new method of attack; the devils pursuing her with screams and inviting her to partake of their abominations. In vain did she close her eyes and ears, she could not banish these horrible spectres, and to crown her affliction, her divine Spouse, who had usually come to visit and comfort her, seemed to abandon her without any relief visible or invisible; hence her soul was plunged into a profound melancholy, without however obtaining from her the cessation of her austerities, or her mental prayer, and she gave this following maxim to souls which she conducted, "When the Christian soul perceives her fervor diminishing on account of some fault or some temptation permitted by Providence, she ought to continue her spiritual exercises and even multiply them, instead of forsaking or lessening them."

Catharine, faithful to the inspirations of God, excited a holy hatred against herself—"O thou vilest of creatures," said she to herself, "art thou worthy of receiving any consolations, recall to mind thy sins, it will be a great favor if thou dost avoid eternal wrath by supporting during a life time these pains and this obscurity. Why then be afflicted; shouldst thou escape hell, Jesus Christ can console thee during all eternity; it was not for present enjoyment thou didst resolve to serve him, but in order to possess him in Heaven: arise then, abandon none of thy pious practices, and celebrate in a more animated strain the praises of thy Creator." Thus by her humility she confounded the prince of darkness, and drew strength from the precepts of Wisdom. Her apartment seemed to be infested with these impure spirits, she therefore left it and staid as long as possible in the Church, because these infernal obsessions tormented her less when there.

This trial continued during several days, when on returning from the Church, being engaged in prayer, a ray of the Holy Spirit beamed upon her soul and recalled to her memory that she had requested, a short time previous, the gift of fortitude, and that God had indicated to her the means for obtaining it. She instantly comprehended the cause of this dreadful temptation and resolved to bear it with holy courage, as long as it pleased her divine Spouse. Then one evil spirit, more malicious than the others, said to her: "Poor miserable soul, what art thou about to undertake—canst thou pass thy whole life in this state—we will torment thee to death. unless thou dost obey us." Catharine remembering the advice she had received answered: "I have chosen sufferings for my consolation; not only will it not be difficult for me, but even delightful to undergo similar afflictions and even greater ones, for the love of my Jesus, and as long as his majesty wills!"

Instantaneously the demons fled in overwhelming shame, and a great light from above descended into her room filling it with heavenly brightness: in the midst of its brilliancy appeared our Lord Jesus Christ, such as he was on the Cross, when he opened heaven with his sacred Blood. "Catharine my daughter," said he, "consider how I have suffered for thee, and it will never be painful for thee to suffer for me." Then he assumed a less dolorous form in order to comfort Catharine, and he spoke to her of the victory that she had just gained; but she, like St. Anthony, said to him: "Lord where wast thou, when my heart was so tormented?" "I was in the midst of thy heart." "Ah! Lord, thou art the everlasting truth and I humbly bow before thy majesty; but how can I believe that thou wert in my heart, when it was filled with such detestable thoughts?" "Did these thoughts and temptations, give thee pleasure or pain?" "An excessive pain and sadness." "Thou wert sad and in suffering because I was *hidden* in the midst of thy heart. Had I been absent, these thoughts would have penetrated thy heart and would have filled thee with joy; but my presence rendered them insupportable to thee: thou didst wish to repel them because thou didst hold them in horror, and it was because thou didst not succeed that thou wert borne down with sadness. I acted in thy soul, I defended thee against thy enemy; I was in the interior and I only permitted these attacks from without, inasmuch as they could prove useful to thy salvation; when the period which I had determined for the combat had elapsed, I sent my beams of light and the shades of hell were dissipated, because they could not resist the light. Is it not I in fine who giveth thee to comprehend that these trials were serviceable to thee for the acquisition of strength, and that it was thy duty to support them cordially, according to my good pleasure? Because thou hast accepted them with thy whole heart, thou art delivered from them by my presence; what pleases me is not *trouble*, but the *will* that supports it courageously. I created thee in my own image and likeness, and I have assimilated myself to thee, in taking thy nature. I never cease rendering thee like to me, so long as thou dost offer no obstacle, and what I did during my mortal life, I strive to renew in your soul as long as your pilgrimage endures. Therefore beloved daughter, it is not by thy virtue, but mine, that thou hast so generously combatted, and merited such an abundant grace; now I will visit thee oftener and more familiarly than ever."

The vision disappeared and Catharine remained absorbed with a joy and sweetness that words cannot express; her heart was especially inebriated with the way in which our Lord addressed her: "*Catharine, my daughter!*" When relating to her Confessor what she then experienced, she besought him to employ the same expressions, in order to renew in her soul their ineffable sweetness.

From that moment the heavenly Spouse visited her with a familiarity which would appear incredible, were we ignorant of what has preceded. But the soul that knows by experience that the goodness of God is above all that man can imagine, will see in the following only things very possible and very probable. The Lord appeared to her frequently and remained a long time with her; sometimes bringing with him his holy Mother, sometimes St. Dominic, and occasionally both together; then St. Mary Magdalen, St. John the Evangelist, St Paul and other Saints, separately or in company, according to his good pleasure. But he came alone most commonly, and conversed with her as one friend with another, when on the most intimate terms. She blushingly avowed to me that our Lord recited Psalms with her, while walking in her room, just as two Religious when reciting their Office. The infinite benevolence of God varies his gifts in each of his saints, so that his magnificence may be made manifest in details as in combination.

Since I have mentioned the recitation of the Psalms, I must inform my readers that Catharine knew how to read without having learned from any one. She narrated to me herself, that having resolved to learn to read so as to recite the *Hours* and follow the Offices, she had studied the alphabet with one of her companions. But after having uselessly consumed several weeks in this labor, the thought came to her to obtain from heaven the grace to lose no more time. One morning while engaged in prayer, she said to Almighty God: "Lord, if it be agreeable to thee that I know how to read, in order to be able to recite the Office and sing thy praises, have the goodness to teach me what I cannot learn alone. If not, thy will be done; I will remain without regret in my ignorance, and I will employ with joy, *in meditation*, the time that thou wilt leave me." Before the end of her prayer, our Lord taught her so well, that when rising from her knees, she knew how to read every kind of manuscript, as rapidly and as perfectly as the most highly educated persons. What astonished me the most was, that she read easily but without being able to *spell* her words, when she was asked to do so; she scarcely knew her letters! Catharine at once procured the "Office books," and read all the Psalms and whatever enters into the composition of the canonical hours. She was particularly fond of the Verse and its response. *Deus in adjutorium meum intende*, etc. She translated it and continually repeated it, She soon made such progress in contemplation, that she gradually omitted her vocal prayers, and her ecstacies became so frequent, that she could scarcely recite the Lord's Prayer without being ravished out of her exterior senses, by a heavenly favor which we will relate hereafter

CHAPTER XI.

OF HER MARRIAGE WITH OUR LORD, AND OF THE MIRACULOUS RING THAT SHE RECEIVED.

THE soul of Catharine became daily more enriched with the grace of the Saviour. She flew rather than walked in the paths of virtue, and she conceived the holy desire of arriving at so perfect a degree of faith, that nothing would henceforth be capable of separating her from her divine Spouse, whom her heart aspired alone to please. She therefore besought God to augment her faith, and render it sufficiently strong to resist any and every enemy. Our Blessed Lord answered her, "I will espouse thee in faith." And each time Catharine renewed her prayer, Jesus Christ repeated the same answer. One day, at the approach of the holy season of Lent, when Christians celebrate the Carnival, or a foolish adieu to the viands which the Church is on the eve of prohibiting, Catharine withdrew into her cell there to enjoy her Spouse more intimately by fasting and prayer: she reiterated her petition with more fervor than ever, and our Lord answered her: "Because thou hast shunned the vanities of the world and forbidden pleasure, and hast fixed on me alone all the desires of thy heart, I intend, whilst thy family are rejoicing in profane feasts and festivals, to celebrate the wedding which is to unite me to thy soul. I am going, according to my promise to espouse thee in Faith." Jesus Christ then spoke once more, when the Blessed Virgin appeared; and with his glorious Mother, St. John the Evangelist, the apostle St. Paul, St. Dominic, founder of her Order, and with them the prophet David who drew from his harp tones of heavenly sweetness. The Mother of God took in her holy hand, the right hand of Catharine, in order to present it to her Son, asking Him to deign to espouse her in Faith. The Saviour consented to it with love, and offered her a golden ring, set with four precious stones, in the centre of which blazed a magnificent diamond. He placed it himself on Catharine's finger, saying to her: "I thy Creator and Redeemer, espouse thee in Faith and thou shalt preserve it pure, until we celebrate together in Heaven the eternal nuptials of the Lamb. Daughter, now act courageously; accomplish without fear the works that my Providence will confide to thee; thou art armed with Faith, thou shalt triumph over all thy enemies." The vision disappeared, and the ring remained on the finger of Catharine. *She* saw it, but it was invisible to others! She acknowledged to me, while blushes mantled her cheek, that it never left her, and that she was never weary with admiring it. There was already one Catharine, queen and martyr, who, after baptism, espoused our Lord. We have here a second, who, after many victories won of the flesh and the devil, celebrated also her regal espousals with Jesus Christ.

Let us admire the beauties of her ring, and observe its mysterious meaning. What is there stronger than diamond? it resists everything by its hardness and penetrates the most solid bodies, nothing but lamb's blood can cause it to sparkle. In like manner, the faithful heart triumphs over all difficulties by fortitude, and only yields to the Blood of Jesus Christ. The four precious stones indicate four kinds of purity practised by Catharine, purity of intention, purity of thought, of word and of action. This marriage seems to me to be a confirmation in divine grace; the ring was a visible pledge of it for her, but not for others. Amid the waves of the sea of life, she was destined to save a great number of souls, by confiding them to the succor of heaven and without dreading for herself either shipwreck or tempest. The holy Doctors explain why God often, by a special favor, reveals to his predestinate that they will persevere in his love and in his grace. It is because he wishes to send them into the midst of a corrupt world, for the glory of his Name, and for the salvation of souls. On the day of Pentecost, the Apostles received a striking evidence of their mission; it was also said to St. Paul, "my grace is sufficient for thee." *Sufficit tibi gratia mea.* (II. Cor. xii. 9.) Catharine, although a woman, was to be an apostle in the world and convert many souls; she received a sensible sign of grace in order to accomplish with more courage the divine work that was entrusted to her. What was most surprising in Catharine, is that the token of grace, transient for others, was permanent and ever visible to her, I think that God bestowed it on her because of the weakness of her sex; the novelty of her mission, and the perversity of our time were to present difficulties greater than any other; and it was necessary that she should be continually sustained in her holy undertaking.

With this first part of her history terminates her silent and retired life. We shall see in the second what she did among men for the glory of God and for the salvation of souls. Her guide was always our Lord Jesus Christ, who lives and reigns with the Father and Holy Ghost, world without end. Amen.

SECOND PART.

CHAPTER I.

OUR LORD COMMANDS CATHARINE TO EMPLOY HERSELF FOR THE SAKE OF HER NEIGHBOR.

Our blessed Lord, had lavished on his favorite Spouse the sweetness of his grace. He had exercised her soul in combat and in victory; he had bestowed on her admirable instructions and enriched her with superior virtues. So shining a light was not destined to remain hidden, but to display its rays abroad. The spouse was about to return with interest the talents that the Lord had entrusted to her: "open to me" was said to her, open to me, by thy zeal, the door of souls, so that I may enter; open the way by which my sheep will go to seek pasture. Open to me, for my honor, the celestial treasure of truth and of grace, so as to shed it upon the faithful. "Open to me, my sister," by conformity of nature; my friend, by interior charity, my dove, by simplicity of spirit; my immaculate one, by purity of soul and body. And Catharine responded to this call, yet, she often acknowledged to me that every time that our Lord ordered her to quit her cell and converse with men, she experienced so lively a sorrow, that it seemed to her, her heart must break.

After the mystic alliance that our Lord deigned to contract with Catharine, he gradually introduced her to the "active life." He did not, however, deprive her of his heavenly communications, but on the contrary augmented them, so as to lead her to a higher degree of perfection. Freqnently in his apparitions, after speaking to her of his Kingdom, and revealing to her some of its secrets, after having read or recited psalms with her, he added: "Go quickly, this is the hour of repast, thy parents are going to take their places at the table, thou wilt stay there with them; and then thou wilt return to me." At these words, Catharine would break forth into sobs: "If I have offended thy Majesty, behold my wretched body, punish it immediately, I cheerfully accept every thing; but spare me the grief of being separated from thee, even for one instant, O my beloved! *What will I do at table?* thou knowest full well that I partake of a food that those whom thou commandest me to seek, know not. Is it in bread only that man finds strength? do not the words that issue from thy mouth better impart vigor and energy to the soul of the pilgrim? Thou knowest far better than I, that I fled the society of creatures to find thee, my Lord and my God. And now that I have obtained thy grace, notwithstanding my unworthiness, must I resign this inestimable treasure, to mingle anew in worldly affairs, to fall again into my former ignorance and perchance become odious to thee? Ah no, no, thy infinite goodness will never command any thing which can separate the soul from thee." Sobs would interrupt her, and she would cast herself at our Lord's feet, in hopes of winning his consent to remain. Then our Lord, would speak, I do not say in *these very words*, but in *this meaning:* "Calm thyself, beloved daughter, thou must accomplish all justice, and cause my grace to fructify in thee and in others; far from being desirous of separating from thee, I desire to become more closely united to thee by *charity towards the neighbor.* Thou knowest that my love has two commandments; to love me, and to love thy neighbor, now I wish thee to observe these two commandments. Forget not that in thy youth, zeal for souls, which I had placed and developed in thy heart, went so far as to give thee the idea of disguising thyself so as to become a Friar Preacher, and labor for the conversion of souls. Why, therefore, wonder and complain that I conduct thee where thou desirest to go, and for which thou didst assume the habit of St. Dominic, that zealous founder of an order for promoting the salvation of souls." Then Catharine said, "Lord not *my* will but *thine* be done, I am only darkness and thou art all light; I am nothingness and *thou art;* I am ignorance and thou art the wisdom of the Father; but, Lord, suffer me to inquire how I shall execute thy commands—my sex presents an obstacle, for women have no authority over men, and propriety interdicts frequent relations with them." Our Lord answered, like the Archangel Gabriel, that all things are possible with God! "Am I not he who formed both man and woman? my spirit breathes where it will; to me there is no difference of sex or condition, it is as easy for me to create an Angel as the lowest insect, and a worm of the earth as a new firmament; it is written of me, that I do what I will, (Ps. cxiii. 3.) and naught that the mind can conceive is impossible to me. I know it is humility and not a disobedient spirit that prompts thee to speak thus, and now I wish thee to know that in this age, the pride of men has become so great, especially among such as believe themselves to be learned and discreet, that my justice can no longer endure them, and is about to confound them by a just judgment; but because mercy is the gentle attendant of all my works, I design at first to give them a salutary confusion, in order that they may acknowledge and humble themselves like the Jews and Gentiles when I sent them stupid persons whom I filled with my divine wisdom. Yes, I will give them *women* ignorant and weak by their nature, but prudent and powerful through my grace, to confound their arrogance. If they recognize their folly, if they humble themselves, if they profit by the instructions which I will offer them in these frail but consecrated vases, I will be full of mercy towards them; but should they contemn this salutary disgrace, I will send them so many humiliations, that they will become the scoff of every one. This is the just chastisement which I administer to pride; the more the proud aim at exaltation the lower will I abase them, even beneath themselves. For thee, delay not to obey me, for I wish thee to apear publicly: I will accompany thee on all occasions, I will continue to visit thee and will direct thee in all that thou must do."

After these words Catharine prostrated herself with filial obedience at the feet of our divine Redeemer; she immediately went forth from her cell, joining her family at table as God had commanded her.

Catharine was corporally with creatures but spiritually she never quitted her divine Spouse. All that she saw and heard was burdensome to her; the strength and ardor of her love rendered like long years, the hours that she passed with men, and she returned into her cell as quickly as she could, in order to meet there Him whom her soul cherished: then she would honor him, and adore him with renewed fervor. Catharine who was favored with an ever-increasing desire of being united to the object of her love, took the resolution of receiving him in holy communion as frequently as she could,—and God prepared her daily for the relations she was destined to hold with men for the salvation of souls. When she drew near to her family again, she determined not to remain unemployed, and began anew to devote herself to the duties of the household.

CHAPTER II.

OF SOME WONDERFUL THINGS THAT OCCURRED AT THE COMMENCEMENT OF CATHARINE'S RELATIONS WITH THE WORLD, AND OF HER EXERTIONS IN SUPPLYING THE NECESSITIES OF THE POOR.

CATHARINE resolved in conformity with the will of her divine Spouse, to live in a manner that would render her useful to her neighbor, and capable of inclining him to virtue. She therefore devoted herself to practices of humility, and by degrees consecrated herself to works of charity, without, however, permitting these to interfere with her fervent prayers and extraordinary penances. She performed the most menial services of the house, as sweeping, washing the dishes, and even the work that strictly appertains to the kitchen department. When the servant was sick, she entirely supplied her place, and also found means to attend to her wants during her sickness; yet these so multiplied occupations did not make Catharine neglect her heavenly Spouse. She was so intimately united to him, that no exterior act nor corporal fatigue was capable of disturbing their delicious interior conversations. Her ecstacies became even more frequent. As soon as the thought of Jesus penetrated her mind, the soul appeared to retire from the sensual part, and the extremities became cold, contracted and insensible. During her ecstacies, she was often lifted above the earth, her body pursuing her soul, in order to show the power of the spirit that attracted her.

Knowing that the surest means of pleasing the divine Spouse was to be charitable towards the neighbor, her heart burned with the desire of relieving him in all his wants. But having promised to observe the three Vows of Poverty, Chastity and Obedience, she would no longer dispose of what belonged to others without their consent. She therefore sought her father, and asked him if she might deduct, according to her conscience, the share of the POOR from the riches that God had deigned to accord her family. The father cheerfully consented, because he saw clearly that his daughter was walking in the way of perfection, and he was even so considerate as to announce to every one in the house, the permission he had accorded. "Let no one," said he, "prevent my beloved child from bestowing alms. I grant her full liberty; indeed she may, if she will, dispense all that is in the house." Catharine used almost literally the permission she had received; however, she had the gift of discernment, and gave only to those whom she knew had a real need, and *then* she did not wait for such individuals to ask. She was acquainted with some poor families, in her neighborhood, who were in great distress, but who were ashamed to solicit alms. She therefore imitated Saint Nicholas, rising early in the morning, so as to carry corn, wine and oil, with whatever else was necessary for them. She went unattended to the houses of the unfortunate persons. God would open the door for her in a miraculous manner, while she would shut it quickly and glide stealthily away, having deposited her provisions in the house.

One day as she was sick and suffering from head to foot, and felt that it was impossible for her to rise from her bed, she learned that a poor widow in the neighborhood was in absolute destitution, having not even a loaf of bread for her little children. Her heart bled, and during the whole night she was begging her divine Spouse to render her sufficient corporal strength to go to the relief of this unhappy woman. She arose before daylight, ran over the house, filled a little sack with meal, took a large bottle of wine, a jug of oil, all the aliments that she could find prepared. She succeeded in gathering these articles together into her cell; but it appeared impossible for her to carry them, all at once to the widow's house. She succeeded however in her pious undertaking assisted by a supernatural strength.

Her maladies followed not the order of nature; God governed them according to his will, as we shall see in the sequel. Catharine imitated several times, notwithstanding her infirmities, the matinal charity of St. Nicholas. In the following incidents we shall see how she renewed the beautiful alms of Saint Martin.

One day while she was in the Church of the Friar Preachers of Sienna, a poor man came to beg an alms "for the love of God." She had not at that moment any thing to give him, as she carried neither gold nor silver. She besought the poor person to accompany her as far as the house, promising to assist him as much as she could But he, who was undoubtedly poor in appearance, answered her: "If you have any thing to give me, give it directly, I entreat you, for it is impossible for me to wait." Catharine would not afflict him more, and sought some means of relieving him. Her eyes fell upon a little silver Cross which was attached to one of those little cords trimmed with knots, on which the Lord's Prayer is recited, and called on that account a "*Pater Noster.*" Catharine instantly broke the cord and offered the little silver Cross to the poor person, who joyfully accepted it, and withdrew at once as though he had not come to ask any thing else. The night following, whilst Catharine was praying according to her custom, the Saviour of the world appeared to her, holding in his hand the little silver Cross all enriched with precious Jewels, and he said to her: "Daughter dost thou recognize this Cross?" "Perfectly well," replied Catharine, "but it was not so handsome when it belonged to me." "Yesterday" said our Lord, "thy heart gave it to me, an offering of love, and these precious stones represent that love. And I now promise thee, that on the day of judgment, in presence of the angels and of men, I will return it to thee such as it now is, so that it may become thy glory: and at that solemn moment in which I will manifest the justice and the mercy of my Father, I will not conceal it, and will never permit that what thou hast done for me shall be forgotten." He disappeared after these words, and left Catharine wholly absorbed with gratitude and ready to continue similar alms, as we shall soon see.

Our Lord, ravished with the charity of his faithful Spouse, tempted her, for our example and urged her on to great things. One day *Tierce* having been recited every body left the church; Catharine alone remained with one of her companions to pray longer, and when she descended from the chapel of the Sisters intending to return home, our Lord appeared to her under the form of a young man only half-clad—he appeared to be a stranger and aged about thirty-two or thirty-three. He implored her, in the name of God, to condescend to give him some clothing. Catharine, more and more ardent in alms giving, said to him: "Wait here a moment, my friend, until I return from the chapel, and I will give you what you ask." And going back into the chapel, she took off, without uncovering herself, aided by her companion, a garment without sleeves which she wore under her dress to protect her from the cold, and went joyfully to offer it to the poor person. The latter was not satisfied and said to her: "Madam, you have given me a woollen garment, but can you not also give me something of linen to cover me?" "Follow me," answered Catharine immediately, "and you shall be content." Our Lord followed his Spouse, without any mutual recognition, when they arrived at the house, Catharine ran to the place in which her father and mother put their linen, took two under garments and carried them quickly to the poor mendicant, who appeared still dissatisfied. "But, Madam" said he, "what shall I do with this garment that has no covering for the arms? give me some sleeves and you will have furnished me with a complete suit." This demand, far from importuning Catharine, augmented her zeal. She ran over the whole house in search of sleeves; she found at length hanging on the wall, a new dress belonging to the domestic; she took it down, and hurriedly removed the sleeves and carried them to the man.

But He who tried Abraham, still insisted and said to her: "Now Madam, you have dressed me, and I thank you in the Name of him for whom you did it; but I have at the hospital one of my companions who is in need of clothing; could not you give him some article that I might take to him on your part."

The multiplied demands had not yet chilled the charity of Catharine and she sought the means of clothing also the other necessitous person who was at the hospital. But she remembered that all the inmates of the house, her father excepted, complained of her donations and put what they had under lock and key, so that she might not distribute them unto the poor. She had already given the sleeves that belonged to the domestic who was far from being in good circumstances; she durst not take the whole gown; then she began to examine serious.y, whether she ought not to give the sole dress that she had reserved: charity whispered yes, modesty said no. Charity triumphed over itself, love for souls was victorious over love for the body. She thought that, if she went out not having on any dress, those who might see her would be scandalized, which must be especially avoided. She therefore answered the poor man thus: "See now, good friend, were it possible for me to remain without this dress, I would most cheerfully give it to you; but as I cannot and I do not find any other just now, I pray you not to wish it of me. If I could, I should be delighted to give you all that you request." The poor man smiled, and said to her: "Yes, I see that you give me most cordially whatever you possibly can; farewell." As he was leaving, Catharine fancied that she recognized by certain signs that it was the heavenly Guest who so frequently appeared to her, and who deigned to converse familiarly with her. Her heart was at once troubled and inflamed, but humility persuaded her, that she was unworthy of such a favor and then she continued her usual daily exercises.

The night following, whilst Catherine was praying, the Saviour of the world, our Lord Jesus Christ, appeared to her, under the figure of the destitute man, holding in his hand the garment that she had given him, richly embroidered with pearls and glittering with precious stones. "Beloved Daughter," said the Lord to her, "dost thou recognize this garment?" And when she replied affirmatively, but that she had not given it so richly adorned—our Saviour added: "yesterday, thou gavest me this article with great love; by charity clothed me, and preserved me from ignominy. Now, I will bestow on thee, from my own body, a garment that shall be invisible to men, but perceptible to thee, because it will preserve from cold both thy soul and thy body, until the day in which I will clothe thee with honor and glory before the saints and angels." And immediately he drew from the wound of his adorable Heart a vestment tinged with the purple hue of his precious blood and beaming with light. He put it on her with his own sacred hands, saying to her; "I give thee on earth this vestment with its exclusive right, as a symbol and pledge of the hope of glory that shall be thine in Heaven!" The vision disappeared. The efficacy of this divine garment was such, not only for her soul, but also in reference to her body, that, from that moment, Catharine wore neither in summer, nor in winter, more than one robe and never added to it even in the most severe cold She has even acknowledged to me, that she did not feel cold—her miraculous garment preserved her, so that she did not think it possible for her to require more.

Let us remark the merit of that faithful servant of God. She follows in her secret alms-deed, the footsteps of St. Nicholas, and imitates in giving her very personal clothing, the glorious St. Martin. Not only did our Lord appear to her and return her thanks, but the infallible Truth also gave her a formal promise of an eternal recompense, and bestowed on her a sensible and perpetual sign of the joy her alms had caused *Him*, who is of all alms-givers the best. He also assures her of final perseverance, and distinctly makes known to her the secret of her predestination and the splendor of her reward. He did not accord similar revelations to the Saints that we have mentioned above, and who had done many, very many charitable deeds—such favors are not to be lightly esteemed; they give the soul a certainty of salvation, and an inexpressible joy and comfort. The surety of possessing Heaven excites her to the practice of every virtue; it augments patience, fortitude, temperance, zeal for pious works, with the theological virtues Faith, Hope and Charity. What appeared difficult becomes easy, the soul "can do all things" for the love of Him who discloses to her, a predestination to glory and fortifies her continually. We have already had striking proofs in the relations just given: the proofs are about to become more numerous and more striking.

At another time, Catharine, always inflamed with the fire of compassion, learned that a poor person, who had voluntarily divested himself of his wealth, for the love of God, was on the point of dying with hunger; she desired again "to feed" Jesus Christ in his poor, and filled with eggs a linen sack which she had sewed under her dress. When approaching the residence of the poor person, she paid a visit to a church; as soon as her soul found itself in the house of prayer it rose towards Him, to whom it was continually united; she fell into an ecstacy, losing the use of her senses: her body sunk down precisely on the side which bore the sack filled with eggs, and weighed on it so heavily, as to crush a large thimble of metal that was in the same pocket, into three pieces, whilst the eggs, which charity had deposited therein, suffered no injury; they bore the weight of Catharine during several hours, without their shells being in the least impaired.

Catharine's charity also glorified God by miracles. The following wonderful fact which was witnessed by about twenty persons; I heard from her mother, Lapa from Lysa, her sister-in-law, and from Friar Thomas, her first confessor. At the period in which she used largely her permission to give to the poor whatever she wished, it happened that the wine of a hogshead which the family was using at table was found to be spoiled. Catharine who in respect to wine, bread and all kinds of food, desired to give to the poor, in honor of God, what was *the best* in its kind, drew some good wine from another hogshead, that no one had yet touched, and distributed it daily. This cask, according to its dimensions could suffice for the family, for fifteen or twenty days, by close economising. Before the family had touched it, Catharine had distributed it plentifully during a long time— No one in the house had leave to prevent her. The one charged with the wine-cellar began also to draw from the cask for the common use, and Catharine was not at all remiss on her side; she even augmented her donations of it, presuming there would be less complaint when every one partook of it. Not only fifteen days, but twenty and even a month elapsed, without the hogshead suffering any apparent diminution in its contents. Catharine's brothers and the domestics told this to her father, and all were delighted to see the same wine answering so long the daily wants of the family. Not only it lasted well, but none of them ever remembered to have tasted any so good or so pleasant. The quantity and the quality were equally amazing. Each and all profited by it, without being capable of explaining the phenomenon; Catharine who was alone in the secret of the Benefactor, drew continually and gave to all the poor that she could find; yet the wine continued to flow, and its flavor was unchanged. A second month passed, and a third, and yet there was no difference. At length the vintage-time arrived and casks were to be prepared for the reception of new wine. The persons in charge were anxious to empty the inexhaustible hogshead in order to fill it with the wine that already flowed from the press; but the divine munificence was not wearied, other vessels were prepared and filled, but all were insufficient; then, a young man who was conducting the vintage gave orders to empty that hogshead, and bring it to the wine press; they answered him that on the previous evening, a large vessel full had been drawn, and that the wine was very strong and very clear, and that consequently there must yet remain a considerable quantity. Annoyed at their perseverance, he replied: "Draw out whatever wine may be in it, open the cask, and prepare it for the reception of the new wine, because we cannot wait any longer." They therefore opened the cask, whence on the eve, wine beautfully clear had flowed: but it was so dry, that it seemed an impossibility that any liquid could have been drawn from it in a length of time. Astonishment seized them all: for they remembered the abundance and the quality of the wine which it had afforded, and they verified the extreme dryness of the hogshead from which it had been drawn. This miracle was known to all the city of Sienna; it is attested by the persons then resident in the house of Catharine, and I have mentioned above, the individuals who related it to me.

CHAPTER III.

OF THE WONDERFUL THINGS CATHARINE PERFORMED, WHEN SERVING THE SICK.

CATHARINE was wonderfully compassionate to the wants of the poor, but her heart was even more sensitive to the sufferings of the sick. To relieve them, she accomplished things apparently incredible, but this is no reason for suppressing them, and I shall therefore relate them to the glory of Almighty God. I have, for proof, the written and verbal testimony of Friar Thomas, whom I have already named, of St. Dominic of Sienna, doctor of divinity, and prior provincial of the Roman Province. I could also cite Lapa and Lysa with several respectable ladies who have affirmed the same things to me.

There was at Sienna a poor sick woman named Tecca; her indigence was so extreme, that she was forced to seek in a hospital the remedies she needed, and which she was unable to procure. The hospital in which she entered was barely able to furnish what was strictly necessary. Her disease grew worse and worse, so that the leprosy covered her whole body; the smell arising from her disease repelled every one, so that no person had courage to take care of her, and preparations were made to remove her outside of the city, as is customary in such maladies. When Catharine heard this, her charitable heart was touched; she hastened to the hospital, visited the leper, kissed her, and offered not only to supply all her necessities, but also to become her servant during the remainder of her life. Catharine literally fulfilled her promise, every morning and every evening, she visited the patient in person and gave her whatever was necessary; she contemplated in this poor leper, the spouse of her soul and assisted her in every possible way, and with an indescribable respect and love.

The exalted virtue of Catharine, however, only inspired the leprous woman with pride and ingratitude; this is quite usual with minds destitute of humility, they exalt themselves when they ought to humble themselves, and offer insults in return for benefits that deserve thanks. Catharine's charity and humility rendered Tecca arrogant and irritable. When she saw Catharine so solicitous in serving her, she considered the charitable attentions due to her, and scolded her benefactress with injurious words, when every thing did not conform to her wishes. Often the servant of our Lord, prolonged her morning devotions in the Church and hence came later than usual to the hospital. On such occasions Teeca would display her ill-temper, in phrases like this: "Good morning, my Lady, Queen of Fonte-Branda (this was the name of the section of the city in which Catharine resided:) your Majesty takes pleasure in staying the livelong day in the Church of the Friars; it is *there* you have wasted all this forenoon I am sure, my fine lady: you are never weary of the *dear* Friars!" She strove to irritate her by such words; but Catharine always calm, appeased her in the best way she could, and answered with as much meekness and humility as if she had been her own mother—begging her to be quiet for the love of our blessed Lord: "I have been a little late it is true, but soon all your little wants shall be attended to"—and quickly lighting the fire and putting on water, she would prepare her food, and arrange every thing with such promptitude that the ill-tempered sick woman herself would be in surprise. This continued a considerable time, her patience and zeal never diminishing. Every body was in admiration except Lapa, who complained : "Certainly my daughter you will take the leprosy; I desire that you will not serve that sick person." But she, who placed all her confidence in God, appeased her mother by assuring her that she had nothing to fear, because Providence had confided this work to her, and would never forsake her. Thus, her charity triumphed over all obstacles, and pursued what it had commenced. Satan then had recourse to other means. Our Lord permitted her hands to become covered with leprosy, in order to render the triumph of his faithful spouse the more striking; her fingers which had touched the body of Tecca contracted the infirmity, and it became evident that Catharine had taken her contagious malady. This misfortune did not arrest her, she preferred being covered with leprosy to renouncing her charitable functions; her body she looked upon as dust; she was not anxious concerning what might happen to it, if what she did were agreeable to our Lord. The leprosy lingered a long time, but divine love hindered her from perceiving it. At last He who heals when striking, who exalts in abasing, and who renders all profitable to those who love him, after rejoicing in the courage of his handmaid, would try her no longer. Tecca died, and Catharine happily assisted her in her last agony. Her body was frightful to behold. Catharine carefully washed it, clothed it, exposed it, and buried it herself. When this last act of charity was terminated, the disease disappeared from Catharine's body suddenly; her hands seemed to be whiter than the rest of her person, as though the leprosy had imparted additional delicacy to them. Let us pause and admire the assemblage of virtues which adorned Catharine in this deed. Charity, their Queen, prompted it, humility accompanied it, rendering her the servant of this unfortunate woman; patience led her to support with joy the violence of the leper's temper as well as the disgusts inseparable from that loathsome malady; the strength of her faith shows to her in this diseased subject, the beloved spouse whom she desired to please, and hope never abandoned her, as is shown by her perseverance to the end. A miracle crowns all these virtues, for our Lord healed instantly those hands that had been attacked with leprosy, in serving Tecca during life and after death.

There was also in Sienna, at the time in which Catharine devoted herself to the service of the sick and indigent, a Sister of Penance of St. Dominic, named Palmerina, and who had publicly consecrated herself with all her wealth to works of mercy. Notwithstanding these two reasons for belonging entirely to God, the devil made her his captive. A secret envy and a remnant of pride had inspired her with a profound hatred toward Catharine: not only did she find it disagreeable to see her, but she could not even hear Catharine's name pronounced without being thrown into a paroxysm of vexation; she even denounced her in public, and was so blinded by passion, that she went so far as to calumniate and execrate the devoted servant of God.

Catharine employed all the resources of meekness and humility in endeavoring to calm her, but all these advances were despised. Catharine therefore addressed herself to her divine Spouse as usual; by fervent prayers she "heaped coals of fire on her head," (Rom. xii. 20,) for these prayers soaring like flames towards God, im plored at once his justice and his mercy. Catharine only asked mercy, but God who cannot separate these two attributes, first manifested justice, and then accorded to the prayers of his faithful Spouse a more striking proof of mercy. He afflicted Palmerina's body, so as to heal her soul, and combatted her rude obstinacy by the sweet charity with which he had enriched his Spouse. He also augmented Catharine's zeal for the salvation of others, by revealing to her the ineffable beauty of that soul which was condemned by her own fault, but which she had miraculously saved by her merits and her prayers. Palmerina's illness did not cure this disposition; on the contrary, her hatred only increased. Catharine tried every means of softening it; she frequently proffered her assistance; sought to console her by testimonies of affection, and rendered her all the services she could imagine; but Palmerina obdurately remained insensible to words and deeds prompted by such tender charity; Catharine's eagerness to serve her even seemed to render her odious, and violent hatred at last provoked her to chase Catharine from the house. Then the supreme Judge laid his hand of justice on that enemy of charity! strength suddenly forsook her, and without being able to receive the last Sacraments, Palmerina found herself in presence of death, and of eternal condemnation!

As soon as Catharine learned this, she shut herself in her own apartment and fervently conjured her Spouse not to allow a soul to perish on her account—"Lord," said she, "shall I, a wretched creature prove the occasion of loss to a soul created in thy image? is *that* the good thou wilt use me to effect? no doubt *my sins* have caused the whole, and yet I will continue to claim thy mercy until my Sister sees her error, and Thou savest the soul of that beloved one from death."

Whilst Catharine thus prayed, more with the heart than with the lips, God, so as to excite a still more inflamed desire for succoring that perishing soul, made known to her, Palmerina's faults and the danger that menaced her: and when our Redeemer declared that he could not endure that a hatred so unjust and so implacable should remain without chastisement, Catharine buried herself anew in profound supplication, and implored our divine and merciful Saviour not to suffer the soul of Palmerina to depart until she had been reconciled with God and her neighbor.

Her prayer was so effectual that the patient could not die; her agony endured three days and three nights: all were astonished and suffered on seeing this last combat so prolonged. Catharine was however continually interceding, and the humility of her tears triumphed over the Omnipotent. A ray of light from heaven mercifully penetrated that soul in the midst of her agony, discovered to it this fault, and gave it all the graces necessary for salvation. Catharine knew it by revelation, and hastened to the house. As soon as Palmerina saw her, she bestowed on her every mark of joy and respect; she accused herself of her fault aloud, and died shortly after having received the Sacrament, with signs of the deepest contrition. Our Lord showed this soul as saved, to his spouse. Our Lord then suggested to his beloved Spouse that if He, the source of all beauty was so captivated with the loveliness of souls, as to descend to earth, and shed for them His precious Blood, how much more should we diligently labor for each other, so that a creature so admirable perish not." "If I have exhibited this soul to thee said our Divine Saviour, it is to awaken in thee a more inflamed desire of promoting the salvation of souls, in proportion to the grace that I have given thee."

Catharine thanked our Lord with effusion of heart, and humbly entreated him to deign in future to show her the beauty of the souls who might have relations with her, so that she could become more devoted to their salvation. God granted this favor, saying: "Because thou hast despised the world, to attach thyself wholly to me, who am the perfect Spirit; because thou hast prayed with faith and perseverance for the salvation of that soul; behold I endow thee with supernatural light, which will show thee either the beauty or the deformity of all the souls that thou wilt meet. Thy interior sense will perceive the condition of minds, as thy exterior senses perceive the state of the body. And that will take place not only in respect to persons present, but for all those whose salvation may form the object of thy solicitude and thy prayers, even though they be absent and thou hast never as yet seen them." The efficacy of that grace which God granted her was such, that from that moment, she actually saw more distinctly the souls than the bodies of persons who approached her.

One day I rebuked her in private for not preventing those who approached her from bending the knee before her, she thus answered me; "God is my witness that I frequently do not perceive the actions of those who surround me; I merely occupy myself with their souls, without passing any attention to their bodies." Then I said to her: "Do you perceive their souls?" "Father," answered she, "I acknowledge that my Saviour deigned to accord me that grace, when he heard my prayers, on withholding from eternal flames, a soul that was pre cipitating herself into them by her own fault. He then clearly showed me the ravishing beauty of that soul, and *since* that time, it is rare for me to see any one, without directly becoming acquainted with their interior state." And she added. "O Father, could you but see the beauty of a rational soul, you would sacrifice your life a hundred times, were it necessary, for its salvation. No, naught in this material world is comparable to its beauty." I then requested her to give me a full account of that transaction, and in consequence she gave me the above narrative : *only*, that she softened as far as possible, the injuries which the Sister had offered to her; Others of the Sisters worthy of confidence, who were witnesses of it, acquainted me with their grievousness.

I will add one fact, which will complete these remarks. I frequently served as interpreter between Gregory XI. and Catharine; she did not understand Latin, and the Sovereign Pontiff did not speak Italian. In one of these interviews, Catharine asked why she found in the court of Rome, in which all the virtues ought to bloom, nothing but the contagion of disgraceful vices. The Sovereign Pontiff asked her if it were long since she arrived at the Court, and on being informed that it was merely a few days since, he said to her: "How have you so soon learned what occurs here ?" Then Catharine quitting her humble posture in order to assume an air of authority, which astonished me, pronounced the following words: "I must declare, to the glory of Almighty God, that I have perceived more distinctly the infections of the sins that are committed in the Court of Rome, while yet in my native city, than those even who committed them, and are still daily committing them." The Pope remained silent ; I could not overcome my surprise, and shall never forget the tone of authority, with which Catharine spoke to that great Pontiff.

It often happened to me and to those who accompanied her in journies, to be found in her company in places that we had never seen, and also to see for the first time, persons of honorable and respectable appearance, but, who were in reality addicted to vice. Catharine knew their interior directly, and refused to look at them or give any answer when they addressed us: and if they would insist, she would say: "first, let us purify ourselves from our faults and become delivered from the bondage of Satan, then we will converse about God." She would by this means soon disencumber us of their presence, and we would very soon discover that these persons were plunged in incorrigible profligacy.

The enemy of mankind, beholding the great merit that Catharine was acquiring, and the good she effected in souls, by taking care of the sick, sought new means of turning her from it; but his malice was again defeated. He desired to render sterile that tree planted by the running waters, yet never, on the contrary, did its branches bear more fruit. There was at that time a *Sister of Penance* of St. Dominic, called Andrèa, who was extremely ill with a cancer in the breast which consumed and gnawed away gradually her whole chest; the odor from this wound was so disgusting that it was impossible to approach her without closing firmly the nostrils, and there was scarcely any one to be found that was willing to pay the unfortunate Sister a friendly visit. Directly Catharine knew this, she comprehended that God reserved to her this poor forsaken one; she hastened to comfort her with a cheerful countenance, and offered to assist her so long as that dreadful illness might last. The Sister accepted her offer the more easily as she found herself neglected by all others.

Behold, therefore, the Virgin serving the widow, youth succoring old age, and her who languished with the love of God, devoted to one who languished with the sorrows of earth. Catharine omits no attention, although the stench becomes more and more insupportable; she remains by the bedside continually, using no precaution, uncovers the wound, cleanses it and changes the linens, and never exhibits the slightest repugnance, whatever be the length of time required or the difficulty in the dressing. The patient admires that constancy and fulness of charity in one so youthful. The enemy of all good, irritated at such exalted virtue, has recourse to artifice, worthy of himself. One day as the saint uncovered the wound, a suffocating odor issued from it; her will, reposing on that of Jesus Christ is not moved; but her stomach turns and endangers vomiting. As soon as she perceives it, she becomes angry with herself, reproaching herself with this weakness: "What," said she, "thou art disgusted at thy Sister who is redeemed by the blood of Jesus Christ! mayst not thou also fall sick, and become in even a worse condition—thou shalt not remain unpunished." And immediately, stooping down over the breast of the cancerous woman, she applied her mouth to the ulcer, until she was sensible of having overcome her disgust, and triumphed over that natural revolt. The sick woman cried out: "Cease, daughter, dearest child, I cannot endure that you should thus poison yourself with that horrible corruption." But Catharine would not rise until she had vanquished the enemy, who then left her in tranquillity for a little while. Perceiving that he could effect nothing with Catharine, he charged his batteries against the unhappy patient, who was not on her guard. This sower of tares commenced with inspiring a certain wearisomeness of Catharine's services, and ended at length by changing it into an inveterate hatred. As no one except Catharine, was capable of continuing these cares, she attributed her perseverance to a species of pride, in desiring to do more than others; and as hatred easily believes evil of those that it pursues, this wretched woman, more diseased in mind than body, listened to the devil to such a degree, as at last to suspect Catharine's purity, and to believe that she was committing some great sin, when she was absent. Catharine remained firm as a column; she only saw her Spouse and continued with joy, before his eyes, the work of zeal that she had commenced, strong in patience, she laughed at the enemy whose snares she recognized, and she took delight in provoking his anger by practising charity which is insupportable to him. Then the devil blinded more and more the mind of the old woman, and succeeded in irritating her so far, that she *publicly* calumniated Catharine in the most shameful manner.

These accusations spread abroad among the Sisters, and some of the more advanced who directed the others, came to visit the sick woman and examine whether these reports had any foundation. Andrèa replied whatever the devil suggested to her: the Sisters being extremely provoked, called Catharine, and, after having addressed to her cruel and cutting reproofs, at last asked her how it was possible that she had suffered herself to be seduced and so lose her virginity. Catharine, always humble and patient, contended herself with answering: "I assure you, Ladies and dear Sisters 'hat by the grace of Jesus Christ, I am still a Virgin." And when they renewed this absurd falsehood, her whole defence consisted in repeating: "Indeed I *am* a Virgin"—"Indeed I am a Virgin!"

This circumstance did not change her conduct at all. However her heart grieved at this frightful calumny, she continued to serve with the same love the author of it: but in the secret of her chamber, she took refuge in prayer: "My omnipotent Saviour, my beloved Spouse, thou knowest the delicacy of a female's reputation and how carefully thy spouses should preserve *their* honor from the slightest reproach. For this cause thou didst confide thy glorious Mother to St. Joseph. Thou art acquainted with the efforts of the 'father of lies,' to deter me from what thy love has urged me to undertake; help me then, my Lord and my God, for thou knowest that I am innocent, and suffer not the old serpent to prevail against me." While she thus poured out before God her tears and prayers, the Saviour of the world appeared to her: he held in his right hand a crown of gold enriched with precious jewels, and in his left a crown of woven thorns: "Beloved daughter," said he to her, "know that thou must bear successively, these very different crowns: choose the one that thou dost now prefer. If thou takest the crown of thorns for this life, I will reserve the other for thee after thy death: but if now thou takest the precious one, hereafter thou shalt wear the thorns." "Lord," replied Catharine, "I have long since renounced my own will, and have promised to follow thine in all things: hence I have no choice to make; but if thou wilt have me to answer, during this life, I desire to be conformed to thy blessed Passion, and find my chief delight in suffering with thee." Saying this she took the crown of thorns with both hands, as the Saviour presented it to her, and pressed it on her head with so much violence, that the thorns entered on all sides. She felt the wounds sensibly after the vision, as she herself informed me. Then the Lord said; "I am all-powerful, and if I have allowed this scandal to occur, I can cause it to cease instantly. Complete the work that thou hast commenced, yield not to Satan who would prevent thee; I will give thee a manifest victory over him; all that he has prepared against thee, shall turn to his shame and thy glory." The servant of God remained filled with consolation and with courage.

However, Lapa, her mother, became acquainted with the reports that the sick women had spread among the Sisters; and being quite certain of the innocence of her daughter, she, indignant at the attempts of Andrea, and in great anger said to Catharine: "How often have I begged thee to leave that wicked woman! this is the recompense that she bestows on thee, *dishonor before all the Sisterhood*; if thou servest her again, if thou dost even approach her, I will no longer call thee my child!" This was a new snare of the demon for arresting Catharine; but she, on hearing her mother, kept silent a moment; and then approaching and kneeling before her, she humbly said to her: "My beloved Mother, does the ingratitude of men prevent God from daily exercising his mercy towards sinners? did not our Saviour, accomplish the salvation of the world on the Cross, without heeding the insults offered him? You are so kind dear mother, and you know very well that were I to abandon that sick person, no one would take care of her, and she would die for want of assistance; would we not indeed become the cause of her death? She is deceived by Satan, but God may enlighten her and lead her to acknowledge her error.

She thus appeased her mother, who blessed her, and she returned to the diseased woman, and served as cheerfully, as though she had said nothing against her. Andrea was surprised at seeing no appearance of trouble: she could not deny that she was overcome, and she began to repent interiorly, and much more as she perceived the zeal of her benefactress augmenting daily.

God at length took compassion on that miserable woman and sent her, so as to glorify his Spouse, the following vision: One day as Andrea was in bed, it seemed to her that the moment in which the servant of Jesus Christ entered the room and approached the bed (on which the sick woman was laid,) a great light came down from heaven, surrounded her and filled her with such sweetness and joy, that she, so to speak, forgot her sufferings: she did not comprehend this new state and looked about on all sides, when she saw the countenance of Catharine, so changed and transfigured, that she no longer beheld the daughter of Lapa, but the majestic figure of an Angel, and the brilliancy that surrounded her, enveloped her as a garment. At this spectacle, regret for her fault increased in her heart, with bitter self-reproach for having so basely calumniated so holy a person. This vision which she contemplated with her corporal eyes, lasted a long time, and when it disappeared, it left the sick woman at once sad and consoled. Her sadness was that which according to the Apostle, accomplishes justice. (II Cor. vii. 10.) She instantly asked pardon of Catharine, amid tears and sobs, accusing herself of having sinned against her, and calumniated her. The exterior light which she had seen, illuminated her soul, and caused her to recognize the imposture of the Demon. Catharine embraced the poor patient, and consoled her the best she could, assuring her that she had not for a moment even thought of abandoning her, or retained the slighest ill-feeling towards her: "Beloved Mother," said she to her, "I knew perfectly well that the enemy of our salvation was the originator of those scandals, and that he had deceived you by his grievous malice. I do not accuse *you* but *him*. I thank you on the contrary, for the kind affections which induced you to be so anxious concerning my virtue." After thus comforting her, she administered to her the usual attentions, and quickly returned home so as not to lose time.

But Andréa wholly penetrated with the consciousness of her fault, caused those persons before whom she had calumniated Catharine to be called; she confessed with moans her deep guilt and how fearfully the devil had deceived her; she proclaimed aloud that she of whom she had uttered so much evil, was not only innocent, but that she was a *saint* filled with the Spirit of God, and that she has now a proof of it. And as they demanded an explanation she responded that she had never felt nor comprehended what were spiritual sweetness and consolation before having seen Catharine transfigured before her and environed with light. This testimony increased Catharine's reputation with the public, and the devil who had endeavored to tarnish it, served on the contrary, through the intervention of the Holy Spirit, to glorify it. But our Saint remained as calm in triumph as in trial; she pursued her charitable work, applying at the same time to the study of her own nothingness. He who alone exists by his own power charged himself with honoring her; but the implacable enemy who may be indeed vanquished, but never destroyed, returned to the charge, and determined again to conquer, by the revolt of nature.

One day as the servant of God uncovered the horrible ulcer, to wash it, the infected odor which arose from it, inspired a violent disgust which the devil strove to increase. Her stomach bounded with nausea. This repulse was so much the more painful to her, as, just then, the new victories which she had gained by the grace of the Holy Spirit had helped her to acquire new virtues. Filled with a holy anger against herself, she said: *"thou shalt swallow what inspires thee with such horror!"* and immediately, collecting in a saucer the water in which she had washed what flowed from the wound, she went aside and drank the whole. I recollect that one day, when others related this circumstance in her presence, she said to me, in an undertone: "Father, I assure you, that in my whole life, I never tasted any thing so sweet and so agreeable."

I found in the writings of Friar Thomas, her first Confessor, that the same thing happened to her, when her mouth was applied to the ulcer; she acknowledged to him that she then perceived a delicious odor. In the night that followed this last victory, the Saviour of men appeared to Catharine while she was praying; he showed her the five sacred wounds that he received for our salvation on the Cross. "Beloved," said he to her, "thou hast sustained for me great combats, and, with my assistance, thou hast remained victorious. Never hast thou been dearer or more pleasing to me,—yesterday in particular thou didst ravish my heart. Not only didst thou despise sensual pleasures, disdain the opinions of men, and surmount the temptations of Satan, but thou didst overcome nature, by joyfully drinking for my sake a loathsome, horrible beverage. Well! since thou hast accomplished an action so superior to nature, I will bestow on thee a liquor above nature." And placing the right hand on Catharine's neck, he drew her to the wound of his sacred side, saying to her: "Drink, daughter, that luscious beverage which flows from my side, it will inebriate thy soul with sweetness and will also plunge in a sea of delight thy body, which thou didst despise for love of me." Catharine thus placed at the very fountain of life, applied her mouth to the sacred wound of the Saviour, her soul drew thence an ineffable and divine liquor; she drank long and with as much avidity as abundance; in fine, when our blessed Lord gave her notice, she detached herself from the sacred source, satiated, but still eager, because she experienced no repletion at being satiated, nor pain at still desiring. O ineffable mercy of the Lord, how delightful thou art to those who love thee! how delicious to such as taste thee! Alas, Lord, I, and those who have not experienced it, can not comprehend it; the blind cannot judge of the beauty of colors, nor the deaf the charms of harmony. So as not to be ungrateful, we contemplate and admire, as far as we are able, the great favors thou dost accord to thy Saints, and, although they far surpass us, we thank thy divine Majesty for them in proportion to our strength.

Dear reader, observe the wonderful virtue of Catharine. Admire that inspiration of charity which inclines her to perform an act so repugnant to nature: consider the zeal which influences her, notwithstanding the revolt of her senses; remark that amazing courage that cannot be intimidated by the shocking calumny and odious ingratitude of the sick woman; contemplate, in fine, that soul which derives its strength from God, which praise cannot render haughty, and which gains over the flesh a last triumph, by *drinking* what it shuddered with horror merely to *see!* All this is noble, and there are very few, especially in our day, who would perform similar deeds. But consider, also, the recompense. After Catharine had subdued her thirst at the side of our blessed Redeemer, grace so superabounded in her soul. that her body experienced its effects; it became impossible for her to take even the insignificant amount of nourishment which she took before. I will give a full account of it ere long, but it is time to terminate this important Chapter, which I could not well diminish in length.

CHAPTER IV.

OF HER MANNER OF LIVING AND OF THE REPROACHES WHICH WERE MADE HER CONCERNING HER COMPLETE ABSTINENCE.

THE incomparable Spouse of souls had tried his beloved daughter in the furnace of great tribulations: he taught her to overcome the enemy of souls in every variety of combat, it only remained for him to crown her in a manner worthy of his own divine munificence; but, the souls that she was destined to succor in their pilgrimage, had not yet profited by her virtues as much as the Saviour desired and had promised, and it was requisite that Catharine should remain in the world, receiving in it the pledges of her eternal reward. Our Lord made known by revelation, to his faithful servant the celestial life that she was to lead in this valley of tears.

One day while she was praying in her little chamber, he appeared to her, and announced to her the kind of new miracle that he was going to operate in her: "Learn my sweetest daughter, that henceforth thy life will be filled with prodigies so amazing that ignorant and sensual men will refuse to believe them. Many even of those persons who are attached to thee, will doubt them and fear an illusion caused by excess of love to me. I will diffuse in thy soul such an abundance of grace, that thy body itself will experience its effects and will live no longer except in an extraordinary manner; thy heart shall become so ardent for the salvation of the neighbor, that thou shalt forget thy sex and its reserve: thou shalt no more avoid as formerly the conversation of men, but thou shalt expose thyself to every species of fatigue in order to save their souls; thy conduct will scandalize many who will contradict thee and accuse thee publicly. But be not alarmed, and be not anxious; I will be ever with thee, and I will deliver thy soul from the deceitful tongue and from the lips that speak falsely. Follow therefore courageously, the inspiration which will enlighten thee; for I shall draw, by thy aid, numerous souls from the gulf of hell, and I will conduct them, with the help of my grace, to the Kingdom of Heaven." Catharine heard these words several times, and when our Lord repeated to her: "Fear nothing, be not troubled"—she answered: "Thou art my God, and I am but thy little handmaid: may thy will ever be accomplished, but remember me and incline unto my aid, according to the greatness of thy mercy." The vision disappeared, and Catharine reflected interiorly what that change could be, that was announced to her.

From day to day however, the grace of God increased in her soul, and the spirit of God so abounded within her, that she sung with the Prophet: "For thee my flesh and my heart hath fainted, O God of my heart, and my eternal inheritance." (Ps. lxxii. 26.) and again, "I remember God, and was delighted, and being exercised my spirit swooned away." (Ps. lxxvi. 4.) God therefore inspired her with the thought of receiving her divine Spouse as often as possible in the Holy Eucharist, since she could not enjoy him yet in Heaven—hence she adopted the habit of daily communion, except when hindered by her own indisposition and by the cares which she bestowed on others.

Her desire for frequent communion was so vehement,

that when it was not satisfied she suffered so violently as to become in danger of death. Her body which participated in the joys of her spirit, necessarily shared in the pain attendant on its privations. We shall hereafter dilate on this subject; at present we intend explaining her miraculous way of living, according to her confessions to me, and the writings of her first confessor.

Heavenly favors and comforts so overwhelmed the soul of Catharine after that last vision, that they inundated, so to speak, her body. Its vital functions became so modified, that food was no longer necessary to her, and aliments caused her serious suffering. When she was obliged to take food, she was so incommoded that it would not remain in the stomach—and it would be quite impossible to describe her grievous pains on such occasions. In the beginning, this state appeared incredible to all, even to her relatives and those who were truly attached to her, they called this extraordinary favor from God, a temptation or a snare of Satan. Even her Confessor commanded her to take food daily and not to give heed to any visions that would give her contrary advice.

In vain, Catharine assured him that she was well and strong, so long as she received no nourishment, and became sick and weak as soon as she used it,—he continually prescribed to her to eat; she obeyed through virtue, as far as she was able, but these endeavors reduced her to such a state that fears were entertained for her life. She therefore caused her Confessor to be called and said to him: "Father, if through excessive fasting, I was in danger of death, would you not prohibit me from fasting, so as to prevent me from committing suicide?" "Without doubt" answered her Confessor. "But," resumed she, "is it not as bad to expose one's self to sin by eating as by fasting ? If therefore you see, by the numerous experiments of which you have been witness, that I am killing myself by taking nourishment, why do you not forbid me, as you would forbid me to fast, if the fast produced a similar result ?" There could nothing be said in reply to this reasoning, and her Confessor, who saw the danger to which he was exposing her, said to her: "Henceforth act according to the inspirations of the Holy Ghost, for I perceive that God is accomplishing marvelous things in you."

Catharine suffered excessively from her parents and friends ! Those who surrounded her, measured her words and deeds, not by God's rule, but by the common one, and their own; *they* were in the valley and wished to judge concerning what was on the summit of the *mountain;* they ignored principles, yet would discourse prudently concerning consequences; the brightness of the light blinded them and prevented them from appreciating colors; they disturbed themselves unreasonably and blamed the rays of that radiant star; they wished to direct her whose lessons they could not even understand; night was reproaching day for its splendor ! They secretly accused her, calumniated her under an appearance of zeal, and forced, as it were, her Confessor to deviate from her way. It would be too lengthy to describe the interior trials and anguish of Catharine. Devoted to obedience and self-contempt, she knew not how to excuse herself and durst not resist the orders of her Confessor, and yet she was convinced that the will of God was opposed to that of men; but in the fear of displeasing him, she could not decide to disobey and thus scandalize the neighbor. Prayer was her refuge, and she poured out at the Saviour's blessed feet tears of melancholy hope, humbly supplicating him to deign to make his will known to those who opposed her, above all to her Confessor, whom she dreaded to offend.

She could not say to him, as did the apostles to the chief priests: "It is better to obey God than men." (Acts v. 29.) She would have been answered that the demon transforms himself into an angel of light : that we should not rely on our own prudence, but follow the counsels given. The Lord heard Catharine on this occasion as in others ; he enlightened her Confessor, and changed his opinion; but that did not hinder others thinking ill of her, and failing in discernment. Had they examined attentively, how God had unveiled to her the artifices of Satan; how he had taught her to combat and obtain glorious victories; had they remarked to what a high degree she was endowed with the gift of understanding, and what reason she had to say with the Apostle : "we are not ignorant of its wickedness." *Non enim ignoramus astucias ejus.* (II. Cor. 11.)—they would have observed silence, and not dared, in the imperfection of their knowledge, to exalt themselves above so perfect a master. Little rivulets ought not to change the course of majestic rivers; I have often said this formerly to those who censured Catharine, and I repeat it here, so that certain individuals may profit by it.

But let us return to our subject. The first time that these extraordinary facts occurred we were at the beginning of Lent, and Catharine supported by the grace of God, remained till the feast of the Ascension, without taking any corporeal nourishment, and without any diminution of strength or gaiety. Are not the fruits of the Holy Ghost, charity, joy and peace ? (Gal. v. 22. Did not the Eternal truth say, that man liveth not by bread alone, but by every word that cometh from the mouth of God. (St. Matt. iv. 4,) and "the just liveth by faith." (Rom. i. 17.) On the day of the Ascension she was able to eat, as our Lord had told her, and as she had announced to her Confessor. She ate in effect, bread and vegetables; she then recommenced her fast, and ended by observing it almost continually, interrupting it sometimes only, and at long intervals. Whilst her body fasted, her soul took a more and more abundant nourishment. She approached as frequently as she could, the holy Table, and there derived every time, with ardor, a new supply of graces. Her organs had suspended their functions; but the Holy Spirit, which was acting in her, vivified at once her soul and body, and he that believes in divine things can affirm that her whole existence was supernatural and miraculous.

Often have I seen that feeble body reduced to the last extreme of weakness; but if in the moment that we expected to see her expire, an occasion presented of rendering any honor to God or aiding a soul, not only life returned to her, but with it such wonderful energy, that she walked, acted and performed more than those who were in good health, and without appearing to suffer the slightest fatigue. How explain this fact otherwise than by the action of the Holy Spirit, which sustained simultaneously the soul and body? When she began to live without taking nourishment, her Confessor asked her if she did not sometimes experience an appetite. "God satisfies me so," she answered, "in the holy Eucharist, that it is impossible for me to desire any species of corporal nourishment." And as her Confessor inquired whether she did not at least experience hunger on the days in which she did not communicate, "his sole presence satiates me," said she, "and I acknowledge even that it suffices for me to see a priest that has just said Mass, to be happy."

Catharine was, therefore, at once satisfied and fasting; deprived of all exteriorly, but abundantly nourished in the interior; thirsty in her body, but inundated in her soul, by torrents of living waters, and always when necessary strong and joyous. But the old and tortuous serpent could not endure such a great favor from Heaven, without seeking to empoison it with the venom of envy. He excited against the servant of God, on the occasion of her extraordinary fast, all those who knew her, whether laymen or Religious. We must not be astonished to find that even religious persons were opposed to her. When the self-love of such is not entirely dead, it sometimes arouses a more dangerous jealousy in them than in others, especially when they behold things which are impossible for them to attain. Let us recal the story of the Fathers of the celebrated Thebaide; one of the disciples of St. Macarius, having taken secular clothes, went out and presented himself at a considerable monastery, which was under the direction of St. Pacomius. At the earnest request of the Superior he entered the community; but the austerity of his life, and his extraordinary penances so frightened the other monks that they almost revolted against Pacomius, and came one day to tell him: "that unless he immediately dismissed this monk, they would one and all quit his monastery on that very day." If men who appeared to be almost perfect spoke in this manner, what might we not expect from those of our day?

Every one murmured against Catharine's fast. Some said: No one is greater than our blessed Lord, who ate and drank. His glorious Mother did the same, as well as the Apostles, for their divine Master recommended them to eat and drink what they could find. *Edentes et bibentes, quae apud illos sunt.* (St. Luke, x. 7.) Who can surpass, or even equal them? Others said that all the Saints had taught, by their words and their examples, that we should never be singular in our way of living. Others pretended that all excess is vicious, and that such as fear God ought to avoid it. Others respected her intentions and only said that she was the victim of an illusion. Others again, more coarse and vulgar, calumniated her publicly, and repeated continually that it was a kind of vanity that prompted her to wish to be noticed; that she did not fast really, but fed herself well in secret.

If I did not refute all these rash and absurd judgments, I should think that I was offending God. I pray, therefore, that it be remarked, that if the objection that is drawn from our Lord, the Blessed Virgin and the Apostles be just, it would follow that St. John the Baptist was greater than our Lord himself: for it is said of him in the Gospel that John neither eat nor drank, whilst the Son of Mary on the contrary ate and drank. (Matt. xi. 18.) it would also follow that Anthony, the Macariuses, the Hilariens, the Serapions and many other hermits, who fasted more than the Apostles, consequently surpassed them. If it be objected that John in the wilderness, and the monks in Egypt did not entirely fast, but took from time to time some food, what shall be said of St. Mary Magdalen, who remained thirty-three years in a grotto, without touching any aliment, as is related in history, and the place in which she dwelt also proves, which was, at that time, inaccessible. What shall be said of the saints who also passed considerable time without eating, and who contented themselves for the most part of the time with receiving holy Communion on Sunday. No, let those who are unaware, be informed that sanctity is not measured by fasting but by holy charity: let them know that we should not decide upon things with which we are not acquainted, and also hear the words of incarnate wisdom on this subject. (Luke, vii. 32.) "Whereunto then shall I liken the men of this generation? and to what are they like? They are like children sitting in the market-place, and speaking one to another, and saying: we have piped to you, and you have not danced: we have mourned, and you have not wept?" And our Lord adds. "John the Baptist came neither eating bread nor drinking wine; and you say: he hath a devil. The son of man is come eating and drinking; and you say, that he is a glutton and a drinker of wine." These words of the Saviour refute those who offered the first named objection to Catharine.

As to the second, those who avoid all extraordinary ways, we may easily reply, that if a soul ought not to adopt these ways through an impulse of self-will, she ought to follow them with gratitude, when God deigns to indicate them; she would otherwise despise his grace, and when the Scripture says that the just man ought not to seek what is above him, he adds directly: For many things are shown to thee above the understanding of men. (Eccl. iii. 25.) That is, thou must not be inquisitive concerning things above thee; but if God reveals it to thee, be thankful. This happened in the case of which we are now speaking; the agency of God was manifest and no one had a right to apply the common rule. The servant of God concealed this under the veil of sincere humility, when she answered those who asked her why she took no nourishment: "God," said she, "on account of my sins, has stricken me with this infirmity which prevents me from taking food; I desire to eat, but it is impossible. Ask God, I entreat you to pardon the sins for which I am suffering." As if she had said, God is the author of this and not myself. So as to destroy even the appearance of vanity, she attributed the whole to her sins, and in so doing she did not speak in contradiction with what she thought, because she was persuaded that God permitted the false judgments of men, for the punishment of her faults: she imputed to herself all the ill that happened, and to God alone all the good. This was her rule in every circumstance. What we have just advanced should also serve as a reply to those who recommend the avoiding of extremes. An extreme is never culpable when God indicates it, and in such a case, man ought not to shun it.

As to such as pretend that she was in illusion, I beg them to be so kind as to answer me—if hitherto Catharine had perfectly triumphed over the snares and temptations of the demon, is it probable that she would have yielded in this circumstance? But admit this, who could preserve the strength of her body: if we say that the devil could do it, who could have maintained her mind in joy and peace, when it was deprived of all interior comfort? *These*, are fruits of the Holy Spirit which the demon *never* could produce; it is written that "*the fruits of the Holy Ghost* are *charity, joy* and *peace.*" (Ep. Gal. v. 22.) and it is impossible to attribute them to the enemy of salvation. May we not on the contrary suspect him who would say the opposite, of being the sport of the evil spirit? If the devil were capable of seducing *her* who had so frequently defeated his wiles in her own soul and in the souls of others, *her* whose body lived and was sustained in a supernatural manner, *her* whose soul enjoyed continual peace and spiritual joy, how much more rational is it to presume that *he is deceived* to whom none of these circumstances have occured. It is highly probable that if any one be deceived, it is not she who had been preserved previously. In fine it is better to answer nothing to skillful calumniators, they merit only the contempt of upright persons. What degree of virtue would they not attack; those who resemble them, called our Blessed Saviour, a demon, why should they not defame his faithful servant.

Catharine full of the spirit of prudence and desirous of imitating her divine Master, remembered that when St. Peter asked him for the two didrachmas that he was obliged to pay for the tax, he proved to him that he was exempt; but that he added: "But that we may not scandalize them, go to the sea, and cast in a hook: and that fish which shall first come up take; and when thou hast opened its mouth, thou shalt find a stater; take that, and give it to them for thee and me." (Matt. xvii. 26) Catharine was willing to appease their murmurs and determined that every day, she would go once and take a seat at the common table, and endeavor to eat. Although she used neither meat, nor wine, nor drink, nor eggs, and did not even touch bread, what she took or rather what she tried to take, caused her such sufferings that those that saw her, however hard hearted they were, were moved to compassion: her stomach could digest nothing, and rejected whatever was taken into it; she afterwards suffered the most terrible pains and her whole body appeared to be swollen; she did not swallow the herbs which she masticated, she only drew from them their juice and rejected their substance. She then took pure water to cool her mouth; but every day, she was forced to throw up what she had taken, and that with so much difficulty, that it was necessary to assist her by every possible means.

As I was frequently witness of this suffering, I felt an extreme compassion for her, and I counselled her to let men talk, and spare herself such torture; she answered me with a smile: "Is it not better to expiate my sins at present, and not be punished during all eternity? The judgments of men are very profitable to me, since they cause me to avoid infinite pains by enduring these transient ones; no! I certainly ought not to shun God's justice, and the great grace he accords me of allowing me to make satisfaction in this world." She was so convinced that she was thus paying a debt of justice to God, that she said to her companions: "Come let us do fit justice to this miserable sinner." In this way all the persecutions of men and all the attacks of Satan contributed to her perfection.

One day as we were conversing together of God's graces, she said to me: "Did we but know how to use the graces that God bestows on us, we would profit by all that happens to us. In favorable events or in contradictions, say always: 'I must reap something from this.' were you to act thus, you would very soon be rich." Alas! how much I might have profited by this lesson and numerous others. But you, my reader, do not imitate me, but meditate her instruction and follow her example. I entreat the Author of all good to enlighten you, and grant me also light to imitate this holy soul with courage and perseverance, with this I terminate this chaper, in which I have just told what I learned from Catharine herself or the Confessor that preceded me.

CHAPTER V.

OF CATHARINE'S WONDERFUL ECSTACIES AND OF THE GREAT REVELATIONS WHICH SHE RECEIVED FROM GOD.

Our Lord, who had bestowed on his Spouse a corporal life so extraordinary, also treated her soul in a marvelous manner, and favored it with ineffable consolations; her physical strength was supernatural and had its source in the abundance of grace, that she received; hence having spoken of the prodigy of her material existence, it is suitable also to speak of the miracles by which her soul was enriched. From the moment in which this holy virgin allayed her thirst at the wounded side of our Lord, grace was so abundant and supreme in her soul, that she was, we may say, in a continual ecstacy. Her mind was so constantly and intimately united to her Creator, that the inferior part of her being ordinarily ceased its functions. A thousand times we have been witnesses of it: we saw and touched her arms and hands, so strongly contracted that they could have been more easily broken than their position changed. Her eyes were entirely closed, her ears heard no noise, however great it might be, and all her corporal senses became powerless. And all this will not surprise, if attention be given to what follows. God began from that time to manifest himself to his Spouse, not only when she was alone, as formerly, but in public, when she walked, or when she was remaining tranquil; and the fire of love that inflamed her heart was so great, that she told her Confessor that it was impossible to find expressions to depict what she experienced.

One day, in the fervor of her prayer, she said with the Prophet: "Create within me O God a new heart," etc. And supplicated our Lord to condescend to take away her own heart and her own will. It seemed to her that her Spouse presented himself to her, opened her left side, took out her heart and carried it with him, so that in reality she no longer perceived it in her breast. This vision was striking and her attendant symptoms agreed with it so well, that when she spoke of it to her Confesssor, she assured him that she had really *no heart.* Her Confessor began to laugh, and rebuked her for saying any thing of the kind, but she only renewed her assurance. "Really, Father," said she to him, "as far as I can judge of what I experience in my person, it seems to me that I have no heart. The Lord appeared to me, opened my left side, drew out my heart, and went away." And, as her Confessor declared to her that it would be impossible to live without any heart, she answered that nothing was impossible with God, and that she had a heart no longer. Some days later, she was in the Chapel of the Church of the Friar Preachers, in which the *Sisters of Penance* of St. Dominic assemble: she remained there alone so as to continue her prayer, and was disposing herself to return home, when on a sudden she saw herself environed with a light from Heaven, and amid this light, the Saviour appeared to her, bearing in his sacred hands a Heart of vermillion hue and radiating fire. Deeply affected with this presence and this splendor, she prostrated herself on the ground. Our Lord approached, opened anew her left side, placed in 't the Heart which he bore, and said to her: "Daughter, the other day I took thy heart, to-day I give thee mine, and this will henceforward serve thee." After these words he closed her breast; but, as a token of the miracle, he left there a cicatrice that her companions have frequently assured me they had seen, and when I questioned her pointedly on this subject, she avowed to me that the incident was really true, and that from that period she had adopted the custom of saying : "My God, I recommend to thee thy Heart."

When Catharine had obtained that heart in so sweet and wonderful a manner, the abundance of grace which her soul possesssed, rendered her exterior actions more and more perfect and multiplied the divine revelations in the interior. She never approached the altar, without seeing some beautiful vision superior to the senses, above all when she received holy communion. She often perceived in the priest's hands a new born infant, or a lovely youth, sometimes a furnace of fire, into which the priest seemed to enter at the moment in which he consumed the adorable Eucharist. Commonly she perceived so delicious and penetrating an odor, when she received the sacred Host, that she was on the point of swooning away. As soon as she approached the Holy Sacrament of the Altar, an ineffable joy was awakened in her soul, and caused her heart to beat so violently, that persons who surrounded her could distinctly hear it. Friar Thomas was advertised of this, and being her Confessor, he verified this circumstance with great care and affirmed it in his writings. This noise, occasioned by the beating of the heart, did not at all resemble any thing that could have been produced by the organs; it was something singular and supernatural, effected solely by the power of the Creator. Did not the Prophet say—"My heart and my flesh shall exult in the Lord." *Cor meum et caro mea exultaverunt in Deum vivum.* (Ps. lxxiii. 8.) The Prophet styles God the living God, because that agitation, that trembling which comes from him, purifies man, instead of putting him to death.

After that wonderful exchange of hearts, Catharine appeared to herself to have undergone an amazing change: "Father," said she to her Confessor, "do you not perceive that I am no longer the same: I am completely changed: Oh! did you but know what I experience! *No*,—certainly, if it were comprehended what passes within my soul, there would be no harshness nor pride that could resist it. All that I can say falls short of reality." She sought however to give an idea: "My soul" said she, "is so inebriated with joy and delight, that I am astonished that it remains in my body. Its ardor is so great, that external fire is as naught in comparison with it; it seems to me that I should find refreshment in *that*. And this ardor operates in me such a renovation of purity and humility, that I feel as though I had returned to my fourth year of age. The love of the neighbor also augments in me to such a degree, that it would be my greatest pleasure to die for any one." All this she told her Confessor in secret, and concealed it as far as possible from others. These confidential interviews display the abundance of grace that the Lord poured into the soul of his servant. If I were to extend the subject, I should fill volumes; but I limit myself to citing some facts which prove more evidently the sanctity of Catharine. Among these facts, I cannot pass in silence the admirable visions which she received from Heaven. One day the King of kings and the Queen his Mother, appeared to her with St. Mary Magdalen, to console and fortify her. Our Lord said to her: "What wilt thou · which wilt thou choose, *thine* or *mine*?"

Catharine wept and humbly replied, like St. Peter; "Lord, thou knowest what I will, thou knowest that I have no other will than thine, and that thy Heart is my heart." Then the thought was suggested to her that Mary Magdalen gave herself totally to our Lord, when she bathed his sacred feet with her tears; and as she felt the sweetness and the love which that Saint then experienced, her eyes remained fixed upon her. Our Lord to correspond to her desires, said to her. "My beloved daughter, in order to sustain thee, I give thee, Mary Magdalen for mother; thou canst address thyself to her in all assurance, I charge her with you in a special manner." Catharine was profoundly moved to thanksgiving and recommended herself with fervor to Mary Magdalen; she humbly implored her to watch over her salvation, since the Son of God had entrusted her to her care. From that moment she enjoyed a tender devotion towards that Saint, and alwaays called her Mother. There is, it appears to me, a signification in these relations with Mary Magdalen that we ought to observe. That Saint passed thirty-three years on a rock, without taking any nourishment and in continual comtemplation; those years represent the life of our Lord upon earth; Catharine, from that apparition, until her thirty-third year, (in which she died,) was so absorbed in divine contemplation, that she had no need of any aliment and lived by the graces that superabounded in her soul. Mary Magdalen, seven times a day was borne towards heaven by Angels, and beheld the secrets of God; Catharine was continually ravished in celestial contemplation, in order to praise God and the Angels, and her body was often raised above the earth, in presence of a multitude of witnesses. Hence she saw, as I will relate, admirable things while in those ecstacies, and she sometimes expressed during them most sublime truths.

I saw her one day ravished out of her senses, and I heard her speaking in an under-tone; I approached her and heard her perfectly say in Latin "*Vidi arcana Dei,*" "I saw the secrets of God," she added nothing to this phrase, but continually repeated, "I saw the secrets of God." Long after, when she was restored to herself she still repeated the same words; I wished to know why: "Mother," said I, to her, "why pray, do you constantly repeat the same words, and not explain them to us by speaking to us as usual." "It is impossible for me" said she "to say anything else, or to say it otherwise." "But why? you are accustomed to tell us what God has revealed to you, when we do not interrogate you, why do you decline answering, when we inquire of you." "I should reproach myself" said she to me, "in undertaking to express to you what I saw, as guilty of vain words: it seems to me that I should blaspheme God and dishonor him by my language. The distance is so broad between what my spirit contemplated, when ravished in God, and whatever I could describe to you, that I should think that I was falsifying, in speaking to you of them. I must therefore not attempt their description; all that I can say is, that I saw ineffable things!"

It was quite natural that Providence should unite Catharine and Mary Magdalen by the ties of mother and daughter, because they so resembled each other in their *fasts,* their *love* and in their *contemplations,* When Catharine spoke of this favor, she merely said, that a sinner had been given for daughter, to a saint that had formerly sinned, so that the mother, by remembering the fraility of nature, and God's plentiful mercy, might compassionate her daughter's weakness and obtain her pardon.

Brother Thomas, her first Confessor, in the notes that he left concerning his vision, relates that it seemed to her that her heart entered into our Lord's side, to be united and blended with his Heart. She felt her soul dissolved as it were, in the flames of his love, and cried out within herself: "My God! thou hast wounded my heart! My God! thou hast wounded my heart!" Friar Thomas says that this apparition took place in 1370, on the feast of St. Margaret—virgin and martyr. The same year, on the day following, St. Laurence, her Confessor, dreading that the priests who were celebrating Mass might be disturbed by her sighs and her sobs, recommended her to subdue and conceal them as much as possible, when she would be near the altar. The obedient Catharine remained apart and besought God to make known to her Confessor, the difficulty of retaining these exterior marks of the love of God; her Confessor declared that she was so perfectly heard, that he declined ever making her any similar recommendation again. I presume that it was through humility, that he would not say any more, and that he learned by a happy experience, how impossible it is to suppress within one's self such transports. Catharine, thus remote from the altar, experienced a burning desire for receiving the holy Communion; her heart cried loudly and her lips softly: "Ah! would that I could receive the body of our Lord Jesus Christ!" The Saviour to satisfy her desire appeared to her, and approaching, suffered her to apply her mouth to the wound of his sacred side, permitting her to content her desire for his sacred body and blood. Catharine eagerly sought the blessed source and drew long-drawn draughts.

The sweets which then filled her soul were so excessive, that she believed she would really suffer death from their exquisiteness, and when her Confessor asked her to describe what she experienced, she replied to him that it would be impossible for her to give him to understand it

There also happened to her a circumstance quite wonderful, in the same year, on the feast of Saint Alexis: whilst she was in prayer the night preceding the festival, and sighed interiorly to receive holy Communion, it was revealed to her that she *should* receive on the morrow. She was often deprived of this favor, through the neglect or fault of the Brethren and Sisters who at that time directed the Congregation. As soon as she had received this promise, she supplicated our Lord to condescend to purify her soul, so as to render it more worthy of so great a Sacrament.

Immediately, she felt descending on her soul, as it were, a rain of blood mingled with fire, and this rain washed her soul so completely that it penetrated to her very body, and banished not only the stains but even the first principles of evil. When daylight dawned, the sickness which she was enduring at that moment was so aggravated, that it appeared unreasonable to think of taking a single step. But Catharine aware of what had been promised her, put her trust in God, arose and directed her steps towards the Church, to the great astonishment of every one.

When she arrived there and had taken a place in a chapel beside the Altar, she remembered that her Superiors had not allowed her to receive the Communion indiscriminately, from the hands of all those who might celebrate Mass: she therefore desired that her Confessor might come to say his Mass at the Altar where she was praying God showed her how much he took pleasure in satisfying her desires. Her Confessor, in his notes which he left, says that he did not intend celebrating Mass on that day, and that he was quite ignorant of her arrival; but grace suddenly touched his heart and gave him such an attraction for the holy Mysteries, that he yielded without delay, and went precisely to the altar at which Catharine awaited him, although it was not the one that he habitually used. There he found his spiritual daughter who asked him for the holy Communion, and he comprehended that he was the instrument of Providence; he therefore celebrated the Mass and gave Catharine the holy Communion. When she advanced towards the altar, her face was red, shining, and bathed in tears and perspiration; she received the Holy Communion with a devotion that deeply moved her Confessor, and filled him with admiration. Then she remained totally absorbed in God, lost in the inebriation of his heavenly communications, and during that day, even after having recovered the use of her senses, she remained incapable of utterance.

On the morrow, her Confessor asked her what had happened to her at the moment of receiving holy Communion, when her countenance was so red. "Father," said she to him, "I know not of what color I was, but I assure you that at the instant in which I partook of the Holy Eucharist, my senses discerned nothing corporal or colored; but my soul contemplated a beauty, relished a sweetness that no expression can render. What I beheld so attracted me, that things of earth seemed to me but emptiness and dust; and this, not only of wealth and sensual pleasures, but also of the enjoyments of the mind and heart. I implored God to deprive me of them completely, so that I might only please him and possess him.

I entreated him to take away *my* will and give me *His*, and he in mercy heard my prayers; for thus he answered me: 'Dearest daughter, I give thee my will, and this shall be the proof of it, that no exterior event can trouble thee or change thee.'" This promise God fulfilled; all who were acquainted with her can testify to it, from that moment Catharine was satisfied in every circumstance and occurrence, and no event however contradictory ever disturbed her.

Catharine said to her Confessor, on this occasion: "Father, do you know what our Lord did to-day in my soul? He acted as a tender mother towards her much-loved babe, she extends her arms from a little distance so as to excite a desire, and when her son has wept a few instants, she smiles, siezes him, clasps him closely to her heart, and then satisfies his craving thirst. Our blessed Lord did the same with me; he showed me in the distance the wound of his side; the desire that I felt to cement my lips to it excited me to burning tears; he laughed during some moments of my grief; then he hastened to me, and took my soul in his arms, and placed my mouth upon his sacred wound, and then my soul was able to satisfy its desires, to hide itself in his sacred breast, and there find heavenly consolations. Oh! did you but know, you would be amazed that my heart is not consumed with love, and that I yet *live* after experiencing those holy ardors!"

In the same year, on the eighteenth of the month of August, God manifested his power again, in Catharine. She communicated in the morning, and, at the moment in which the Priest, holding the sacred Host, invited her to say: "Lord, I am not worthy thou shouldst enter" into my heart, etc., she heard a voice answering: "And

I, I *am* worthy of entering into thee." When she received the Communion, it seemed to her, that, as the fish which is in the water is penetrated by the water, her soul was in God, and God in her soul. She was so absorbed in her Creator, that she could scarcely return to her cell; she laid down on the planks that served as her bed, and remained there a long time motionless; then her body was raised in the air, and remained there without any sort of support. Three persons, whose names I will give, were witnesses of that prodigy and have affirmed it. At length her body lowered to the bed, and she began to say in a low voice such sweet and admirable things, that her companions, on hearing them, could not restrain their tears. She afterwards prayed for several persons,—she named some of them, her Confessor among others, who was then in the Church of the Friar Preachers, and who was not thinking of anything capable of exciting him to a particular fervor. He wrote, himself, that he was at the moment in nowise disposed to experience sensible devotion. But suddenly while she was praying, (it being unknown to him,) a wonderful change was effected in his soul; he became wrapt in an extraordinary fervor such as he had never experienced, and he examined his own dispositions to learn whence came this grace. Amid these reflections, one of Catharine's companions came, by chance, to speak to him, and she said to him: "Father, at such an hour Catharine prayed most fervently for *you*." Then the Confessor understood why, at that very hour, he had experienced such a special devotion. He then questioned the person more particularly, and was informed by her, that, in the prayer for him and others, Catharine had asked of God the promise of their eternal salvation. She had stretched forth her hands saying:

"Promise me that you will grant it." And whilst her hand was extended, she appeared to feel a sharp pain which obliged her to exclaim, with a sigh: Praise be to our Lord Jesus Christ! She was accustomed to this aspiration in her most poignant sufferings. Then her Confessor went to see her, and required her to narrate the whole vision. She was obliged to obey, and after telling what we have related above, she added: "When I implored your eternal salvation with earnestness, God promised it to me, but I desired to retain a testimony of it, and I said to him: 'Lord, grant me a token of what thou wilt do,' and he replied: 'Reach hither thy hand.' I extended my hand; he took a nail, and putting the point in the middle of my hand, he pressed on it with such power, that it seemed to me that my hand was transpierced; I felt just such a pain, as it seems to me, would be felt, if a nail had been driven with a hammer. Hence, thank God, I now have his holy stigma in my right hand; no one sees it, but I feel it very sensibly and suffer from it continually."

In continuation of the same subject, I will here relate what occurred a long time after, at Pisa, and in my presence. When she came to this place I, with certain other persons, accompanied her. She received hospitality at the house of an inhabitant, near the the little Church of St. Christina. On Sunday I celebrated Mass there, and gave her the holy Communion. She remained afterwards a long time in ecstacy, according to her custom; her soul which sighed after her Creator, separated itself, as much as it could, from the body. We waited until she had resumed her senses, in order to receive some spiritual consolations, when on a sudden we saw her body that was prostrate on the ground, rise a little, kneel, and extend its hands and arms. Her countenance was inflamed; she remained a long time motionless and with her eyes closed. Then, as though she had received a deathly wound, we saw her suddenly fall, and resume a few moments after the use of her senses. She sent for me and said to me in a low tone: "Father, I announce to you that, by the mercy of our Lord Jesus Christ, I bear his sacred stigmata in my body." I answered her, that I suspected after what passed in her ecstacy, and I asked what our Lord did to her. "I saw," said she, "my crucified Saviour who descended upon me with a great light; the effort of my soul to go forth to meet its Creator, forced my body to arise.

"Then from the five openings of the sacred wounds of our Lord, I saw directed upon me bloody rays which struck my hands, my feet and my heart. I understood the mystery, and cried out: Ah! Lord my God, I entreat thee, that these cicatrixes may not appear exteriorly on my body. Whilst I was speaking, the bleeding beams became brilliant, and reached in the form of light, these five places on my person, my hands, my feet and my heart." Then I said to her, did no beam of light reach your right side? She replied to me: "No, on the left side and directly above the heart. The luminous line that emanated from the right side, did not strike me obliquely but directly." "Do you feel," said I, "a sharp pain in each of those places?" she then answered me, heaving a deep sigh: "I feel at these five places, and especially in my heart, a pain so violent, that without a new miracle, it appears to me impossible to live in this state."

These words filled me with grief, and I examined whether I could observe any signs of her grievous sufferings. When she had finished what she had confided to me, we went out of the chapel, in order to repair to the house where she resided. Scarcely had we arrived than she retired into her apartment, and fell unconscious. We collected around her, and seeing her in this state we all wept, and feared losing her, whom we loved in the Lord. We had frequently witnessed her in ecstacies which deprived her of the use of the senses, and which weighed down her body, under thanksgiving, but we had never seen her in such a profound suspension of the vital powers. A little after, she came to herself and repeated to me that she was certain, that if God did not come to her aid, she would soon die. I immediately assembled her spiritual children and I conjured them with tears, to ask with united prayers that God would spare us yet a while our beloved Mother and mistress, and not leave us orphans amid the tempests of the world, before we were strengthened in virtue. All promised with generous hearts, and went to her dissolved in tears and said: "O Mother we know that you languish for the presence of your Spouse; but your recompense is secured. Rather take compassion on us; we are yet too weak to be abandoned to the fury of waves. We know that your beloved Spouse refuses nothing to the ardor of your prayers and we entreat you to ask him not to deprive us of your presence yet, because we may be lost if you cease to conduct us. We ask it ourselves with all our strength; but alas! we feel that we are unworthy to be heard; you so ardently desire our salvation, obtain for us what *we* cannot obtain." She replied to our tears and lamentations: "It is long since I have renounced my own will, and I have no wish for myself nor for others except what God wills. I desire your salvation with my whole soul, but I know that He who 's the salvation of all, can secure it better than any creature whatsoever; therefore let his will be accomplished in all things. However I will cheerfully ask that he will do what is for the best." On hearing these words we remained in the deepest affliction—but Almighty God despised not our tears. On the following Saturday Catharine sent for me, and said: "It appears to me that the Lord is disposed to grant your petition, and I trust that you will soon be satisfied." All happened as she had said. On the following day, Sunday, after having received holy Communion she fell into an ecstacy, as on the preceding Sunday; but her body, instead of appearing reduced under the divine action seemed on the contrary to resume its vigor. Her companions were astonished at not seeing her suffer as much as in her other ecstacies; she appeared rather to revive and renovate her strength by a natural slumber. I told them, that I hoped according to the promises she had made to me yesterday, our tears which had implored God for her recovery, had gone up favorably before God. She was hastening to join her Spouse but it was necessary to retrace her steps, in order to assist us in our misery. In effect, when she resumed her consciousness, she appeared so strong that no one doubted that she had been heard. O Father of mercies! what wilt thou not do for thy faithful servants and thy beloved children, if thou dost compassionate with so much bounty those who have offended thee! So as to be more certain of what had transpired, I said to her: Mother, do you continue to suffer the same anguish in the wound that you received? She answered—"The Lord has granted your prayers, to the great regret of my soul. Not only my wounds do not cause my body to suffer, they sustain and fortify it, I see, that what formerly weakened me, now relieves me."

I have recounted these details to collect them with other celestial favors received by this holy soul, and I add that it must be remarked that sinners who pray for their salvation, are heard by Him who wills in his love, the salvation of the whole world.

Were I to recount all Catharine's ecstacies, time rather than materials would fail me. I therefore hastened to arrive at a circumstance which surpasses all the others, and which will terminate this chapter. I found *four* written books of Friar Thomas her Confessor, entirely filled with her admirable visions and revelations the most sublime. Sometimes our Lord introduced her soul into the wound of his side, and initiated her into the mysteries of the adorable Trinity: sometimes his glorious Mother imparted refreshing beverage to her from her virginal breast, and filled her with unspeakable delight; and again Mary Magdalen came to converse familiarly with her, and related to her the divine communications which she received seven times a day in the desert. Sometimes the three came together to pay her a friendly visit, and infused into her soul ineffable consolations. Other saints did not neglect her, particularly Saint Paul, whose name she never heard pronounced without evidencing a visible delight. St. John Evangelist, sometimes St. Dominic, frequently St. Thomas Aquinas and still oftener the blessed Agnes of Monte Pulciano, whose life I wrote twenty-five years ago. It had been revealed to her that she would be her companion in Paradise, as we shall see in the sequel. But before giving my promised narration, I ought not, for the utility of my readers, pass in silence, a circumstance relative to St. Paul. Catharine had an ecstacy on the day of that Saint's conversion, and her spirit was so absorbed in the contemplation of heavenly things, that during three days and three nights her body remained insensible; several persons present thought that she was dead, or at the point of death. Others better informed, believed that she was ravished with the Apostle to the third heaven. When the ecstacy had terminated, her mind remained so filled with the remembrance of what she had seen that she returned with difficulty to things of earth, and remained in a kind of slumber or ebriety from which she could not be aroused. In the mean while, Friar Thomas, her Confessor, and Friar Donato of Florence, determined to pay a visit to a venerable monk of the Order of Hermits, who resided in the country. They first came to see Catharine, whom they found in her holy somnolence and all inebriated with the spirit of God. To try to awaken her, they said "We are going to visit the Hermit, who lives out in the country—will you come with us?" Catharine, who liked such pilgrimages, answered *yes*, in the midst of her drowsiness. But scarcely had she uttered this word, than she began to repent of it, as of a falsehood. The grief that she suffered, restored her completely to her senses, and she mourned this fault as many days and nights as she had been in ecstacy. "O the most wicked and guilty of women," said she to herself "is it thus thou dost recognize the graces that God's infinite bounty has just granted thee; is it thus thou dost profit by the verities that thou hast learned from heaven! Have the sublime instructions of the Holy Ghost only taught thee to lie, when returning to earth. Thou knowest full well, that thou hadst no intention of acccompanying those Religious, and thou didst answer them, '*yes.*' Thou hast told a falsehood to thy Confessor and to the fatners of thy soul; what a grievous and aggravated fault!" She remained without drinking or eating as long as her ecstacy had endured

Let the Reader here remark how "admirable are the ways of God, and how worthy to be praised." That the sublimity of her revelations might not swell her with pride, God permitted Catharine to fall into this deceit, if we may call *falsehood*, a word without intention of deceiving and without attaching any importance to it; this humiliation served to induce her to be more vigilant over the treasure entrusted to her, and her body which had been so to speak, oppressed by the elevation of the mind, was restored in a manner by its abasement. Although the joy of the soul is sensible to the body, on account of their intimate union, still the ravishment to the third heaven, that is to say, to the intellectual vision, so deprives the body of its particular life, that a new miracle is necessary to preserve it from death. It is certain that the act of the understanding does not require the mediation of the body, except to represent to itself the immaterial object; but if this object presents itself supernaturally to the mind, by the omnipotent effect of grace, the understanding finds the plenitude of its perfection in Christ and endeavors to unite itself to him, by abandoning the body. Sometimes the Dispenser of all good elevates the intelligence that he created, by showing to it his light; sometimes he humbles it by permitting some fall, in order to exhibit to it at once the divine perfection and its own weakness He thus sustains it in a happy mean, which saves it and conducts it through the storms of this world to the port of a blessed Eternity, "for virtue is perfected in weakness." (I Cor. xvi. 9.) and also, *Ne magnitudo revelationum extollat me datus est mihi stimulus carnis meæ.* (I Cor. xvi. 7.) To return to our subject, Catharine did not disclose to any one, not even to her Confessor as was usual with her, what she beheld in this ecstacy, because as she afterwards told me, she could find no expression for rendering things, which according to St. Paul, it is not permitted to man to recount: but the ardor of her heart, the continuity of her prayer, the efficacy of her teaching, proved sufficiently that she had seen heavenly secrets which none can understand without witnessing them.

At the same time, she told her Confessor, who transferred her relation to writing, that St. Paul, the Apostle, had appeared to her and warned her to apply continually to meditation. She obeyed with earnestness. On the vigil of the Feast of St. Dominic, while she was praying in the church she received great revelations concerning St. Dominic and several saints of his Order. These revelations or visions were so vivid, that she often thought that she still saw them when she was describing them to her Confessor; this was a proof that God wished her to make them known for the benefit of the faithful. On that day, therefore, a little before Vespers, whilst she was receiving these revelations, Friar Bartholomew of St. Dominic, of Sienna, happened to enter the church. He is now a doctor in theology; he was then the friend of Catharine's Confessor, who placed great confidence in him also, and took him for her Confessor when her own was absent. She was aware of his arrival more by an effect of her mind than of her exterior senses; she arose directly, and went and informed him that she had something to communicate to him. When they had gone aside in the church, she related what God had shown her concerning St. Dominic. "At this moment," said she to him, "I see St. Dominic more distinctly and perfectly than I see you. He is more intimately present to me."

But as she was conversing on the subject, *her* brother, whose name also was Bartholomew, passed by: his shadow or the noise he made in passing by, attracted during an instant, Catharine's attention, who scarcely turned her eyes, but yet sufficiently to recognize him; she afterwards resumed her position, but suddenly her moans and tears prevented her from speaking.

The Religious waited some time before engaging her to continue what she had commenced; but her sobs rendered it impossible for her to continue. At length, after a tedious interval, she began to utter these interrupted phrases: "Alas, wretch that I am, who will take vengeance on me for my iniquities? who will punish me for such an enormous fault?" And as the Religious inquired what sin she had committed: "Did you not see," said she, "that at the very moment in which God was showing me his wonders, I turned my head and eyes to look at a person passing by?" "But," said the Religious, "you looked so short a time that I did not even perceive it." "If you knew," replied she, "the reproaches that the Blessed Virgin made to me, you would assist me to weep for my fault!" She immediately ceased speaking of her vision, wept until she had confessed, and then retired to her cell, still weeping.

St. Paul appeared to her, according to what she told her Confessor, and rebuked her severely for the time she had lost in turning her head. She afterwards declared that she preferred confusion before the whole world, rather than experiencing the shame excited by the reproach of the blessed Apostle. She said to her Confessor: "Imagine what it will be to bear the reproaches of Jesus Christ at the last judgment, if the reproach of his Apostle occasioned me so much shame." She added that she would have died of shame, if, during the time that the Apostle was reproving her, she had not continually seen a Lamb, all radiant with a sweet mild light. This imperfection which God permitted, was also a means of rendering her more humble and more prudent in preserving the graces that she had received. I have cited these two facts before concluding this chapter, because I think they are very capable of teaching humility, both to the perfect and to the imperfect.

St. Dominic called me to enter his Order in a miraculous manner. I acknowledge that I was not worthy of it; but I should be an ungrateful son, did I pass in silence the glory of my blessed Father, and hence I intend relating the revelation that Catharine had concerning him. Friar Bartholomew, of whom I have just spoken, and who is at present with me, related it to me exactly as she had related it to me on that very day.

Catharine asserted that she saw the Eternal Father producing from his mouth, his co-eternal Son, such as he was, when he clothed himself with human nature; and whilst she was contemplating him, she saw the blessed Patriarch St. Dominic come forth from the breast of the Father, all glittering with brightness, and she heard a voice which said: "Beloved Daughter, I have begotten these two Sons: one by nature, the other by a sweet and tender adoption." As Catharine was amazed at a comparison so elevated, which rendered equal so to speak, a saint with *Jesus Christ*—he who uttered these surprising words, explained them himself: "My Son engendered by nature from all eternity, when he assumed human nature, obeyed me in all things *perfectly*, until his death. Dominic, my son by adoption, from his birth until the last moment of his life, followed my will in all things. He never transgressed one of my commandments, never violated the virginity of either soul or body, and always preserved the grace of Baptism which regenerated him. My SON by nature, who is the eternal WORD from my mouth, preached publicly to the world whatever I charged him to say, and he rendered testimony to the Truth as he himself declared to Pilate. My adopted Son Dominic also preached to the world the verity of my words; he spoke to heretics and to Catholics, not only personally but by others. His preaching continued in his successors, he still preaches and will always preach. My Son by nature sent his disciples, my son by adoption sent his religious; my SON by nature is my Word, my son by adoption is the herald, the minister of my Word. Therefore I have given a quite particular intelligence of my words to him and to his religious with fidelity to follow them. My SON by nature did all things in order to promote by his teaching and his example the salvation of souls. Dominic my son by adoption, used all his endeavors to draw souls from vice and error. The salvation of the neighbor was his principal thought in the establishment and development of his Order. Hence I have compared him to my Son by nature, whose life he imitated, and thou seest that even his body resembles the sacred BODY of my divine SON." It was while Catharine related this vision to friar Bartholomew that the circumstance above related transpired. Let us now pass to the vision which must terminate this chapter.

Abundance of graces and revelations so filled the soul of Catharine, at this epoch, that the excess of her love threw her into a state of real languor. This languor augmented so that she could not rise from her bed; and her illness was ardor for her holy Spouse, whom she continually called, as if beside herself: Sweetest, most amiable youth, SON OF GOD and she sometimes added: And of the blessed Virgin Mary. These words were the flowery couch of her love, and on it she reposed without sleep and without food. But the Spouse who had excited in her soul this enthusiasm, so as to influence her more and more, visited her incessantly. Catharine all vehement with sacred desires said to him: "Oh! why, my beloved Master does this miserable body deprive me of thy heavenly embrace? Alas! in this melacholy life naught can afford me pleasure. I seek but thee; for if I indeed love any thing, it is simply on thy account. I implore thee, let this miserable body no longer prove an obstacle to my happiness. Oh! the best of Masters draw my soul from this prison and deliver me from this body of death!" The Lord thus answered these words that were interrupted with sobs: "Beloved daughter, when I dwelt among men, I accomplished not my will but my Father's; my disciples have rendered testimony of this; I desired greatly to eat with them the last Supper, and yet I waited with patience the moment fixed by my Father. Therefore notwithstanding the ardent desire that you have to be entirely united to me, you must wait my hour with resignation." And Catharine replied: "Since thou wilt not consent, thy holy will be done. But yet, deign I conjure thee to hear a simple prayer: whatever be the duration thou shalt fix to my existence, grant me to participate in all the sufferings that thou hast endured until death. If I cannot be with thee now in Heaven, let me be united to thee at least in thy Passion on earth."

God accepted her prayer, and what she had asked was liberally granted to her; for she began, as she acknowledged to me, to suffer more and more in her soul and in her body, all the dolors that Our Lord had experienced during his life; and, that it may be better understood. I will relate what she told us on the subject. She frequently conversed with me on the sufferings of our Lord, and assured me that from the moment of his conception, he had always borne the Cross in his soul, on account of the desire that he felt for the salvation of souls. He must have suffered cruelly until he had established, by his Passion, the honor of God and the happiness of the neighbor—and this torment of desire, is very great, those who have experienced it, know that it is the heaviest of crosses.

She also gave on the words of our Lord in the garden of Olives, an explanation that I do not remember to have read in any author. She said that by the words: "*Father, let this chalice pass from me,*" (Matt. xxvi. 39) persons enlightened and fortified by grace ought not to believe, like feeble souls who fear death, that the Saviour implored to be spared his Passion: he had drunk from his birth, and according as the hour approached he drank more deeply that chalice of desire which animated him for the salvation of men. He rather implored the accomplishment of what he so ardently wished, the filling up of that Cup whose bitterness he had so long tasted. He was far from dreading his Passion and death, he on the contrary wished to advance the moment; he expressed this clearly when he said to Judas: *Quod facis, fac citius* "*what thou doest, do quickly.*" (St. John xiii. 27.) But although that chalice of desire was the most painful to drink, he added in his filial obedience; "Nevertheless not my will but thine be done." *Verumtamen non mea voluntas, sed tua fiat.* He thus offered to suffer all the delays that it would please God to require in his Passion.

I observed to her that ordinarily the Doctors explained this passage otherwise, and that according to them, the Saviour pronounced these words, as man, because he feared death naturally; and as chief of the elect, of those who are feeble as well as those who are strong; so as not to discourage the weak who dread death and present to all a salutary example. Catharine responded: "The actions of the Redeemer are so fruitful in instruction that by carefully meditating on them, each one finds the nourishment best suited to his soul's salvation. The weak can find consolation in our Saviour's prayer; but the strong and more nearly perfect soul should derive encouragement from it, and this would be impossible without the explanation that I have given you. It is more profitable to present several meanings, so that each individual may adopt the one most appropriate to the soul's necessities." I kept silent and simply admired the grace and wisdom she had received from God.

I found also another explanation of these words in the manuscripts that Brother Thomas, Catharine's first Confessor, left concerning her. She said during one of her ecstacies, that the cause of our Saviour's sadness and bloody sweat in the Garden of Olives, was the foresight of so many souls failing of participation in the fruits of his Passion. But as he loved justice, he added: "*Not my will but thine.*" Without that, said she, all men would have been saved, for it is impossible that the will of the SON of GOD should remain ineffectual. Which agrees perfectly with what the Apostle said to the Hebrews: *Exauditus est pro sua reverentia,* (Heb. v. 7.) The Doctors commonly apply this passage to the prayer in the Garden of Olives

She also told me on this subject that the dolors suf

fered by the Son of God, in his body, were so great, that they were sufficient to produce death a thousand times in any one who would have endured them. The Saviour's love being infinite, the dolors that his love induced him to bear were also infinite and greatly surpassed all those that man's nature and malice could have caused him. The thorns of the mock crown pierced his head to the very brain, all his members were disjointed. (Ps. xxi. 18.) And still so great was his love, that he not only supported these dolors, but he procured himself still more terrible ones, in order to manifest himself to us more perfectly. Yes, this was one of the principal motives of his Passion: he desired to exhibit to us the immensity of his love, and he could not prove it more effectually. Love and not nails fastened him to the Cross; love and not men triumphed. How could *they* have been masters, since with one single word, he could have thrown them to the earth.

Catharine gave admirable explanations concerning the Passion of the Redeemer: she said that she had undergone in her body a portion of his sufferings, but it would be impossible to endure them completely. The greatest torment that Jesus Christ suffered on the Cross, was, she thought, the dislocation of the bones of the breast. She believed this, because the other tortures which she suffered in imitation of the Saviour, were transient, *that* alone was permanent; the pains in the side and head which she daily suffered were considerable, but those in the breast far surpassed them; and I easily believe it, both in reference to her and to our Lord, on account of the vicinity of the heart. The bones which are disposed in that portion of the human frame, for protecting the heart and lungs, cannot be displaced without gravely wounding the precious organs that they contain, and without a miracle this displacing must necessarily produce death. Catharine endured this torture during several days; her corporeal energies became enfeebled, but the ardor of her love only increased. She experienced in a sensible manner, how deeply the Saviour had loved *her*, and had loved all mankind, by undergoing such a dolorous Passion, and this produced such a vehement love, that the heart of Catharine was separated or literally broken and the links that bound it to life were supernaturally destroyed.

The reader of these pages may perhaps doubt that such a death really took place, but let him know that it occurred in presence of several witnesses who have affirmed it. I also doubted: I went to Catharine in order to examine what she had experienced, and I requested her to manifest the whole truth. She then broke forth into sobs and moans, and after having obliged me to wait for her answer a considerable time, she at last said: "Father, would you not pity a soul that had been delivered from an obscure prison, and then plunged anew into darkness, after having enjoyed an extraordinary light? This misfortune happened to me; divine Providence willed it on account of my faults."

These circumstances increased my desire of learning these details from her, and I added: "Mother, then your soul has been really separated from your body?" "Yes," said she to me, "the ardor of divine love was so vehement, the desire that I felt of being united to my BELOVED was so forcible, that no heart, had it been composed of stone or of iron, could possibly have resisted, nothing created is sufficiently powerful to counteract such a force. Yes, be sure of it, the heart that beats in this poor frame was sundered by charity. I feel the place where it is divided. In consequence, my soul actually quitted my body, and I saw secrets of God, that I am incapable of telling on earth, because memory is too feeble, and language too poor for adequately rendering such noble themes. It would be presenting clay for gold. Only when I hear this state spoken of, I instantly feel a profound sorrow, on seeing, that I could descend from those heights to relapse again into the miseries of the world and I have only tears and sobs to express the keenness of my anguish."

Desiring to have a more complete knowledge of all that transpired, I said, "Mother, since you cheerfully confide to me your other secrets, I entreat you not to hide this, and to give me a full description of this wonderful event. I have been favored," said she "with many spiritual and corporeal visions: I had received ineffable consolations from our Lord, and the violence of pure love, had so weakened me physically, that I was obliged to keep my bed. There I prayed incessantly and supplicated God to deliver me from this body of death, in order to unite me more intimately to him. I did not obtain this grace, but it was granted me to be united, as far as I could be, to the dolors of his Passion." And she told me what I have given above concerning our Lord's sufferings; then she added: "This share of pain that he condescended to impart to me, made known more distinctly and perfectly to me, my Creator's love; and mine augmented so, that I fell into a state of languor and my soul knew no other desire but that of quitting the body. How shall I describe it to you? my Saviour daily animated more and more the fire which he had enkindled; my heart of flesh yielded, and love became strong as death. Yes my heart broke, my captive soul was freed from its bonds; but ah me! for only too short a space of time."

"Mother," I rejoined, "how long did your soul remain separated from your body?" She answered me: "Persons who witnessed my death, say that I remained four hours without returning to life. A great many persons came to offer consolations to Mother and my family, but my soul had entered into eternity and indulged no thoughts of time."

I said: "What did you see, mother, during that time, and why did your soul return into the body. I beseech you do not conceal aught of this from me." She answered: "Know, father, that my soul entered into an unknown world, and beheld the glory of the just and the chastisement of sinners. But here also memory fails, and the poverty of language prohibits a full description of these things. I tell you however what I can; be assured therefore, that I saw the divine ESSENCE, and for this I suffer so much in remaining enchained in this body. Were I not retained for the love of God and love of the neighbor, I should die of grief. My great consolation is *to suffer*, because I am aware that by suffering, I shall obtain a more perfect view of God. Hence tribulations, far from being painful to my soul, are on the contrary its delight. I saw the torments of HELL and those of PURGATORY; no words can describe them. Had poor mortals the faintest idea of them, they would suffer a thousand deaths rather than undergo the least of their torments during a single day. I saw in particular those punished who sin in the married state, by not observing the laws it imposes, and seeking in it naught but sensual pleasures." And as I inquired why this sin, which was not worse than others, still received so rude a chastisement, she told me:

"Because little attention is given to it, and consequently less contrition is excited for it, and it is more easily committed." And then she added: "Nothing is more dangerous than a fault, however small it may be, when he who commits it does not carefully purify his soul by penance."

Catharine afterwards continued what she had commenced: "Whilst my soul contemplated these things, its celestial Spouse, whom it believed it possessed forever, said: 'Thou seest what glory they lose and torments they suffer who offend me. Return therefore to life and show them how they have strayed and what appalling danger menaces them." And as my soul was horrified at the idea of returning to life, the Lord added: "The salvation of many souls demands it; thou shalt no longer live as thou hast done, henceforth thou must renounce thy cell and continually pass through the city, in order to save souls. I will always attend thee, I will conduct thee and re-conduct thee, I will confide to thee the honor of my HOLY NAME, and thou shalt teach my doctrine to the lowly and the great, to laymen, priests and monks, I will impart to thee speech and wisdom which none can resist, I will place thee in the presence of Pontiffs, and the Rulers both of the church and of the people, so as to confound, in my way, and by this means the arrogance of the mighty.' Whilst God thus addressed my soul, I suddenly found myself, without the capacity of explaining how, re-united to my body. Then I was so overcome with keen sorrow, that I shed copious and burning tears during three days and three nights: and when my mind dwells upon it, I cannot refrain from weeping, and father, it is not astonishing; what is much more so, is, that my heart is not crushed anew on recalling that glory which I then possessed and of which I am now deprived. The salvation of the neighbor is the cause of it; if I love so ardently the souls whose conversion God has confided to me, it is because they have cost me dear; they have separated me from my God, and deprived me of the enjoyment of his glory during a period to me unknown. But they will prove 'my glory and my crown and my immortal joy.' (Phil. iv. 1.) I tell you these things, father, so as to console you for the anxiety caused you by those who murmur at the confidence I repose in you."

After God had bestowed on me the favor of hearing these things, I asked myself whether it was my duty to publish them at a time in which self-love renders men so blind and so incredulous. My Brethren and Sisters did not approve of my disclosing them during Catharine's life-time, and I remarked that several of those who at first followed her, when this circumstance, which they could not comprehend, was related to them went away. But now that she has gone to the home of the blessed, I thought myself obliged to speak; and I have revealed the whole, so that so great a miracle be not concealed through my fault. The following particulars give all possible authenticity to this event: at the approach of Catharine's death, the women who were with her and who were her daughters in the Lord, sent for Friar Thomas, her confessor, to assist her in her agony: he hastened there without a moments delay, with another Religious Friar Thomas Antonio, and began with tears to recite the customary prayers; the news spreading, another Religious, called Friar Antonio Bartholomew of Montucio, came speedily with John, a lay-brother of Sienna, now residing at Rome. These four Religious, all of whom still live, wept and prayed around the expiring Catharine.

At the moment in which Catharine was breathing her last sigh, Brother John felt such an intense grief, that the force of his sobs and cries ruptured a vein in his breast. He was immediately attacked with a violent cough and such a large hemorrhage that his state appeared desperate. This spectacle augmented the sorrow of the assistants: those who were grieving for Catharine's death, were soon also to be called to mourn that of the poor lay-brother. Then Friar Thomas, Catharine's Confessor, said, with strong faith, to Brother John: "I know the influence of that holy woman with God, you need only apply her hand to the place in which you suffer such violent pain, and you will certainly be cured." The Brother did it before the eyes of all present, and at the same moment he was as perfectly cured as if he had experienced no accident. Brother John related this incident to all who wish to hear it, and affirms it by an oath. Besides the Brothers whom I have just named, there were for witnesses her companion and her spiritual daughter Alessia, who now dwells with her in Heaven, whither she followed her shortly after her death. Nearly all the neighbors also saw Catharine dead, as well as the numbers of men and women who commonly present themselves in such circumstances, and no one had a doubt but that she had truly exhaled her last breath. As to the fact of the elevation of her body, which we described at the beginning of this chapter, it had for witnesses several *Sisters of Penance of St. Dominic*, among others, Catharine, daughter of Ghetto of Sienna, who was during a long time her inseparable companion.

CHAPTER VI.

OF MIRACLES WROUGHT BY CATHARINE'S INTERCESSION FOR PROMOTING THE SALVATION OF SOULS.

WERE I obliged to recount all the miracles that God performed through the intercession of Catharine, for the salvation of souls, a chapter would not suffice, but several volumes would be necessary. In order not to be too lengthy, I have abridged as much as possible—what I relate will enable what I suppress to be comprehended; spirit is superior to matter, and miracles accomplished for the salvation of souls, surpass those performed for the health of the body. I will commence with the more noble, following generally the order of time in my recital, but I shall be occasionally forced to depart from the division I have attempted. These miracles, particularly which refer to souls have been ignored by men; they have sometimes no other proof than the confidence that she gave to me and to a few others; but this will not prevent pious persons from crediting them.

Catharine's father, Jacomo, (James) had recognized the holiness of his daughter, and entertained a respectful tenderness for her; he recommended all the members of his household not to contradict her in anything and to allow her to act according to her own views. Hence their affection daily grew stronger; Catharine prayed incessantly for the salvation of her father, while Jacomo delighted in the sanctity of his child, by whose merits he hoped to obtain grace before our Lord. At length

Jacomo's term of life was drawing to a close, and he took to his bed being very seriously ill. Catharine began to intercede with her divine Spouse to obtain the restoration of one so tenderly loved, but He answered her that Jacomo was very near death, and that it would not be useful to him to live longer. Catharine therefore repaired to the bedside of her cherished parent, and found him wholly disposed to quit the world without regret, and she thanked God with all the fervor of her heart.

But her filial affection was not yet satisfied: she endeavored to obtain from the Source of all grace not only that her father's faults might be pardoned, but also that at the hour of death his soul might be borne to heaven without passing through the flames of purgatory. It was answered her that justice could not lose its rights, and that the soul must be perfectly pure to enjoy the splendors of glory. "Thy father has lived well in the conjugal state, has done many things acceptable to me, and I am in particular pleased with his conduct towards thee; but justice demands that his soul pass by the fire, to purify it from the stains that it has contracted in the world." "O most amiable Saviour," responded Catharine, "how can I endure the thought of seeing him whom thou gavest me for father, who nourished me and brought me up with care, and who has been so kind to me, burning in such cruel flames! I entreat thy divine bounty, not to permit his soul to leave his body, before by some means or other it is perfectly purified and has no need of the fire of Purgatory." God in his amazing mercy yielded to this prayer, and to the desire of his creature. Jacomo's strength was extinct, but his soul could not depart so long as the conflict lasted between Catharine and our Lord, the Redeemer alleging his plea of justice and Catharine invoking mercy. At last Catharine said: "If I cannot obtain this grace without satisfying thy justice, let this justice be exercised towards me; I am ready to undergo for my father whatever thy goodness will deign to send me." Our Lord consented to this, "I cheerfully accept thy proposition, on account of thy love for me, and I exempt the soul of thy father from all expiatory pains, but during thy whole life thou shalt be the victim of a pain which I send thee." Catharine joyfully gave thanks to God, and asked that his divine will might be accomplished. Catharine hastened to the couch of her dying father, who was just sinking into agony; she filled his heart with joy and strength, by giving him the assurance of his eternal salvation from the mouth of God himself, and never left him until he expired. At the instant his spirit quitted his body, Catharine was attacked with an acute pain in her side which she endured without relaxation until the day of her death. I had the declaration of it from herself, and all those who had relations with her saw many evident proofs of it—but her patience was greater than her pain. All that I have related here I learned from Catharine, when compassionating her sufferings I inquired their cause. I should add that at the moment her father breathed his last, she exclaimed with a gladsome countenance and a serene smile on her lips: "Bless God! Father; how happy were I now like thee!" Whilst they celebrated the funeral ceromonies and all around wept Catharine appeared gay and cheerful. She consoled her mother and every one else, and acted as calmly as if the deceased had been a stranger to her. It was because she had seen that dearly-loved soul joyfully escape the prison of the body, and soar unfettered to eternal light;

and this sight had inundated her soul with comfort, because a few days previous she had tasted the bliss of celestial glory.

Here let us admire the wisdom of divine Providence: the soul of Jacomo could certainly have been purified in another way and have been immediately admitted to glory, like the soul of the good thief on Calvary, who confessed our Lord on the Cross; but God willed that Catharine should request it, not to try her, but to augment her merits and her crown. Hence Catharine always spoke of her sweet, dear sufferings; and she was correct, because sufferings augment the consolations of grace in this life and the delights of the glory to come.

Having admired what Catharine did for the soul of a just man, let us see what happened in the soul of a sinner. In 1370, there was at Sienna a citizen named Andrêa of Naddino; a man rich in worldly and perishable goods, but poor in interior and eternal wealth. Without either the love or the fear of God, he subjected himself to the slavery of every vice. Gaming was his predominant passion, and he had a habit of blaspheming horribly. In the month of December of that same year, the fortieth of his age, he was attacked with a serious malady; the physicians entertained no hope of his cure, and death threatened both the soul and body of this wretched impenitent. The curate of the parish came to visit him, hoping to prepare him for his last great change, but the sick man, who had never frequented the Church, nor respected its priests, despised his charitable warnings and repulsed him who gave them. Then his wife and and children, who ardently desired his salvation, invited several pious persons to come, who all endeavored to overcome his hardness of heart; but neither the threats of eternal flames, nor the hopes of divine mercy could bend this unfortunate man, who was plunging into hell with all his crimes. The curate who saw death approaching, was absorbed in grief: he returned with the morning dawn, and renewed his pressing efforts: but all proved useless. The unhappy man repulsed his discourse and refused him presence. He sunk deeper and deeper into final impenitence, and committed that sin against the Holy Ghost, by which the mercy of God is turned aside—naught awaited him but the chastisements of an irrevocable justice.

Friar Thomas, the Confessor of Catharine, was acquainted with what was passing. Grieved at the loss of this soul, he hastened to his penitent, and asked her, in the name of obedience and charity, to interest herself in this miserable man, and cry to God until she would procure his pardon. When he arrived Catharine was in ecstacy, and it was impossible to draw her from her heavenly contemplations. As he could neither speak to her nor wait for her, on account of the approaching night, he recommended one of her companions, named Catharine, and who is still living, to explain to the servant of God, as soon as she came to herself, the object of his visit. Catharine did not recover from her ecstacy until near five o'clock in the morning: her companion immediately gave the Confessor's commission and enjoined her, in virtue of holy obedience, to ask for the conversion of the hard-hearted sinner. At this news Catharine, all inflamed with charity and compassion, began to pray to God with her whole strength, protesting that she could not allow her equal, her countryman, and her *brother*, because redeemed by the same Saviour, to perish in eternal flames.

The Lord answered. "This man's iniquities have mounted to Heaven—not only has he poured forth injuries against me and my saints, but he threw into the fire a picture representing me and my blessed Mother. Do not intercede for him; it is just that he burn in eternal flames; he merits death a thousand times."

Catharine prostrated herself at the feet of her divine Spouse, and bathed them with her tears—and prayed in aspirations like these: "Didst thou not, O loving Jesus! bear this man's sins with ours on thy venerable shoulders? Am I here to dispute thy justice, or to invoke thy mercy? Remember Lord thou didst promise to aid me in saving souls; I have no other consolation but that of seeing them return to thee; it is the only circumstance that renders me capable of enduring thy absence. Repel me not, O most clement Jesus! restore to me my brother; draw him from his hardened state!" Catharine continued, during several hours her vigil and her tears to obtain the salvation of that soul.

God opposed the number and enormity of his crimes which demanded vengeance, and Catharine invoked the mercy that led him to come down to earth and die for sinners. At last mercy triumphed over justice, and our blessed Saviour said to Catharine: "My beloved daughter, I suffer myself to be softened by thy tears; I am going to convert him for whom thou prayest with such fervor."

At that same instant our Lord appeared to Andrèa (Andrew) who was in extremities: "Friend," said he to him, "why will you not confess the sins that thou hast committed against me? Confess them and I am ready to pardon thee all thy faults."

These words suddenly softened that obstinate heart, and he cried out to those that served him: "Send quickly for a priest, because I wish to confess. I see my Lord and Saviour who is inviting me to do so." The assistants filled with joy hastened to obey. The priest came, he performed all his last duties calmly, confessed perfectly, and died in wonderful sentiments of contrition and repentance.

These, Lord, are the works that display thee in thy saints. To show the favor Catharine had before thee, thou didst make known to her the danger of a man with whom she was not acquainted, but who had received from thee the same country and the same baptism. Thou didst grant naught to the prayers of the others, because thou wouldst grant all to those of thy beloved Spouse. Oh! who would not love thee!

There were at Sienna, two notorious brigands that justice had decreed to arrest—and they were condemned to expiate their crime in the most fearful torments. They were going to death, attached to a stake, on a cart, and the executioners, armed with red hot pincers, tore their flesh in every part of their bodies. Neither in prison, nor at the approach of death, could they be induced to repent, nor persuaded to listen to a clergyman; and at the very moment in which they were led through the town in order to inspire a wholesome dread of the laws, instead of recommending themselves to the prayers of the faithful, they blasphemed against God and his Saints. The fiery tortures which these wretched men endured were but a prelude to the torments that awaited them in hell; but that Infinite Goodness who wills the death of none, and who does not twice punish the same faults, delivered these poor souls, by means of his faithful handmaid.

Providence permitted that on that very day, Catharine

should be at the house of Alessia, her companion and her spiritual daughter. Alessia, hearing in the morning the noise of the crowd, approached the window, and saw at some distance, the unhappy criminals who were conducted and tormented by the executioners. She ran to Catharine, "O Mother!" cried she, "what a frightful spectacle directly before the house: here are two men who are condemned to be torn with heated pincers passing by." Catharine, moved not by curiosity but by pity, advanced to the window, perceived the unhappy men, and retired at once to prayer. She informed me that she saw around them a troop of demons which were tormenting their souls still more than the executioners tortured their bodies. Hence she had recourse to fervent prayer, and conjured her Divine Spouse to save those souls who were on the eve of perishing. "Ah! Lord," said she, "who art so clement, wilt thou so far abandon creatures formed to thy image, and redeemed by thy precious blood. The thief who was crucified at thy side really merited his punishment; but thy grace visited him because at the moment in which thy apostles doubted, he confessed thee publicly, amid the ignominies of thy Passion, and he merited the hearing of thy promise ' *To-day thou shalt be with me in Paradise.*' In that word, thou didst give hope of pardon to those who might resemble him. Thou didst not abandon Peter who denied thee, but gavest him a look of compassion; thou didst not contemn Mary the sinner, but attracted her to thee; and Matthew the publican, the Cananean, and Zaccheus, the rich, thou didst not refuse to receive, but didst invite them to return. I entreat thee by all thy mercies, hasten to relieve these souls."

At length she persuaded *Him* who desires to be inclined

mercifully, and streams of pardoning grace flowed in a wonderful manner over the souls of these two miserable men. Catharine obtained the grace of assisting them in spirit, and of accompanying them as far as the city gates. She prayed and wept continually for their change of heart: the demons who saw her, said to her in fury: "if thou dost not cease, we and these two reprobates, will torment thee to such a degree, that thou shalt become possessed." Catharine answered: "Whatever God wills, I will, I shall not discontinue what I have commenced."

When the two criminals halted at the gate of the city, our merciful Redeemer appeared to them covered with wounds and bathed in blood. He exhorted them to conversion and promised them pardon. A ray of divine light immediately penetrated their hearts—they earnestly implored the assistance of a priest and confessed their sins with heartfelt sorrow. Their blasphemies were changed into pious aspirations; they accused themselves, acknowledged that they merited even more terrible torments and marched onward to death, as joyously as if they were going to a festival: instead of loading their executioners with insults, they thanked the Saviour, who in mercy permitted them to acquire, by these transient sorrows, a never-ending glory. All the assistants were in admiration at such a change: the torturers themselves were deeply affected, and dared no longer increase their cruelties, on seeing them in such sentiments, but no one knew whence came this miracle of grace. The good and zealous clergyman who accompanied these hardened sinners endeavoring to convert them, gave these details to Friar Thomas, Catharine's Confessor. The latter, having questioned Alessia, was able to certify that at the very moment in which Catharine concluded her prayer and came forth from her ecstasy, the two condemned gave up their last sighs. I also received Catharine's entire confidence concerning all the particulars, and I found them in every circumstance conformed to what Friar Thomas had written. He only adds that a few days after the death of the two converted brigands, the companions of Catharine heard her say, whilst she was praying. *"Lord I thank thee for having delivered them from a second prison."* Brother Thomas asked her what these words signified; she answered that the two malefactors enjoyed the glory of heaven; that they entered Purgatory, but she had obtained their deliverance.

These circumstances can scarcely fail of surprising those who read them, because they do not fall under the corporeal senses; but if we consult St. Augustine and St. Gregory, it will be seen that this miracle is greater than if those unfortunate men had been resuscitated after death; for, according to the expression of St. Gregory, a body raised to life must die again, but in this case the soul is revivified for all eternity: in the resurrection of the body, the divine power meets no obstacle; but in that of souls, the free-will of man can resist and repel the action of grace: hence the convertion of a sinner displays the divine power more gloriously, than the creation of the entire world. It is related of St. Martin, that by the virtue of the Holy Trinity, he had the glory of raising three individuals from death to life, and St. Nicholas is also admired for having saved three innocents condemned to the worst torments. What then shall be said of Catharine who, by the power of her prayers, suddenly saved two guilty souls from everlasting death, and who drew from purgatorial fires, their souls which were plunged into them. Is not this greater and more amazing? Believe me reader, I saw many prodigies effected by this holy woman; but I find none comparable to this which I have just narrated: no, never in any case was the power of the Most High so largely manifested, never did the unction of grace flow so abundantly.

Catharine obtained another extraordinary grace of conversion, which I must not bury in silence. There was in Sienna, a man named Francis Tholomei, and who still lives: his wife is named Rabès; they had several sons and daughters. The eldest, Jacques, led a criminal life; he was excessively proud, and such was his ferocity, that although young, his hand had twice been imbrued in the blood of his neighbor; his horrible deeds made him the terror of all who knew him; no idea, no fear of God withheld him, and he added crime to crime. He had a sister named Ghinoccia, who was passionately *fond of the world*, in the worst sense of that expression; she was continually occupied in vainly adorning her person, and if she were not wholly lost, it was because she merely dreaded human opinion. Their pious mother Rabès feared for the salvation of her children; she went to Catharine and implored her to be so charitable as to speak on religion to her two daughters, especially to Ghinoccia. Catharine, who so ardently loved souls, consented, and succeeded so well with Ghinoccia, that Jesus triumphed in her affections, and she renounced all the senseless joys of the world—she cut off her long and glossy hair, that had proved a source of vanity to her, took the habit of the *Sisters of Penance of St. Dominic*, and persevered, as I can affirm, in the most admirable practices of devotion. I was frequently obliged to moderate the rigor of her austerities. Her sister Francoise, (Frances) followed her example closely; she also assumed the holy livery of penance, and it was an affecting sight to behold those two sisters so lately captivated with vanity, contesting suddenly its every form in their own persons and that with courage and perseverance.

At the moment of their conversion, Jacques Tholomei was absent; as soon as he learned this, he returned to the city in a paroxysm of rage against his youthful brothers; in his arrogance he uttered the most terrible threats and menaced tearing off his sister's holy habit, and conducting her back with him, to withdraw her from the influence of those who had converted her. But his little brother said, in an inspired tone: "Jacques, I assure thee, that wert thou to go to Sienna, thou wouldst be converted and wouldst confess thy sins." But he ill-treated the child, and replied that he would sooner *kill* all the priests and the religious. The child reiterated his prophecy, and Jacques his threats and maledictions. They at last arrived at the city and Jacques entered his home in a perfect fury, declaring that he would commit the worst violence, did not his sister renounce her habit and follow him without delay.

Rabès, succeeded in appeasing and calming his passion until the morrow. In the morning she sent word to Friar Thomas, the Confessor of Catharine, who providentially took as companion, Friar Bartholomew of St. Dominic. He sought Jacques, conversed with him, yet apparently obtained nothing favorable—but Catharine by a supernatural light, knew all that was passing, and supplicated God for the wicked youth's conversion. The Lord heard her prayer, and touched that obdurate heart. He **yielded to the exhortations of Brother Bartholomew, after** having obstinately repelled those of Brother Thomas; and not only did he permit his sister to serve God as she wished, but humbled himself and confessed his faults with lively sorrow; to use Catharine's expression, he ejected all the poison that defiled his soul, and accused himself of sins that he would never before acknowledge. The wolf was changed into a lamb; the fierce lion had become docile as a child, and all the witnesses were filled with admiration. His mother could find no explanation for this astonishing change; his sisters congratulated him, and the whole household returned thanks to God. The two Religious, full of joy, hastened to bear the joyous news to Catharine.

The Saint, who had seen all in spirit, and who had obtained that grace from the Lord, had not yet come out of ecstacy, but continued to enjoy the caresses of her Divine Spouse. Before the religious brethren entered her room, however, she said: "We must render thanks to God, because Jacques Tholomei, who was a slave to Satan, was delivered this morning; he has confessed to Friar Bartholomew." When the Religious described their joy, Catharine's companion replied: "She was just relating it to me as you entered." Catharine then said to them with her usual edifying manner: "Fathers, we must give thanks to God who never disregards the prayers of his servants, and the good desires which his own divine Spirit inspires. The enemy of salvation, had resolved to rob us of that dear sheep, but the Father of mercies defended his own; he imagined that he had also gained Ghinoccia from our Lord; and he has lost Jacques of whom he had become master. Indeed, our divine Shepherd assures us in the Gospel: 'that no one can take from him his own.'" (St. John v 28.) Ghinoccia was indeed a constant example of piety and mortification; she persevered until death in the service of God, and slept joyfully in the Lord, after having supported with the most admirable patience, a long and painful illness.

Her sister Frances who imitated her, survived her but a short interval. Always satisfied, even amid the most excruciating pains, she expired with a smile on her lips. Matthew, the brother next in age to Jacques, renounced the world, and entered the order of St. Dominic, which he still edifies by his virtues. As to Jacques, he married, *but* he never relapsed into his attacks of passion, being always peaceful and meek. All this good was accomplished by means of Catharine, who obtained from her Spouse the graces appropriate to each individual.

The narrative which I now present was not less wonderful: I was alone witness of the attendant circumstances, but God knows my veracity, and besides, its results were made public. There dwelt, in Sienna, a man perfectly well known among persons of the world, and possessed of surprising genius, which was not regulated by the law of God. His name was NANNI or VANNI. As is frequent among his countrymen, he indulged private hatred, and he knew how to satisfy vengeance by striking in the dark. Several murders had been committed, but they who were their authors dreaded Nanni more than others, because they were acquainted with his deadly malice They had often employed mediators to induce him to be reconciled, but he always answered with hypocrisy, that he was a complete stranger in those affairs, and that it did not depend on him to make peace. He alone, however, offered an obstacle, so as to be able to satiate his vengeance when he could find an opportunity.

Catharine was aware of this disorder and was desirous of arresting its progress, by conversing with Nanni; but the latter carefully avoided her. In fine, a holy man, Brother William of England, of the Order of Hermits of St. Augustine, pressed him so much, that he consented to see and hear Catharine; but at the same time refusing to pledge himself to do what she might desire: he came in effect, to the house at a moment in which I was myself awaiting the arrival of the servant of God, who was occupied somewhere in the salvation of souls. They informed me that Nanni was waiting to converse with Catharine. I went down with a glad heart, because I knew how much Catharine desired this interview; I announced her absence, but pressed him to wait a little, and to beguile the time, I introduced him into the little cell, sanctified by the spouse of JESUS CHRIST. After a few moments Nanni became weary and said: "I promised Friar William to come here and listen to this lady; she is absent, and my occupations prevent me from remaining longer; will you be so kind as to excuse me,— but really I have too much to do to admit my tarrying longer."

I was quite distressed by Catharine's absence, but so as to restrain all sign of impatience, I began to speak of reconciliation, but he said to me: "See, now, you are a priest and a religious, and this good lady enjoys a great reputation for sanctity; I must not deceive you. I therefore tell you frankly, and declare to you that I will do nothing of what you request from me; it is true that I prevent peace, but I wish that it be kept secret. Did I but give my consent, all would be arranged; I refuse; and it is useless to preach to me on that subject, you will obtain nothing; it is already considerable to have told you with so much freedom what I concealed from others. Do not torment me further on the subject." I would insist, and he refused to hear me, when God permitted that Catharine should become the instrument of reconciliation. Her arrival was as disagreeable to Nanni, as agreeble to me. As soon as she perceived us, she saluted this man of the world with angelic charity; she seated herself and then inquired the motive of his visit. Nanni repeated to her what he had just told me and declared also that he would make no concession. Catharine represented to him with as much force as sweetness, the danger to which he exposed his soul; but the unhappy man would hear nothing and closed his heart to her moving solicitations. Then, the holy woman went alone to pray and implore God's assistance; I hoped that she would be heard, and began to discuss with NANNI so as to gain time. Only a few moments had expired ere the obstinate man said to us: "Through politeness I will not refuse you totally, *I have four enmities;* I consent to sacrifice the one which will afford you the greatest pleasure." And he arose to withdraw, when on a sudden he exclaimed "O my God, what consolation my heart feels for this sole word of peace that I have pronounced," then added: "O my Lord and my God! what power retains and triumphs over me; I cannot go away and I have not the force to refuse. What can it be that exerts such an influence over me? Yes, I confess that I am vanquished—I cannot draw my breath"—then falling on his knees, he said, sobbing "Holy Virgin behold me ready to do whatever you command relative to peace, and all else. I see now that Satan held me in chains; henceforth I resign myself to thy counsels; in pity direct my soul and draw it from the snares of the enemy."

At this moment Catharine who had entered into ecstacy, as was usual, returned to herself and gave thanks to God: "Dear Brother," said she, "the mercy of God has at length manifested to you your danger, I spoke to you and you refused to listen; then I turned *to God* who has not despised my petition." NANNI confessed to me without delay and with humble contrition; Catharine reconciled him with all his enemies, while I restored him to peace with God whom he had so long offended!

A few days after his conversion, Nanni was arrested by the Governor of the city and thrown in a close prison; a report was current that he was to suffer decapitation; this news afflicted me, and I went to find Catharine. "Nothing unfortunate," said I, "occurred to Nanni when he obeyed Satan, and now that he has given himself to God, heaven and earth appear to declare against him. I fear, Mother, that this plant is yet too young for supporting such a storm; the poor man may fall into despair, I entreat you, pray for him; you have delivered him from sin, now you must sustain him in his misfortunes." Catharine answered me: "Why are you alarmed on his account? you should rather rejoice. Do you not see the evidence that God has pardoned him the debt of eternal punishment, because he sends him temporal troubles. Our Lord's word is accomplished, the world loves what belongs to it; but now that he has quitted the world, the world detests him. God was preparing endless chastisement for him, but his mercy is satisfied with punishing him in this world. Fear not that he will fall into despair, He who saved him from hell, will also draw him from this danger."

It happened as she announced. A short time after, Nanni came out of prison, but he was obliged to pay very heavy sums, and Catharine rejoiced, saying: "That God was taking away the venom that impoisoned him." Tribulation only augmented his fervor; he desired to give Catharine, by an authentic act, a beautiful residence which he possessed, about two miles from the city, so that she might establish a monastery of females. Catherine did this with the special authorization of Gregory XI. of happy memory, and bestowed on it the name of "*Holy Mary of the Angels.*" I assisted at the consecration with all her spiritual family; the commissary designated by the Sovereign Pontiff was Friar John, abbot of the convent of St. Anthimè. This conversion, operated by the omnipotent hand of God, is due to Catharine's prayers. I can myself render testimony of it. I was during several years NANNI's Confessor, and I know that he made great progress in good, during the time that I knew him.

Volumes would not suffice for relating all that our Lord accomplished by his faithful Spouse, for the conversion of sinners, the spiritual advancement of the good, the encouragement of the weak, the consolation of the afflicted, the warning of souls in danger, etc. Who could compute the miserable whom she saved from hell, the hardened hearts that she has touched, the worldlings detached from vanity, persons tempted that she assisted by her prayers and freed from the demon by her counsels, the elect whom she directed in the path of virtue, those whose good desires she aided in progress towards perfection, those whom she saved from the abyss of vice and conducted to heaven, by bearing them, so to speak, in her arms, suffering and praying for their salvation? Yes, I may say as St. Jerome said to St. Paul: "Were

I gifted with a thousand tongues, it would be impossible for me to enumerate the fruits of salvation borne by this virginal plant, and cultivated by the Father in Heaven." I have often seen thousands of men and women hastening to her from the summits of the mountains and from the surrounding country, as though a mysterious trumpet invited them; they came to see and hear; her words were even sometimes useless, while her presence sufficed to convert them and inspire them with a lively contrition; all renounced their sins, and sought the tribunal of penance; then I was witness of the sincerity of their repentance, and it was evident to me that a superabundant grace acted in their hearts; and this happened not once, nor twice, but very often.

The Sovereign Pontiff, Gregory XI., consoled and delighted with the good effected in souls, granted to me and two companions, the powers reserved to Bishops, for absolving all those who went to Catharine and confessed. We, therefore, heard men and women of heinous guilt, soiled with every variety of crime, who had either never confessed, or who had not done it in suitable dispositions. We sometimes remained fasting until the evening, and yet we could not suffice to all who presented themselves. I acknowledge to *my* shame and Catharine's honor, that the multitude was frequently so considerable, that I was fatigued and discouraged. As to Catharine, she did not interrupt her prayer, and rejoiced in conquering souls for our blessed Master: she simply recommended to those who accompanied her to take care of us, who held the nets which she knew so well how to fill. It would be impossible to describe her joy; what we saw exteriorly, consoled us greatly and induced us to forget our fatigues

I will not enlarge further on the miracles that God wrought through Catharine; perchance the reader may have found this chapter lengthy, yet it is short in comparison with what we had to say.

CHAPTER VII.

OF SOME MIRACLES OBTAINED BY CATHARINE, FOR THE LIFE OR HEALTH OF THE NEIGHBOR.

I INTEND now to relate a circumstance amazing indeed, in our time, and yet very easy to HIM, with whom all things are possible. Lapa, Catharine's mother, was very simple and very kind, but not very desirous of invisible goods; she always had a great terror of quitting this life. After the death of her husband she also fell ill, and soon excited serious anxiety. Catharine, had recourse as usual to prayer, and entreated the Lord to deign to relieve her mother. It was answered her that Lapa would be saved if she died *then*, and that, thus, should avoid many heavy trials which menaced her. Catharine went to her mother and made the sweetest exhortations in order to prepare her, if God were to call, by engaging her to a compl te submission to his holy will; but Lapa, too deeply attached to earthly things, was horrified at the thought of leaving them; she conjured her daughter to plead with our Lord for her cure, and not to mention death. The Spouse of our Lord saw with pain these dispositions, and prayed in anguish that our Lord would not permit her to die, before she was perfectly submissive to his will. God complied with Catharine's prayer; the malady of Lapa became more alarming, but death was still averted. Catharine intervened between God and her mother, by her prayers and exhortations; she entreated God not to take her kind mother from the world, without her own consent; she exhorted her mother to submit to the good pleasure of God; but her prayers were more prevalent with our Lord, than with the mind of the patient. Hence our Redeemer said to his Spouse. "Announce to thy mother who is unwilling to die at present, that a day will arrive in which she will ardently sigh for death, without obtaining it." I can testify, with many others, the fulfillment of this prophecy. Lapa attained an extreme old age, and had so much to endure in persons and things that she loved, that she was continually saying: "God has riveted my soul to my body, so that it cannot be separated from it; how many children and grand-children have I already lost? it is only I that cannot die, I am left to feel the sufferings and death of all the others."

Lapa's heart was so obstinate, that she did not think of her soul's salvation. God then appeared to refuse his Spouse what he granted her at first. After having deferred, in accordance with her petition, the death of her mother, he permitted, in order to display her merits, that Lapa should die without having confessed. Her daughter, at the view of this misfortune cried to heaven, dissolved in tears: "Ah! Lord my God, are these the promises thou gavest me that none of mine should perish? Was not thy mercy pledged not to withdraw my mother from the world but when she would consent to it; and behold she is dead without receiving the Sacraments of the Church; in the name of thy infinite Bounty, suffer not my hopes to be thus deceived. I will not leave thy presence, until thou dost restore to me my mother." Three Ladies of Sienna, whose names we will give, were then present and heard these words. They saw Lapa breathe her last, and touched her body which gave no signs of life; they would have made every preparation for her interment, had they not waited for Catharine to complete her prayer. The Most High beheld the anguish of Catharine's heart and her humble and fervent supplications penetrated to the mercy-seat. The God of mercy and of consolation heard her, for the body of Lapa suddenly recovered motion; life returned completely and she soon resumed her ordinary occupation. She lived until the age of eighty-nine years, in the midst of affliction, privations and trials, just as her daughter had announced to her on the part of God.

The witnesses of this miracle were, Catharine Getti, Angela Vannini, (actually a *Sister of Penance of St. Dominic*) and Lysa, Catharine's sister-in-law: and Lapa's daughter-in-law: they still live and are all in Sienna; they heard Catharine when she said beside her dear mother, "Lord are these thy promises?" Thousands of persons knew Lapa after that period. All this shows Catharine's merit before God, for she preserved her father's soul from purgatory and recalled to life the inanimate body of her mother. This miracle took place in the month of October, 1370.

The following fact I can particularly attest. Seventeen years ago, that is 1373 or 1374, religious obedience summoned me to Sienna, where I exercised in the Convent of my Order, the functions of Lector. I was serving God in a lukewarm manner, when the plague declared itself, and raged as it had done in many places during our time, but never so fearfully as in Sienna. The contagion attacked men and persons of all ages; one day, two or even three days at most, sufficed to make one the victim of its empoisoned breath. In consequence terror reigned everywhere; zeal for souls, which is the spirit of the Order of St. Dominic obliged me to devote myself to the salvation of the neighbor. I therefore visited the sick, and I went very often to "Sainte Marie de la Misercorde." The director of that house was at that time Father Matthew who still lives. This man of holy life and reputation, was extremely attached to Catharine, and the virtue which heaven had accorded to him had inspired me with a warm affection for him. I was in the habit of seeing him once every day. One morning after the Conventual Mass, I went out to visit my sick and as I passed the HOUSE OF MERCY, I inquired whether any one in the establishment had been attacked with plague. On entering, I found Father Matthew whom the brothers were carrying like a corpse from the church to his room; his countenance was pale, his strength had forsaken him to such a degree, that he was incapable of speaking: when I inquired what he suffered he could not answer me. I therefore addressed myself to those who were accompanying him, and questioned them concerning what had happened to my friend: "Last night," said they to me, "about eleven o'clock, whilst he was watching near a sick person, he perceived himself stricken with the epidemic; and in a few moments, he fell into extreme weakness." I followed them to the sick man's bed, I bent over him, and when he had reposed a short time, he called for me and confessed as he was accustomed to do. After giving him absolution, I asked him what he suffered: He explained to me in what region he felt the pain; adding that it seemed to him that one of his legs was breaking and that his head was separating into four parts." I then felt his pulse, and saw in effect that he was suffering a violent fever. I recommended those who were taking care of him to explain certain things to doctor Senso, his physician, who is still living and was deeply attached to him.

I returned to visit him a short time after. Doctor Senso declared to me that my friend had the plague, and that every symptom announced the approach of death. "It is evident that the blood is inflamed in the liver; it is the reigning malady, and I greatly fear that the House of Mercy is soon to be deprived of its good director." I asked him if the medical art could not furnish some remedy? "We shall see to-night," answered he, "whether with the 'quintessence of cassia,' we can succeed in purifying the blood; but I have only a faint hope in this remedy, as the disease is too far advanced." After this response of the medical adviser, I withdrew, being very sad, and directed my steps towards the residence of the patient, praying God, mercifully to retain in the world, a man of so useful an example.

However, Catharine had learned the illness of Father Matthew whom she loved sincerely, on account of his many virtues; her heart was touched, and she speedily repaired to him whom she was unwilling to lose. Hardly had she entered the apartment, than she cried: "Get up Father Matthew, arise, this is not the moment to repose indolently in your bed." At the very instant in which she uttered these words, the fever and the marks[*] of the pestilence disappeared; Father Matthew found himself as free from pain, as though he had not been sick. Nature had obeyed her Master, who commanded by Catharine's mouth; and his word had restored the sufferer to perfect health. Father Matthew arose joyfully, and blessed the Lord for the power he had bestowed on his handmaid. Catharine modestly retired, to avoid the admiration of men; but at the moment in which she

---

[*] The plague spots.

withdrew from the house, I entered it, ignorant of what had passed, and believing my friend to be still very sick. As soon as I saw her, my grief urged me to say, with deep anxiety: "Mother, will you allow a person so dear and so useful to die?" *She*, wishing to conceal what she had done beneath the veil of humility, appeared to be annoyed at my words. "In what terms do you address me," said she, "am I like God, to deliver a man from death?" But I, beside myself with sorrow, continued: "Say that to others if you will; as to me who am well acquainted with your secrets, I know that you obtain from God whatever you ask with fervor." Then she bowed her head and smiled a little; after which she looked at me with a joyous countenance, saying: "Well, let us take courage, he shall not die this time."

At these words I banished all fear; I understood that she had obtained some grace from heaven. I left her, and went very contentedly to my sick friend, whom I found seated at his bedside and recounting to everybody the miracle that Catharine had just effected. I informed him that she had that moment assured me that he should not die of this malady. "Are you ignorant," replied he, "of what she has just done for me?" When I told him that I was not aware of anything, and that all she said to me was contained in that pleasing assurance, he stood up, much surprised, and joyfully narrated what I have here written. To attest the miracle more solidly the table was laid, and Father Matthew seated himself at it with us: they served him with food scarcely suitable for a sick man—vegetables and some *raw onions*—he, who an instant previous could not take anything, shared them with us; he chatted and laughed gaily; whilst that very morning he could scarcely pronounce one audible word.

Admiration and joy were general; all praised God who had bestowed so great a favor, and conversed approvingly and with holy envy of the merits of the saint who had obtained them. This miracle had also for witness, brother Nicolas d'Andrea of Sienna, of the Order of the Friar Preachers; he yet lives, and accompanied me on that day. Those who were resident in the house, pupils, priests, and more than twenty persons besides, saw what I have related.

Such as have not had their hearts touched may perchance say: what is there astonishing in the cure of a malady, even though it be serious? does not that happen naturally every day? I will respond to them by asking them: Why the Gospel recounts that our Lord healed Simon's mother-in-law, who was ill with a fever? Do we not continually see men relieved of violent fevers? Why then does the Evangelist cite this fact as a miracle? Let him who sees nothing beyond the letter, give attention to what the sacred writer has deigned to observe· "He approached her," says he, "he commanded the fever, the fever immediately left her, rising *instantly* she served them." (St. Luke iv. 39.) The proof of the miracle lies in the sudden disappearance of the fever, at the sole command of the Saviour, and without any natural remedy; she who had been so long sick and bed-ridden, arose without any exterior help; therefore, in what I have said, the eyes must be closed voluntarily, if the truth is not perceived. That God who had healed the mother-in-law of Simon, dwelt in Catharine; she did not approach, but afar, she commanded fever and pestilence, and without remedy and without delay, Father Matthew was delivered. Open, therefore, the eyes of the mind; be not incredulous but believing.

There was, near the HOUSE OF MERCY, a very pious woman, who wore, if I remember rightly, the habit of the *Sisters of Penance* of St. Dominic. In her admiration of Catharine's virtues, she desired to consecrate herself to her service; she followed her counsels with docility, was edified by her examples, and entertained towards her sentiments of profound veneration. It happened one day, that this woman being at home, the floor gave way beneath her, and dragged her downward in its descent; she was covered with contusions; her whole body was one general wound. The neighbors assembled in all haste, to draw her from amidst the fallen stones and timbers; they thought her killed. However, thanks be to God, they were able to remove her to her bed, where by degrees her consciousness returned; but it was to suffer horribly. The pain drew from her both tears and shrieks, and she detailed what she was enduring to those who surrounded her. Medical aid was obtained, and all was done for her that was possible; yet the poor woman could not move, and suffered a martyrdom in every limb.

As soon as Catharine heard it, she was filled with compassion for one who was her Sister, and who had made herself her servant. She went immediately to visit her, and exhorted her to patience by devout instruction. When she saw her suffering so excessively, she began to touch, (as though she would administer relief,) the places of which she complained; the patient willingly consented because she knew that those blessed hands could not fail of doing her good. As soon as Catharine touched any place, its pain vanished: hence the sick woman showed her the other parts that were tormented so that she might apply the same remedy, and Catharine lent herself to this charity with so much care, that she finished by completely healing her. In proportion as her virginal hand glided over her bruised body, the pain disappeared, and the sick woman who could not move a single member, recovered little by little her liberty of motion : she kept silence whilst Catharine was present lest she might alarm her humility, but afterwards she said to the physicians and neighbors that were surrounding her :—"Catharine, Lapa's daughter, has cured me by touching me." All were in admiration and gave glory to God ; for it was immpossible not to admit that this restoration proceeded from a divine virtue : I have related this miracle on the testimony of others, because when it was wrought, I was not yet acquainted with Catharine and did not even reside in Sienna.

During the same pestilence, a hermit called "*The Saint,*" and who *was so indeed*, was attacked by the contagion. As soon as Catharine heard it, she caused him to be carried from the cell in which he lived outside of Sienna, to the HOUSE OF MERCY ; she visited him with her companions, and was attentive to see that he had all necessary care. She approached him and said in a low tone. " Do not fear, however ill you may become you will not die this time." But she told us nothing similar, when we requested her to pray for his cure. She on the contrary, appeared like ourselves to fear his death ; and we were much grieved being sincerely attached to this pious man. The illness grew hourly worse, and we were beginning to despair of the safety of the body, and think only of the salvation of the soul. All physical energy appeared extinct, and we awaited his expiring sigh. Catharine said again in the patient's ear, "Fear not, you will not die." He who appeared to be unconscious, understood her perfectly, and believed more strongly in her word than in death whose presence he felt. And in effect, Catharine's word triumphed over the laws of nature; and divine virtue, more powerful than all human remedies, saved the dying man against all hope.

We were already preparing for his interment, and several days elapsed without amelioration. Catharine arrived and said in the ear of the sick man: "I command you, in the name of our Lord Jesus Christ, not to die." Life and strength immediately returned. The saintly man rose from his bed and asked for something to eat. A few moments sufficed for a complete cure: he related to us what Catharine had said to him, and that he had felt a divine energy retaining his soul which endeavored to escape. He affirmed that he was not cured by any natural cause, and believed this miracle to be as great as though he had arisen from the dead.

Having spoken of others, I must not pass in silence what Catharine did for me. When the plague was raging in Sienna, I resolved to sacrifice my life for the salvation of souls and not to avoid any pestiferous patient whatever: it is certain that the malady is contagious; but I also knew that our Lord Jesus Christ, is more potent than Galen and that grace is superior to nature. I also saw that many had taken flight, and that the dying remained without assistance; and as the blessed Catharine had taught me that charity obliges us to love the soul of the neighbor more than our own body, I was desirous of assisting as many sick as I could, and I did so by God's grace. I was almost alone in that vast city, and had scarcely time to take a little food and sleep. One night as I reposed, and the time approached to rise and recite my Office, I felt a violent pain in the region of the body first attacked by the reigning epidemic; my hand discovered to me the fatal swelling; frightened at this discovery I dared not rise and began to think seriously of death. I longed for the day, so that I could find Catharine before the disease made progress: the fever and pains in the head soon seized me; my fears augmented; I had however sufficient strength to recite my prayers. When morning came, I dragged myself with my companion, to Catharine's residence; but she was absent, having already been visiting a sick person. I decided to wait, and as I could no longer support myself, I was obliged to lie down on a bed which was there: I besought the person of the house not to delay sending for her. When she came, and saw my excessive suffering, she knelt down by my bed, placed her hand on my forehead, and began to pray interiorly as usual; I saw her enter into an ecstasy and I thought that there would soon result some good both for my soul and body. She remained thus, during nearly an hour and a half, when I felt a universal movement in my every limb: I was persuaded it was a prelude to vomitings, such as those I had witnessed in several persons that I saw die; but I was in error, it seemed as if something escaped from all the extremities of my body with a violent impulse; I began to feel an amelioration which augmented at every moment: before Catharine had recovered the use of her senses, I was completely cured, there only remained to me a certain weakness, a proof of my illness, or an effect of my want of faith. Catharine, aware of the grace that she had obtained from her Spouse, came to herself and caused them to prepare for me the ordinary nourishment common to the sick. When I had taken it from her virginal hands, she ordered me to sleep a little; I obeyed, and on awaking I found myself as active as if nothing had happened to me: then she said to me, "Now go and labor for the salvation of souls and render thanks to the Omnipotent who hath delivered you from this danger." I returned to my habitual fatigues, glorifying the Lord who had bestowed such power on his faithful Spouse.

At the same epoch, Catharine worked a miracle on Friar Bartholomew of St. Dominic of Sienna, my friend, he who at present governs the Roman province, and this miracle was more remarkable, because that Religious had been long and grievously sick with the plague.

When the contagion had passed to Sienna, many persons, but above all the sisters of a Convent of Pisa, having heard the praises of Catharine celebrated, evinced a lively desire of seeing her, and profiting by her instructions. They, therefore, entreated her to repair to Pisa, promising, in order to attract her, that her presence would be profitable to many souls. Catharine did not like journies; but she had recourse to her divine Spouse, and humbly deferred the case to his decision; she had consulted the opinion of those who surrounded her, and their sentiments were divided; some days after, our Lord appeared to her, and commanded her to yield to the requests of his servants, who were expecting her in the city of Pisa. "My NAME," said he, "will be greatly glorified by this journey, and souls will derive much benefit, according to the promise that I made thee, when thy soul separated from thy body, and was united to it anew."

Catharine obediently made known to me the divine will, and repaired directly to Pisa. I accompanied her, with several Fathers of my Order, so as to hear confessions; many of those who visied her had their hearts moved by her fervent words; and Catharine, in order that the devil might not resume his conquests, ordered them to seek a Confessor, and ask directly the sacrament of penance.

On our arrival at Pisa, Catharine was received hospitably at the house of an inhabitant named Girard Buonconti. Her host one day brought a young man of twenty years, and presented him to her, requesting her to be so kind as to pray for the recovery of his health informing her that during eighteen months fevers had never left him, and although he had none at that moment, they had been so violent, that his health was completely ruined notwithstanding all the efforts of medical skill and science. And indeed his pale attenuated countenance was sufficient proof.

Catharine moved with pity, enquired of the youth how long a time had elapsed since he had been to confession. On his replying that several years had found him remiss in this duty: "God," said she to him, "sends you this affliction, because you have remained so long, without purifying your soul in the Sacrament of Penance; go, therefore, my dear son, and confess; cleanse your soul from the corruption of sin whch has empoisoned your body." Then she sent for Friar Thomas, her first Confessor, and confided the sick youth to his care that he might hear his confession and give him absolution; when this was terminated, the youth returned to Catharine who said to him, while putting her hand on his shoulders: "Go, my son, with the peace of our Lord Jesus Christ, it is my will that you should have this fever no more." And it happened as she willed.

From that moment the young man had no more attacks of fever. In Catharine resided the power of Him of whom it is written : He spoke and it was done, commanded and creation sprung from chaos. Some days after the youth came and thanked her who had healed him, and he assured us that he had not been troubled with the slightest indisposition since that hour.

I was witness to this, and can say like St. John : "He who hath seen beareth testimony." There were also with me, Catharine's host, and Lapa, and also the inmates of the house, also Friar Thomas, confessor of Catharine and of the patient, Friar Bartholomew of St. Dominic and all the devout women of Sienna, who had accompanied Catharine. The youth who had been restored to health, published the miracle throughout the city, and when I was passing through Pisa several years after, he visited me and it was with difficulty I recognised him, so robust and manly was he in health and bearing : he recounted in presence of those who accompanied me, what has occurred, and attributed the glory of it to God's faithful servant Catharine.

A miracle similar to this, had taken place at Sienna ; only the illness was more dangerous. A *Sister of Penance* of St. Dominic named Gemmina, was much attached to Catharine : she had a quinsy, in consequence of a cold in the head which she had neglected, and her sickness made such rapid progress that the remedies employed proved inefficacious : the throat was so much inflamed that there was danger of suffocation. In this position, she made an extraordinary effort and went to Catharine, saying, as well as she could, as soon as she beheld her, "Mother, I shall die, unless you help me." Catharine had pity on the poor sister who could scarcely breathe in holy confidence, she applied her hand to the throat, made over it the sign of the Cross, and the pain disappeared immediately: she who had come in much pain and suffering, returned in perfect health, and with joy and gratitude, ran to Friar Thomas and related to him what had occurred; the latter took note of it, and from his manuscripts I extracted what I have just narrated.

When the Sovereign Pontiff, Gregory XI., quitted his abode in Avignon to return to Rome, Catharine arrived at Gênes, before him, and remained there to meet him. Two young persons from Sienna accompanied us; they were very pious, and are still living. The first was called Neri de Landoccio of Pagliaresi: he despised the world and its vanities and sanctified himself in solitude; the other was Etienne Corrade of Maconi: Catharine, when leaving this exile to soar to heaven, ordered him to enter the order of the Carthusians, and the grace of God so truly accompanied him, that he now directs a great portion of his Order, by his visits, teaching and example. He was successively placed at the head of several monasteries, and is now Prior of the Chartreuse of Milan. They were witnesses, as myself, of the greater number of miracles related in this *second part*; but in the city of Gênes the divine power was manifested in regard to themselves, by means of the blessed Catharine.

Whilst we were there, Neri was taken with an acute pain, which caused him much suffering and inconvenienced us greatly; he could neither walk nor yet be in bed; he crawled about on his hands and knees in the apartment, where other persons slept, and this irritated his pains, instead of soothing them, and an inflammation ensued.

Catharine having heard it, appeared to be moved to pity, and desired me to have physicians called and proper remedies given him: I obeyed promptly, inviting two medical advisers whose orders were faithfully accomplished; but the patient instead of obtaining relief, suffered more. I presume God permitted this, because he desired to display in an admirable manner, the power of his Spouse. The physicians perceiving their prescriptions useless, told me that they had no hope of saving him.

When I gave this news to the religious and the companions who were at table with me, Etienne Maconi left his repast, with a melancholy heart, and hastened to Catharine's room. He threw himself at her feet, melting into tears, conjuring her not to suffer his companion and brother, during a journey undertaken for God and her, to die far from home and be buried in a strange land. Catharine, deeply affected, said to him with maternal tenderness: "Why, my son, do you suffer yourself to be troubled? If God wishes to recompense your brother Neri's labors, you ought not to be afflicted, but on the contrary, rejoice." But Etienne insisted, "O dearest, kindest mother, I conjure you, hear my petition help him; I am perfectly convinced that you can, if you will." And Catharine, incapable of concealing her tenderness, replied: "I only exhorted you to conform to God's will; but since I see you so sad, when I receive holy communion at to-morrow morning's Mass, remind me of your request and I promise to pray God for your intention—you must yourself pray that he may hear me."

Etienne, quite joyous at having obtained this promise, failed not to present himself to Catharine just as she was going to Mass; he knelt humbly, and said to her: "Mother, I entreat you not to deceive my expectation." Catharine communicated at the Mass and as usual remained a long time in ecstasy. When she had resumed the use of her senses, she smiled on Etienne, who was waiting by her side, and said to him: "You have obtained the grace that you asked." Etienne said: 'Mother, will Neri be cured?" "Assuredly he will be saved," answered she, "for God desires to restore him to us." Etienne hastened to impart his joyful hopes to the sick person. The physicians afterwards arrived, and having recommenced their observations, began to say that, although they had given him up, his symptoms demonstrated that he might yet recover. In effect, according to Catharine's promise, convalescence commenced, and the recovery was soon complete.

But Etienne Maconi, overcome by the fatigue and sorrow occasioned by Neri's illness, was attacked by a violent fever, attended with vomiting and violent pains in the head. He kept his bed, and as he was generally beloved, we assisted him, and sought to console him. When the blessed Catharine heard of his state she was much afflicted; she visited him, and interrogated him concerning his malady, and perceiving that he was suffering from a fever, she said in a tone of authority: "I command you in virtue of holy obedience to have this fever no longer." Wonderful to relate! nature obeyed this order as if the the Creator of all things had pronounced it from high heaven; without employing any remedy, and before Catharine left his bedside, Etienne was completely delivered from his fever. We were all delighted to have our friend restored to us, and gave thanks to God for having so promptly manifested his power.

To these two miracles I will add a third, of which I was not witness, being absent; but she in whose favor it was performed, is yet living, and can testify to it. Jeanne de Capo, was a Sister of Penance of St. Dominic, and belonged to Sienna, but did not reside there. When the

Sovereign Pontiff Gregory XI., had returned to Rome, he sent Catharine to Florence in order to establish peace and reconcile the common father of the faithful with his revolted children. Catharine succeeded as I will narrate in a special chapter; but the infernal serpent who creates and entertains discord, because he is the enemy of unity, excited a sedition in the city against the Spouse of Christ, who was endeavoring to make peace. Her friends and those who accompanied her, advised her to withdraw for a time, and allow this tempest to pass. She, always humble and prudent, submitted to their views, but said that God had forbidden her to quit the neighborhood of the city, so long as peace and concord were not concluded between the Sovereign Pontiff and the people of Florence.

Catharine was therefore making preparations to retire from the city: but it was discovered that Jane was indisposed: one of her feet was very much swollen, and the pain in it, created a high fever, which prevented her from setting out. Catharine would not leave her alone, exposed to the ill-treatment of the impious, and she had recourse to prayer. She implored our Lord to condescend to lend an ear to her necessities, and while she was praying a gentle slumber took possession of the sick woman, and when she awoke, she was perfectly cured, without feeling any effects of her illness. She arose, and when daylight dawned, she set out with the others; her companions who had seen her suffering were in amazement, and blessed God for his mercies, towards Catharine.

To this miracle, I will add another which occured at Toulon, in Provence. We stopped at an Inn of that City, at the time of the return of Gregory XI. to Rome;

Catharine withdrew as usual to her apartment; we had not spoken of her, but the very stones appeared to announce her arrival. First women, and then men, came to our residence and asked where was the saint who returned from the Pontifical Court. The hostler having told them, it became impossible to hinder the crowd, and we were obliged to admit the women. One of them brought an infant whose body was so swollen that it excited pity in the beholders, and some persons present asked Catharine to be so obliging as to hold the infant a moment in her arms. Catharine refused, because she desired to shun the admiration of men; but in fine, overcome by compassion, she consented to what was demanded with such lively faith. Hardly was the babe placed in her virginal hands, than the swelling disappeared, and the little invalid was completely restored. I was not present when this miracle was performed; but it was so evident and so well certified, that the Bishop of the City sent for me, and when relating it, informed me that the child was the nephew of his vicar: he requested me to obtain for him an interview with Catharine.

Our Lord Jesus Christ produced many other miraculous cures, by the intervention of the blessed Catharine: it would be impossible for me to recount them all in one book, but I have recounted some, which will suffice to prove how Jesus, the Son of God and of Mary, acted in her. The deliverance of those that were tormented with devils naturally refers to the healings of the body: but as this chapter is sufficiently lengthy, and as Catharine enjoyed a special grace for those unfortunate souls, I will treat this subject separately.

CHAPTER VIII.

OF MIRACLES PERFORMED BY CATHARINE BY DELIVERING SUCH AS WERE POSSESSED BY THE DEVIL.

Our divine Lord continually exhibited exteriorly the graces with which he interiorly adorned his Spouse. Fire cannot remain concealed, and a tree planted by the water courses, always bears its fruit in due season. The virtue of Jesus Christ, or rather Jesus Christ himself, dwelt in Catharine's heart, and displayed its presence there more and more each successive day, not only by obtaining for sinners the conversion of their souls, and for the sick health and corporal restoration, but in commanding evil spirits, and chasing them from those whom they possessed; and thus for the Name of Our Lord residing in her, every thing in heaven, on earth, and in hell bent the knee before her.

There was in Sienna, a man named Ser. Michel de Monaldo, a very skillful notary, whom I have seen a hundred times, and from whom I received the following facts. Being advanced in years, he took the resolution with his wife's consent, to consecrate himself wholly to the service of God and to offer to him the virginity of his two daughters. He made application to a monastery established in the city, under the invocation of St. John the Baptist; he confided his daughters to the religious Sisters who resided there, gave them his fortune, and lodged with his wife outside of the enclosure, and there directed the temporal affairs of the convent.

This arrangement lasted a considerable time when by a just, but incomprehensible judgment of God, one of the daughters of Ser. Michel, called Laurencia, aged about eight years, became possessed by the devil; the foe of salvation tormented her cruelly and troubled the peace of the entire monastery. The Nuns being unable to retain the child longer, obliged Ser. Michel to resume his charge. When she had retired from the Convent the devil ceased not to manifest his presence in an extraordinary manner. He spoke Latin by her mouth, although *she* had no idea of that tongue; he answered the most difficult questions, and manifested the sins and secrets of a great number of persons; in fine, it was evident to every one that God permitted the devil, for a motive concealed from man, to torment this poor little innocent.

Her parents were in the deepest distress and sought every method of relieving her; they brought her to visit the relics of saints whose merits could put the devil to flight. They had above all confidence in the intercession of the blessed Ambrose of the Order of Preaching Friars, whom God has glorified during more than a century by a great number of miracles, and who is endued with a special power for chasing out malignant spirits; his cope or his scapular which are still preserved, have often sufficed for delivering the possessed when clothed in them; I have myself witnessed this effect on several occasions. The parents of little Laurencia led her to the church of the Preaching Friars, placed her on the tomb of Blessed Ambrose, covered her with his habit or sacerdotal ornaments, and fervently implored God for her deliverance, but they were not heard: *this* possession was undoubtedly not to punish the child who had not sinned, nor her parents who had always led an exemplary life;

but God I presume suffered it, in order to increase the honor of his faithful servant. The blessed Ambrose who already enjoyed beatitude, desired to leave the credit of the miracle to Catharine who was continuing her earthly pilgrimage, and thus make known her virtues to the faithful, even before her death: several of Catharine's acquaintances advised the parents of Laurencia to present their child to her, but when they attempted it, Catharine answered: "Alas! I am myself daily tormented by the demons: how do you imagine that I can deliver others?" And as she could not escape by the door, without meeting those who came, she hid herself so completely in the attic that they could not find her. The parents retired, without having obtained anything; but this proof of humility and this flight from human esteem, inspired them with greater confidence in her sanctity, and induced them to demand her assistance with greater ardor.

As they could not procure access to her, because she forbade all her companions to speak to her of this affair, they had recourse to Friar Thomas, as her confessor, to whom they knew Catharine was very submissive. They exposed their misfortune to him, and entreated him to oblige Catharine in the name of holy obedience to help them in their affliction. Friar Thomas felt an extreme compassion for their trouble, but he knew that his authority did not extend so far as to oblige Catharine to the performance of miracles, and as he feared to wound her humility, he made use of the following expedient: one evening while Catharine was absent, he conducted the little possessed into her oratory, and said to one of her companions who remained in the house: "Tell Catharine, when she will return, that I command her in virtue of holy obedience, to allow that child to remain here during the night, and to keep her until morning near herself." Catharine returned a short time after, and found little Laurencia in her room; she recognized that she was possessed by the demon, and suspected that it was the child that she had refused to see: Having questioned her companion and learned the order of her Confessor, she perceived that there was no means of escape; she therefore had recourse to prayer, and forced the child to kneel and pray with her. The whole night was consumed in thus combating the enemy by a holy vigil: before daybreak, the demon, was, notwithstanding his resistance, overcome by the divine virtue, and the delivered child felt no ill. In the morning, as soon as Alessia, Catharine's companion, was informed of it, she told her Confessor that Laurencia was no longer possessed. Friar Thomas, with the parents, repaired directly to Catharine's house; they found Laurencia completely cured, and with tears of joy, thanked God, and her whom he had deigned to use as his merciful instrument. They intended taking their daughter with them; but Catharine knew by a divine light what was to happen and bade them: "Leave the child there a few days, it being necessary to her salvation." They accepted this proposition with eagerness and joyfully withdrew. Catharine profited by this time to give holy counsels to Laurencia; she taught her by word and example to pray frequently and fervently, and prohibited her leaving the house, under any pretext, until her parents came for her. The child was docile, and showed herself day by day better disposed; the house in which she was staying, was not Catharine's, but that of her companion Alessia, and it was not very remote. It happened that Catharine remained a whole day at home with Alessia, having left Laurencia in charge with the domestic. After nightfall, Catharine suddenly called Alessia, and told her to put on her cloak and go with her at once to the child that had been entrusted to them; the latter observed that it was unbecoming for females to go out at that hour; but Catharine answered: "Hasten, for the infernal wolf has caught the lamb that we have saved." She and Alessia set out without delay—and when they reached the house they found Laurencia furious, her countenance totally distorted and inflamed. "Ah! serpent," exclaimed Catharine, " thou hast dared to enter anew into that innocent child; but I have faith in Jesus my Saviour and Spouse; thou shalt make thy exit, no more to return." Pronouncing these words, she led the child into the place where the prayers had been offered, and after some instants, she brought her back perfectly delivered, and recommended her to take some repose. When morning arrived, she sent for the parents, and said: " Now, you may take your child in all security; she will not be tormented in future." The prophecy has so far been accomplished; Laurencia returned to her monastery and has served God in it, in peace, for more than sixteen years.

Being desirous of knowing more fully what had passed, I interrogated Catharine herself, and I asked her how the demon had been so audacious as to resist the power of relics and even exorcism: she answered that the obstinacy of the evil spirit was so great that she had been forced to dispute with him until four o'clock in the morning: she ordered him to come out in the Name of the Redeemer, and he obstinately refused, but after a prolonged contest, the demon perceiving himself on the point of being driven out, said: " If I leave her, I will enter thy soul." Catharine said: "If God allow it: for I know that thou canst do naught without his permission, and I refrain from opposing his holy will in the least."

Then the spirit of pride, overcome by this trait of sincere humility, lost his power over that child; however he held her by the throat and provoked a swelling in it: Catharine raising her hand to the neck, made over it the blessed sign of Redemption; the devil then lost his grasp entirely.

The following miracle will exhibit more clearly to what a degree the blessed Catharine had received from God the power of driving out Satan; I was not present, for she had sent me to the VICAR of JESUS CHRIST, Pope Gregory XI., on affairs relative to the church; but brother 'Saint,' the hermit whose cure I related above, Alessia and other accompanying friends are witnesses.

Catharine had gone with the noble, and venerable Lady Bianchina, widow of John Agnolino Salimbeni, to la Roche Castle, where I had passed several weeks with her: a woman near this castle was seized with the demon, who tormented her shockingly. When Lady Bianchina knew this, she, through compassion, wished that Catharine would succor the unhappy victim: but she knew her humility and her annoyance, when they spoke to her of such subjects. Having taken counsel from her companions, she had the possessed person brought into Catharine's presence, in order that the sight of her might inspire charity and excite her to deliver her. When they conducted her there, our blessed Catharine was laboring to reconcile two enemies who were at war, and she was disposing herself to go into the neighborhood to terminate the quarrel. As soon as she beheld the possessed woman, she comprehended that escape was inevitable, and expressed her sorrow to Lady Bianchina; "May God forgive you, Lady, for what you have done! Do you not know that I am often tormented by the devils; how can you oblige me to expose myself to them, by leading before me a possessed individual?" then she turned towards the demoniac, saying: "You cursed spirit, who are resolved to prevent this reconciliation, place your head here, and wait in that position until my return!"

At that order, the possessed woman with great docility placed her head as Catharine had commanded, and the Blessed Catharine went to terminate the work her charity had begun. Satan cried out, by the mouth of the possessed: "Why do you retain me here, let me go, I am too cruelly tormented." The persons present said: "Why do you not leave the room, the door is open?" And the evil spirit said: "I cannot; that woman has enchained me." When he was asked whom he meant, he either would not or could not name her; he only said: "*My enemy.*" Brother Saint who supported the head of the possessed woman, asked him: "Is thy enemy very powerful?" He answered "I have none greater in the whole world." When those present desired to prevent his screams, they tried to silence him by saying: "Be quiet, Catharine is coming." The first time he rejoined: "She is not coming yet, she is in such a place," and indicated the exact place where she actually was. On being asked what she was doing: he said, "Something that displeases me sovereignly, and which she often does"—and with that saying, he shrieked still louder: "Why keep me here?" Still he never moved the head of the demoniac, from the position in which

Catharine had commanded it to be placed. After a few moments he said: "The one I hate, is returning here." They asked where she was; he answered: "She is no longer in that place; she is in *such* a place," then added: "now she is *there*," and indicated all the different localities through which Catharine passed; at length he said, "now she is on the threshold of the house;" and it was correct.—When Catharine entered the room, he cried still more loudly: "Why do you keep me here?" "Get up, wretch," said Catharine to him, "go forth quickly, and leave in peace this creature of our Lord Jesus Christ, and never presume to torment her anew."

At these words, the evil spirit forsook every portion of her body, except the throat which he caused to swell in a fearful manner. Catharine applied her virginal hand and making the sign of the Cross over it, chased the demon away completely. The woman was relieved in presence of all the spectators; and being weak and overcome, by excess of suffering, Catharine sustained her some time by allowing her to recline upon her breast and in her arms; after ordering her some refreshing diet, they led her to her own house. When the poor invalid, who was delivered, had opened her eyes after sleeping, she was astonished to perceive herself surrounded by so many persons, and in the house of her mistress; and she inquired of her relatives, "who carried her there, and when?" When they informed her that she had been tormented by the demon, she said that she had no remembrance of it, only she felt as though she had been beaten violently in every limb, and that her body felt universally bruised. She rendered humble thanks to her liberator, and went on foot to the house whence they had been forced to carry her on a litter.

Our Lord Jesus Christ delivered several other possessed, in a miraculous manner, by Catharine's intercession. I did not recount these cures in this chapter, but those that I have cited suffice to give a clear view of the grace the Blessed Catharine had received for casting out demons; she obtained it by triumphing in herself over these malicious spirits, with God's help, in many a striking circumstance.

CHAPTER IX.

OF ST. CATHERINE'S GIFT OF PROPHECY, AND IN WHAT MANNER SHE DELIVERED SEVERAL PERSONS FROM DANGER WHICH THREATENED THEIR SOULS AND BODIES

WHAT I am about to offer may appear incredible; but the infallible TRUTH is my witness, that such has been my experience, that there is nothing of all that has ever occurred to me, of which I am so certain. Catharine possessed a prophetical spirit so perfect and so constant, that nothing could escape her; she knew whatever referred to herself or to those who approached her, or who sought her counsels for the benefit of their souls; it was impossible for us to do anything good or ill in her absence, without her having at the very instant a knowledge of it; we experienced it, so to speak, at each moment; and what is more admirable, she often told us our inmost thoughts, as if they had been hers. I know that for myself, and I confess it before the whole church militant, she rebuked me for certain thoughts which were troubling me in the very moment, and that I was obstinately concealing from her. I am not ashamed to declare it for her glory. "Why hide from me," said she to me, " what I see more clearly than you think." And she directly gave me wholesome advice on that subject. This happened to me very often. He who knoweth all things is my witness. But let us enter into some details; and for the sake of order, let us commence with things spiritual.

There was in Sienna a knight, who to nobility of birth

added glorious exploits, and who had acquired in the neighborhood the title of "*My Lord Nicolas des Sarrasius*." After passing a great portion of his life in battles he had returned to his domestic fireside, intending to administer his estate, and enjoy a fortune; he made merry with his friends, and promised himself a long career. Eternal Goodness, who wills the death of none, inspired the knight's lady, and some pious relatives with a design of engaging him to go to confession and do penance for the sins committed in the lengthy wars, which had occupied the former portion of his life; but he, all devoted to visible things, derided these prudent counsels, and cared little for his eternal salvation.

At this period, the blessed Catharine enlightened the city of Sienna by her virtues, and was particularly remarkable by the conversion of sinners the most hardened, who were either completely converted, or at least renounced a portion of their evil customs. The individuals who were interesting themselves in the salvation of the knight, perceiving the futility of their efforts, requested him to hold a conversation with Catharine. "What have I to do with that good woman? Pray, what service could she render me?" His wife who was strongly attached to Catharine went to her and informed her how hardened was her husband, and entreated her to pray to God for his conversion. It happened one night that the blessed Catharine appeared in a dream to our chevalier, and warned him to listen to the good advice of his wife, if he would avoid eternal damnation. On awaking, he said to his lady: "Last night, I saw in my dreams, *that* Catharine of whom you so often speak with me; I should like to have an interview with her, and see if she really looks as she appeared to me." His wife overjoyed at this news, hastened to Catharine, thanked her, and agreed upon the time in which her husband might converse with her. In fine, the knight conversed with Catharine, was perfectly converted, and promised to go as soon as possible to confess hiss ins to Friar Thomas; he was faithful to grace and fulfilled his promise.

One morning after he had concluded, this man, whom I knew already, met me when I was returning from the city to my convent, and inquired of me where he would probably find Catharine at that time. I said: "I presume in our church." "I pray you," added he, "be so kind as to conduct me there, because it is necessary for me to speak with her." I cheerfully consented; and entering the church with him, I called one of Catharine's companions and charged her with the commission of the chevalier. Catharine arose from the place in which she was praying, and advancing to meet him, graciously and respectfully saluted him. The aged knight said to her with a profound inclination: "Madame, I have done what you prescribed to me; I confessed all my sins to Friar Thomas, who assigned me a penance, and I am resolved to accomplish it, such as it is imposed on me." Catharine responded: "You have acted wisely for the salvation of your soul, now avoid all your former practices and combat as valiantly for Jesus Christ, as you have done for the world." She added: "My Lord, have you confessed all that you did?" And as he assured her that he was certain of having told all that came to his memory, she repeated to him: "Examine well, whether you have omitted nothing?"

He affirmed anew that he had confessed all that he recollected. Catharine took leave of him, and allowed him to remain alone a few moments, and then called him by means of one of her companions, and said: "Examine your conscience I entreat you, and see whether you did not forget some sin." And as he again affirmed that he had confessed all, she drew him aside, and recalled to his memory a grievous sin that he had secretly committed when in la Puglia. The soldier, much astonished, acknowledged that he had indeed committed that sin; he went in search of his Confessor and completed his confession. Afterwards he could not keep silence in regard to this miracle, and narrated its particulars to all those that wished to hear him, as though he would say like the Samaritan woman of old: " Come and see this virgin who revealed to me my most secret offences; is she not a saint and a prophetess? How do otherwise than recognize it, for the fault which she recalled to me, could be known to no one but myself." From that hour, the brave knight obeyed Catharine as a pupil obeys his master, and death soon manifested the necessity of this happy change. Ere that year had winged its flight, a painful illness concluded his days, and he rendered his soul to God in the best dispositions.

There are several points worthy of remark in this event; first, the apparition during sleep, the supernatural revelation of a sin, and then the salvation of a man, long habituated to offending. Let us, while blessing God for the use he made of Catharine's intercession, turn our attention to another species of revelation and a miraculous help obtained from heaven by her means.

Before enjoying the privilege of a particular acquaintance with the blessed Catharine, I dwelt a long time in a fortified place, called Montepulciano, and I directed there during four years, a monastery of Nuns of my Order. During my sojourn in this place, where there was no convent of Preaching Friars, I had with me but one companion, and I found great pleasure in receiving the Religious men who came from the houses in the vicinity, especially those for whom I felt a stronger spiritual friendship. Friar Thomas, (Catharine's Confessor,) and Friar George Naddo, now professor of Theology, proposed coming to see me in the convent of Sienna, in order to exchange spiritual consolations. So as to return more promptly to Catharine, (who always required Friar Thomas,) the two Religious took horses that were lent them by persons of their acquaintance. Arrived at about six miles from the place where they intended going, they had the imprudence to halt and rest themselves : the people of the place were not thieves by profession, but when they saw travellers alone and without defence, they allured them apart, robbed them, and sometimes killed them, so that justice might not discover their crimes.

Having observed these two Religious, unaccompanied and taking rest in an inn, they went before, to the number of ten or twelve, and awaited in the winding paths of a solitary place. When the Religious passed by, they attacked them roughly with swords and lances, dragged them from their horses, robbed them completely, and conducted them with abusive treatment into the depth of the forest : there they held council, and the two Religious comprehended perfectly well that there was question of killing them, and concealing their corpses in order to destroy all trace of their criminal conduct.

In the midst of such a pressing danger, Friar Thomas spared not entreaties, and promises of "*saying nothing ;*" but when he saw that all was useless, and that they were conducting them farther and farther into the deep and entangled forest, he comprehended that God alone could succor them and began to pray. Knowing how agreeable his spiritual daughter was to God, he said interiorly: "O Catharine, meek and devoted servant of God, help us in this peril." Scarcely had he uttered these words in heart, than the Robber nearest him, and the one too who appeared to be charged to kill him, said: "Why should we kill these poor friars who never did us any injury? it would be indeed an enormous crime! let us suffer them to go, they are good hearted men, who will never betray us." All accepted this opinion so suddenly advanced, with such unanimity, that not only they allowed the Religious their lives, but even restored to them their garments, horses and all that they had stolen, except a little money, and suffered them to go at liberty: they arrived at my house on the same day and related these preceding circumstances. When Friar Thomas returned to Sienna he certified, as he wrote, and as he recounted to me, that at the same moment in which he had invoked her assistance, Catharine said to one of her nearest companions: "My father Confessor is calling me, and I am aware that he is in great danger," and rising immediately she went to pray in her oratory. It cannot be doubted, that it was at that moment by the efficacy of her prayers, that a change so wonderful was produced in the dispositions of the robbers; and she did not, we may believe, desist from praying until they had restored to those Religious their liberty and their goods. It is evident that Catharine possessed the spirit of prophecy, for she knew at a distance of twenty-four miles, a mental prayer addressed to her, and was capable of granting so promptly and perfectly the help implored.

How advantageous is it to be in the friendship of

persons who see like the angelic spirits, and who being clothed with power divine may aid us in every danger; and if Catharine's prayers were so powerful while she was yet in this terrestrial vale, what must be her influence now in Heaven.

I here present another circumstance to which I was witness with Friar Pierre de Velletri of my Order, actual Penitentiary at St. John Lateran: it was a renewed proof of Catharine's gift of prophecy. At the moment in which the greater portion of the cities and of the lands which belonged to the see of Rome, had revolted against the Sovereign Pontiff, Gregory XI. (viz. in 1375), Catharine was at Pisa, whither I had accompanied her. When the news of the defection of Perouse reached us, I was distressed at beholding in Christians, neither the fear of God, nor love for his holy Church, since they despised the sentences of excommunication pronounced against them, and had the audacity to usurp the rights of the SPOUSE of JESUS CHRIST. I went therefore to Catharine, with Friar Pierre de Velletri, my heart drenched in grief, and with tearful eyes announced to her this melancholy event. At first she mingled her sorrow with ours and deplored the loss of souls and the great scandals which afflicted the Church; but after a little, perceiving that we were too much dejected, she said in order to calm us: "Be not in haste to shed tears; you will have worse things to excite your lamentations; what you now mourn is mere *milk* and *honey* to what will follow." These words instead of administering comfort awakened a deeper grief, and I said to her: "Mother, can we possibly witness greater misfortunes, than beholding Christians lose all love and respect for the Church of God, and fearless of her censures, separating from her union openly?

the next step will be to deny our Lord himself!" Then she said to me: "Now Laymen behave thus; but ere long you will find that the clergy will also render themselves culpable." And as, in great astonishment, I exclaimed, "how dreadful;—will the clergy also rebel against the Sovereign Pontiff?" She continued, "When the Holy Father will attempt to reform their morals, the ecclesiastics will offer the spectacle of a grievous scandal to the whole church; they will ravage and divide it as though they were heretics." These words overwhelmed me with emotion, and I asked "Mother, will a new heresy arise?" She answered: "It will not be an actual Heresy, but it will divide the Church with all Christendom; hence arm yourself with patience, for you will be obliged to witness the misfortunes."

I was silent and waited, because I fancied that she was disposed to disclose many other things to me: but not to increase my trouble she declined further predictions. I confess that I did not comprehend these correctly, at the moment, on account of the obscurity of my understanding: for I thought that all this would happen during the pontificate of the reigning Pope Gregory XI. At his death I had nearly forgotten that prophecy, but when Urban VI. succeeded, and the Church was rent with schism I beheld the verification of what she predicted to me. Reproaching myself for the obtuseness of my intellect, I endeavored to hold another conversation with her on this subject, and God allowed me this privilege, when in obedience to the Order of the Supreme Pontiff, Catharine repaired to Rome, in the commencement of the Schism. I then reminded her of what she had said to me, several years previous: she had not forgotten it, and added: "I then told you that what was transpiring would prove but milk and honey; I now declare to you that the present transactions are children's sport in comparison with what will take place in the neighboring territories." She thus designated Sicily, the Roman province, and the surrounding country: heaven and earth can testify the accomplishment of that event. Queen Jeanne then reigned; but after, who can describe the misfortunes which lowered on her and her kingdom, on her successor and on foreigners who entered her States. The ravages which desolated that unhappy country are universally known. It is evident to any one in possession of reasoning faculties, that the Blessed Catharine was indued with the gift of prophecy in so high a degree that she read in the future, whatever of importance was destined to occur.

But that it may not be said, as Achab formerly said of Micheas: (IV. Kings, xii. 8.) "His prophecies always announce evil and not good." I will present you sweets after the bitter, drawing for you from the pure treasures of things past and future belonging to the Blessed Catharine. At Rome I requested her to inform me what would happen in the Church after all these miseries.— She replied. "After these tribulations and trials will have passed, God will purify the holy Church by means unknown to men; he will arouse the souls of elect from lukewarmness and the reform of Holy Church will be so beautiful, the renovation of her ministers so perfect, that the future prospect of all this rejoices my soul in God. I have often spoken to you of the wounds, and of the nudity of the Spouse of Christ: but then she will be radiant with beauty, sparkling with jewels and crowned with a diadem of VIRTUES; the faithful will rejoice in the holiness of their pastors, and unbelievers attracted by the good odor of Jesus Christ, will return to the sheepfold, and will surrender themselves to the Chief and Bishop of their souls. Give thanks to God for the great calm, that he will grant to the Church, after that tempest." She said no more; and I who know that the Almighty is more prodigal of his kindness than of his rigors, I have a firm hope that after the ills which are happening, the blessings foretold by the Blessed Catharine will arrive; and that all the tribes of Israel shall know that she is truly a prophetess from God.

As there is here question of Catharine's prophecies, I think it the best place to confound the ignorance of those who presume to contest her sincerity, and spread shameful calumnies against her sanctity. To give a specious coloring to their falsehoods, they say that she predicted a general Crusade of Christians which she and her disciples were to follow into the Holy Land. She being dead many a year, as well as those who followed her, it is impossible that this pilgrimage should be accomplished, and they concluded thence that all her sayings were no prophecies, but discourses unworthy of attention.

I acknowledge, first, that it is very true that Catharine always desired a Crusade, and that she acted with diligence in the hope of realizing this desire: it was, it may be said, the ruling motive of her journey to Avignon; she intended engaging Pope Gregory to organize a holy War; and I am witness that she did so; because when she conversed with the Sovereign Pontiff on that subject, I acted as interpreter; Gregory XI. expressed himself in Latin, and Catharine in the dialect of Tuscany. The Sovereign Pontiff said to her: "First of all, peace must be established among Christians, and then we might organize a Crusade." Catharine replied to him : "Holy Father, there is no better means for re-establishing peace among Christians, than the undertaking of a Crusade. All the turbulent soldiers who now entertain division among the faithful, will go cheerfully and combat in the holy cause ; very few will refuse to serve God in the profession which pleases them, and it will be a means for expiating their offences : the fire will be thus extinguished for want of fuel. You will thereby, Holy Father, accomplish several excellent things at once ; you will bestow peace on such of the Christians as require it, and you will save great culprits by removing them. Should they gain important victories, you could act, in consequence, with Christian Princes ; if they yield, you will have procured salvation to their perishing souls ; and besides, many Saracens might be converted." These words show with what zeal the Blessed Catharine labored to organize this crusade.

Now, I declare to these calumniators that I never heard Catharine indicate in any manner whatsoever that a Crusade would certainly take place ; I always found her on the contrary very reserved concerning it, never determining an epoch, but resigning the whole to divine Providence ; she expressed a hope that God would cast a look of mercy on his people and thus save many believers and unbelievers ; but none can truthfully advance that she ever fixed the period of that Crusade, and declared that she would follow it with her disciples : should any one appear to have thus understood her, they have conceived an incorrect interpretation of her words.

The person who was the subject of the following prophecy, relates it daily to any one desirous of hearing it. There lived in Sienna, at the period of my acquaintance with Catharine, a youth of noble birth, but at that time of vile and contemptible manners; he was called then as now, François Malevolti. He lost his parents at an early age, and the too great liberty he possessed led him into the most vicious practices. He espoused a youthful wife, and this union ought to have incited him to a reformation of life, but he could not resolve to break off his wretched customs. One of his companions who was a disciple of Catharine, took compassion on his soul, and invited him to go and hear the holy counsels of the " Blessed," and he succeeded in leading him there occasionally; after which François would repent and moderate his disorders for a time, but without being able to forsake them totally. I have often seen him with us; he relished Catharine's salutary lessons and admirable examples, and took pleasure in adopting them; but he would return to his former habits, especially to gaming, of which he was passionately fond.

Catharine, who often prayed for his salvation, said to him one day in the ardor of her zeal: " You frequently come to visit me, and then like an untamed bird you return to your vices; but fly away as much as you please, the moment will come when God will allow me to throw a noose around your neck, which will prohibit your future flight!" François and all present observed these words. Catharine died without seeing their accomplishment— poor François relapsed into his former faults; but his faithful friend did more for him in heaven than her counsels could effect for him in earth. François first lost his wife, by an early death; then his mother-in-law, and other individuals who presented obstacles to his salvation. He was thus led to consider his ways, and renounced the world to enter into the Order of the Olivetains. He persevered therein, by God's grace and Catharine's merits;

he always attributes his conversion to her who had predicted it, and continually tells the tale to every willing listener.

To make a recapitulation here, of all that has reference to souls, I am about to relate a fact of which God rendered me the witness, but which is better appreciated by dom Bartholomew de Ravenne who was then, and is still, Prior of the Carthusians, in Gorgone Island, thirty miles from the port of Livourno. This Religious, who possessed fervent piety joined to a consummate prudence, was greatly attached to Catharine, and extremely edified by her admirable instructions; he often pressed her to come and pass a day in his island, that he might conduct his Brethren to her and let them profit by God's holy word, and he entreated me to support his petition. Catharine consented to it; we made the voyage to the number of about twenty persons. The night of our arrival, the Prior lodged the " Blessed " and her companions about a mile from the monastery; and the following morning he conducted all of his monks to Catharine and requested her to favor them with some words of edification. Catharine refused at first, excusing herself on the grounds of her incapacity, her ignorance, and her sex; saying that it was meet that she should *listen* to God's servants, rather than speak in their presence. Overcome at last by the earnest prayers of the Father and of his spiritual sons, she began to speak, and said what the Holy Ghost inspired her in reference to the numerous temptations and illusions which Satan presents to solitaries, and concerning the means of avoiding his wiles and of gaining a complete victory, and all this she did with so much method and distinctness, that I was filled with amazement, as indeed were all her audience. When she had terminated, the Prior turned towards me and said with admiration : " Dear Brother Raymond, I confess these Religious,—and, consequently, know the defects of each. I assure you, that if this saintly female had heard as myself all their confessions, she could not have spoken in a more just and profitable manner ; she neglected none of their wants, and did not utter a useless word. It is evident that she possesses the gift of prophecy and that she speaks by the Holy Ghost."

In fine, I will add, that I am positively certain in reference to my own case she predicted many things that I did not suspect, and of which I now see the full accomplishment ; but I decline entering into further details. I will restrict myself to what happened to others : she had announced the terrible chastisements that would befall some persecutors of the Catholic Church : I say naught concerning them because of the wickedness of the people of our time, and to avoid exciting against her glorious name the venom of detractors.

CHAPTER X.

OF THE MIRACLES THAT OUR LORD PRODUCED BY MEANS OF CATHARINE ON THINGS INANIMATE.

SUPREME JUSTICE wills that all things obey those who are pefectly obedient to God. Catharine obeyed her Creator faithfully, and all creatures in return fulfilled her commands. At the period in which our Saint lived in Sienna, and previous to my acquaintance with her, there was a young widow, Alessia by name, who indulged such an affection to Catharine that life was unpleasant when deprived of her society. She was anxious to be clothed with the holy livery which Catharine wore, and deserted her own house to occupy one near Catharine's, and thus be able to commune with her more frequently : hence our Blessed Catharine neglected somewhat the paternal roof, often tarrying with Alessia several days, and sometimes weeks and entire months. One year grain was scarce ; many inhabitants had purchased wheat that was spoiled by humidity and it being impossible to find any other for any price, Alessia was forced to do the same. At the approach of harvest, before their provision of flour was exhausted, new and excellent grain was brought to the market : and hence Alessia intended throwing away the remains of the bad flour, and make bread of the new wheat just purchased, and mentioned her intention to Catharine. The latter said, " Why throw away what God has given for man's sustenance ? if you do not like to eat of that bread distribute it to the poor who have none." Alessia said that she scrupled giving them bread that was of such bad quality, and preferred giving them plentifully of that formed out of the good flour, to which Catharine replied: " Prepare the water, and bring hither the flour that you intended throwing away, I will myself make some loaves of it, to distribute to the poor of Jesus Christ."

Catharine first kneaded the paste, and then formed from a small quantity of the bad flour, such a number of loaves, and with such promptitude, that Alessia and her domestic who were looking on, could not recover from their astonishment; four or five times the amount of flour would have been requisite for making all the loaves which the blessed Catharine presented to Alessia that the latter might arrange them on the boards; and these loaves of bread had not the disagreeable odor of those that had been hitherto made from this flour. When the whole was used, Catharine sent the bread to the oven and caused it to be served at table. All who partook of it not only found it free from bitterness or any unusual odor, but on the contrary declared they " had never eaten any so pleasant." The affair was reported to Friar Thomas, Catharine's Confessor, who came with other learned Religious to examine these particulars; those pious men were in admiration at the view of the multiplied quantity of the loaves and their quality so marvelously corrected. A third prodigy succeeded these two: Catharine caused the loaves to be distributed; they were given copiously to the poor and to the Religious: no other bread was consumed in the house, and yet a great quantity was ever in the Pantry. Thus the Lord, by the intervention of his handmaid, signalized his power in three ways, on the occasion of her loaves;

first he corrected the corruption and bad odor of the flour; then he increased the paste from which it was formed, and in fine he so multiplied the bread that it served for distribution during several weeks. Many pious persons kept portions of this bread through devotion, there are some still provided with it, although twenty years have elapsed since the occurrence of this miracle.

Catharine was yet living, when I became acquainted with the above prodigy, and as I felt anxious to know more perfectly what passed I interrogated her in private concerning the details of this event, and she gave me the following answer: "I experienced an ardent wish to avoid throwing away what God had designed to bestow on us, together with an extreme compassion for the poor; I went therefore with fervor to the chest (or bin) containing the flour. My gentle Queen, the Blessed Virgin, appeared to me accompanied by Saints and Angels, she ordered me to do what I projected and deigned in her affectionate kindness to work with her royal hands in the kneading of the paste, and it was the virtue emanating from her sacred hands which so multiplied the loaves; she presented them to me as she finished each one, and I handed them to Alessia and her maid-servant." I said therefore, "Mother, I am no longer astonished that this bread tasted so delicious, being composed and moulded by the glorious hands of that great Queen in whose virginal womb the august Trinity condescended to make the *bread that came down* from *heaven*, and which '*gives life*,' to the believer." By thus assisting Catharine, the Mother of the Word designed to show us that she gave us by her intercession the spiritual bread of salvation; just as she gave us a material and miraculous bread. It was God who had inspired us to call her MOTHER and truly she gave us birth amid sighings and sorrow, until she had formed Christ within us, and daily distributed to us the wholesome bread of her excellent instructions.

Having spoken of this multiplication of bread we will continue the same subject, recalling what happened in the latter period of her life. My witnesses are, two Sisters of Penance of St. Dominic, who are still living and at present in Rome. The first is Lysa, whose name is familiar to the reader, the second is Jeanne de Capo who was also at Sienna. They accompanied Catharine when Urban VI. of happy memory, bade her come to the Eternal City. She lodged in the section of the column of Antonius, with a great number of her spiritual children. Her disciples had followed her, as it were, without her permission; some to visit the holy places, others to ask some favor from the Sovereign Pontiff, but all more particularly to enjoy the attractions of her conversations, which were so profitable to souls; and it must also be said that the Sovereign Pontiff caused several servants of God to go to Rome, in consequence of a request from Catharine, and she took pleasure in showing them hospitality. She possessed naught in the wide world having "neither money nor purse," but begged for a support with her companions; yet she would have received a hundred persons as easily as one alone, so confiding was her heart in God; she knew that God's treasures were inexhaustible; hence, at that epoch she had at least twenty-four persons with her and the number was at intervals considerably increased. Catharine established an admirable system in the house; one of her associates was designated each week to provide for and survey the domestic arrangements, so that the others might be occupied with God and accomplish the pious works and holy visits which had induced them to come to Rome.

Jeanne de Capo had her turn in fulfilling the functions of housekeeper. The bread consumed in the house was procured from the daily alms ; and Catharine had recommended to the person in charge that each week she should give notice, one day in advance, when the bread would probably fail, in order that she might send other mendicant Religious, or go in quest of it herself. God permitted Jeanne to forget this recommendation on one occasion ; in the evening the bread was nearly all consumed ; she had not forewarned Catharine and had no means of procuring any. There was scarcely enough of bread for the repast of four persons. Jeanne acknowledged her negligence, and went pensive and mortified to confess her fault and her embarrassment to Catharine. The latter said to her : " Sister, our Lord forgive you for having reduced us to this position, notwithstanding the order I gave you. Now, the whole community are hungry for it is already quite late ; and where can bread be procured for so many at so short a notice." Jeanne lamented, confessing her fault, and saying that she had sinned through negligence and merited a penance. " Warn the servants of God to take their places at the table," said Catharine. And when Jeanne observed that there was so little bread, that by dividing it no one would have sufficient, Catharine answered " Tell them to commence with the little that is served, and wait until God provides for their necessities ; "—and then she went to prayer.

Jeanne accomplished her orders, and apportioned among them all, the scanty supply of bread. The guests weakened and famished by the continual fasts which they observed (for the greater part,) found their shares very insignificant and thought they must quickly disappear; but in vain they ate, they never saw the last piece, for *some* bread continually remained on the table, and in this there was nothing to excite surprise, since it was the will of HIM who, with five loaves, satisfied five thousand men in the wilderness.

Each one was astonished at herself and her neighbors, and all inquired in what manner Catharine was occupied; it was answered *in fervent prayer*. The sixteen persons who were then present agreed in saying: Her prayer has called down bread from heaven; we are all satisfied; the little that was served us, far from being diminished is instead increased. After the repast such a quantity of bread remained on the table, that it sufficed to the Sisters in the house and others who afterwards partook of it plentifully; and they were also able to give an abundant alms to the poor. Lysa and Jeanne, eyewitnesses of this marvel, recounted to me one similar to it, which God accomplished by means of Catharine in the same house and in the same year, during the Lenten season and in a week that François (a Sister Penitent of St. Dominic and spiritual companion of Catharine on earth, and I trust now in the better land) was housekeeper.

I am unwilling also to pass in silence what happened to myself when Catharine had gone to the home of the blessed; my witnesses are, *all* of the Friars who were at that moment in the convent of Sienna.—It is nearly five years ago; I was in that city and at the earnest petition of Catharine's spiritual children, I had commenced writing her life: it occurred to me that the head of the Saint, which had been brought from Rome to Sienna, and which I had ornamented to the best of my ability, had not yet been publicly exposed and honored. I thought that a day might be selected, for a solemn reception of this precious relic in the convent, as though it had just arrived, and that the Religious might chant the Office of the day, as a particular one could not be allowed as long as the Sovereign Pontiff had not yet inscribed her in the catalogue of the Saints. The festival took place to the great satisfaction of the Religious and the citizens, but especially of those persons of whom she had been the spiritual directress. I invited her most faithful disciples to dine in the refectory and recommended the lay Brother to give an extra attention to the serving of the repast.

When the Office was concluded, and the moment for breakfast arrived, the Brother in charge of the Pantry came to the Prior and told him with a melancholy air, that there was not sufficient bread for the Brethren at the first table, and none at all for the twenty invited guests. On this information, the Prior determined to ascertain the real situation of affairs, and having verified it, he immediately sent the Friar steward with Friar Thomas (Catharine's first Confessor) to several friends of the Order, to bring the bread required; but they delayed coming so long, that the Prior ordered the bread that was in the house to be taken to the strangers who were with me, and consequently very little bread remained in the Pantry; and as the mendicants did not appear, he bade the Religious seat themselves at the table, and in the mean time begin their meal. Then, either in the pantry, or at table, or elsewhere, the bread was so multiplied by Catharine's intercession, that the whole Convent was abundantly supplied both at the first and the second tables, and they gathered up many remains: fifty Religious were nourished with what could scarcely have sufficed for five among them. When the mendicant Friars returned, it was announced that their collection would serve another time, because God had perfectly provided for the necessities of his servants. After the repast, I conversed with our invited friends; I was talking at length of the virtues of Saint Catharine, when the Prior with some other Religious arrived, and recounted to us the miracle that had just taken place: I consequently observed to my hearers: "Our blessed mother would not deprive us on her feast of a prodigy which she often effected during her sojourn on earth: and this is a new proof that she accepts our homage and is continually with us; hence let us return thanks to God, and to *her*, for her maternal kindness."

Besides the above wonders, God worked many miracles by his Spouse,—on flowers for example (for the Saint was very fond of this poetry of nature;) on broken, or injured articles, and indeed on every grade of inanimate objects; but I observe silence concerning them in order to avoid prolixity. I must however indulge myself in narrating a circumstance, testified by twenty persons, as well as myself, and well-known to the citizens of Pisa in general. In 1375, Catharine and her suit lodged at the house of Ghérard Buonconti—and during her sojourn there her continual ecstasies so enfeebled her body that we thought her at the point of death. I dreaded losing her, and reflected upon what means I could adopt for reviving her: she held meat, eggs and wine in abhorrence, and for a stronger reason she would certainly decline any kind of cordials. I asked her to suffer them to put a little sugar in the cold water that she was taking: she directly answered: "Would you extinguish my feeble remains of vigor and life: whatever is sweet is poison to me."

Ghérard and myself sought with anxiety some remedy against her swoons: I remembered having seen in similar cases the temples and wrists of the invalid bathed in the wine of Vernaccia and a sensible relief thus afforded. I proposed to Ghérard the administering the exterior remedy, as we could do nothing for the interior. He informed me that he had a neighbor who was supplied with a cask of this kind of wine, and that he could easily send and procure some of it. The individual sent on this commission, described the fainting fits of Catharine, and asked in Ghérard's name a bottle of the desired wine. The neighbor, whose name I forget, answered: " Friend I would willingly give Ghérards, the whole cask; but it has been completely empty during the last three months; I am sorry for it, but to be very sure, come with me and see." He then conducted him to the wine-cellar—the messenger saw only exteriorly that the hogshead was empty, yet the proprietor to give a greater certitude drew the wooden peg which served for drawing off the wine; when immediately an excellent wine of Vernaccia come forth in abundance and moistened the surrounding earth. The astonishment of the owner was at its height, he closed the opening, called all the inmates of his house, and asked whether any one had put new wine into the cask. All declared that their had been no wine in it during the last three months, and it was impossible for any one to have poured any into it. The news was spread in the environs and everybody saw the miracle. The messenger overjoyed and filled with wonder, brought back a bottle of the marvellous wine, and recounted to us what had transpired. Catharine's numerous spiritual children rejoiced in the Lord, and gave thanks to the Spouse of virgins for this miracle.

A few days after, Catharine, being re-established, went to visit the Apostolical Nuncio just arrived at Pisa; the whole city was in commotion; all the mechanics left their workshops to go out and meet her. Behold! said they, one who does not drink wine, and who has yet filled an empty CASK with miraculous wine. As soon as Catharine became aware of this general movement, she poured out her tears and prayers before God. She thus complained to him interiorly: "Lord, why wilt thou afflict the heart of thy lowly servant, and render her the sport of everybody? All of thy servants can live in peace among men, except me! Who did solicit this wine from thy bounty? For many long years, by an effect of thy inspiration, I deprive myself of wine, and now behold wine covers me with ridicule. In the name of all thy mercies, I conjure thee to dry up, as quickly as possible, this wine, and in such a manner as to destroy this report and unbecoming excitement." God seemed incapable of supporting her trouble longer, and produced a second miracle, greater in my opinion than the first. The hogshead was filled with superior wine, and many of the inhabitants procured quantities from it through devotion, and yet its contents had not diminished, but on a sudden the wine changed into a thick sediment, and what had been lately so delightful and exhilarating, became disgusting dregs similar to mud, and utterly unfit for drinking. In consequence, the master of the cellar and those who went to obtain wine, were forced to be silent, being ashamed to relate any more the circumstance that had excited their boasting. Catharine's disciples were also contradicted by this change, but she appeared quite gay. and happy at the event, and thanked her divine Spouse who had delivered her from the attentions of men.

In the former miracle, our Lord showed how very agreeable Catharine was in his sight, and in the latter, how profoundly submissive she was towards HIM; in the former appeared the grace which adorns her; in the latter her wisdom; for where humility dwells there also is wisdom found: for this reason, St. Gregory, in his first book of Dialogues, esteems wisdom above prodigies and miracles. It is clear that the virtue of humility, without which there is no prudence, was the cause of the second miracle, and rendered it more admirable than the first; but the carnal heart cannot comprehend these things, and it is not astonishing, because the prudence of the flesh is not and can never be submissive to God. (Rom. viii. 7.)

CHAPTER XI.

OF CATHARINE'S FREQUENT COMMUNIONS, AND OF THE MIRACLES PRODUCED BY ALMIGHTY GOD FOR HER, RELATIVE TO THE HOLY EUCHARIST AND THE RELICS OF THE SAINTS.

DEAR READER, God knows I would willingly conclude this biography, particularly on account of the numerous occupations which press me on every side; but when I meditate on Catharine's life, so many wonderful circumstances present themselves to my mind, that I am conscientiously obliged to add daily new facts, and extend this volume beyond the limits that I primarily prescribed to it. It is well known to all who were acquainted with Catharine what profound respect and devotion she entertained for the Body of our Lord in the Blessed Eucharist. It was publicly rumored that Catharine communicated every day, and that she could live without taking any other nourishment. *That*, was not perfectly exact; but those who said so, piously believed it, and glorified God who is always wonderful in his Saints. Catharine *did not* receive holy communion daily, but very often; and some haughty persons, more heathenish than Christian, murmured at these frequent communions. In consequence I defended the " Blessed," and they found naught to reply to the arguments that I offered, because they were all drawn from the lives and writings of the Saints, and from the tenets of the Church.

It was proved in the work of St. Dennis on the ecclesiastical Hierarchy, that in the primitive church, when the fervor of the Holy Ghost abounded, the faithful of both sexes approached daily to the Holy Sacrament of the Altar; this appears to be the meaning of St. Luke, when in the *Acts of the Apostles* he speaks of the breaking bread; and once he adds " *cum exultatione,*" with gladness (Act. ii. 46.) which can only be applied to the Eucharistic food. In the fourth petition of the *Lord's Prayer*, in which we solicit our daily bread, this is explained of the holy Communion, and such interpretation, far from being rejected, ought to be accepted with love, as a token of the daily Communion of the faithful. Our Holy Mother, the Church, has in the Canon of the Mass, a prayer for those who communicate with the priest, and it is not without reason that she says: *Supplices te rogamus, omnipotens Deus, jube hæc perferri per manus sancti angeli.* " And we humbly implore thee, Almighty God, grant that this Host be borne by the hands of the holy angels." And she adds: *Ut quot quot ex hac altaris participatione sacro sanctum Filii tui corpus et sanguinem sumpserimus, etc.* " So that, by this participation in the altar, we may receive the body and blood of thy divine Son." Hence all the holy Fathers teach that the faithful who have not the conscience defiled with mortal sin, and who feel a devotion not only can, but also do right to approach this Sacrament, which is so profitable to their salvation. Who, therefore, would presume to interdict a person of holy and irreproachable life, the means of making rapid progress in perfection? I have no hesitation in saying that a refusal to a person who humbly asks, the sacrament commemorative of the Passion of our Lord, would be doing her a considerable injury, for this is to the privileged the viaticum of her pilgrimage. After all that I have here advanced, there still exist persons who will insist that it is not permitted to any among the faithful, whatever be their degree of tendency to perfection, to receive the Holy Eucharist so frequently: some even, (not understanding well,) will say that it must be received but once in the year; but I rely more on the testimony of the sacred Writings than on all their reasonings.

As a support to their ridiculous opinions, some of those haughty spirits, who are destitute of devotion, and of intelligence of the Holy Scriptures, cite a passage from St. Augustine, wherein he says, that he neither blames nor praises those who communicate daily. That great DOCTOR intended saying that daily communion is good; but, that it may sometimes be dangerous: he leaves its appreciation to the judgment of the Omniscient God, and refrains from giving any decision on this point. If that splendid genius, that prince among DOCTORS, is so reserved, I am at a loss to comprehend how those who quote him can resolve the question with so much assurance. I remember Catharine's response to a bishop who alleged the authority of Saint Augustine, *against* frequent Communion. "If," said she, "Saint Augustine does not censure it, why my Lord, will you censure it? By thus quoting him, your Lordship places yourself in opposition with him."

The great Doctor, St. Thomas Aquinas, examines the utility of the faithful communicating frequently and daily, and thus replies: frequent communion increases the devotion of him who receives it, but it *sometimes* lessens respect. Hence, every Christian should cultivate and possess the devotion and respect due to this greatest of the SACRAMENTS; and when he perceives that frequent communion diminishes that respect, he should in prefer to renew and increase it, abstain sometimes ; but if he perceives that his respect, far from diminishing, increases, he should receive the Eucharist often, because a soul well-disposed necessarily acquires great graces by the reception of that admirable and efficacious Sacrament. This is the opinion of the angelical DOCTOR, whose doctrine Catharine followed in every respect. She communicated often, and sometimes denied herself the consolation, although she always desired to be united to her divine Spouse in the adorable Eucharist. Her burning charity unceasingly inclined her towards HIM whom she had seen really, and whom she loved with all her heart and will.

Such was the vivacity of her desires, that on the days in which she was deprived of holy communion, her body suffered in the same manner as one that had long undergone a violent malady : she frequently endured interior troubles which re-acted exteriorly : and she owed this to some unenlightened Religious who directed her, as to the Superior of the SISTERS OF PENANCE, and sometimes to persons for whom she entertained the warmest attachment. This was one of her reasons for finding greater consolation in my ministry than in that of my predecessors. I used every possible effort to obtain the consolation she so much desired—she was conscious of this, and when she sighed for the BREAD of ANGELS, she used to say to me : " Father, I am hungry ; for the love of God feed my soul ! " Therefore the Sovereign Pontiff, Gregory XI. by a special Bull gave her a permission to have a Priest and a portable Altar, so that, she could everywhere and always, without any permission, hear Mass and receive holy Communion.

After these explanations, I purpose narrating a miracle

of which I was sole witness; when in my ministry at the Altar, (unworthy though I was of that dignity;) I presume that Almighty God intended glorifying his NAME in my presence, and gave me to understand how agreeable the fidelity of his hand-maid was in his sight. I confess that I prefer *not* relating the fact, but in conscience I cannot remain silent, because there is question of God's honor and that of blessed Catharine.

After our return from Avignon to Sienna, we visited in the environs of the city, some servants of God, in order to console ourselves together in the Lord. We came back on the festival of St. John the Evangelist, and when we arrived at Catharine's the hour of Tierce had already passed. She turned towards me and said: "O father, did you but know how hungry my poor soul is." I understood her meaning, and rejoined: the hour of saying Mass is nearly elapsed, and I am so fatigued that it is very difficult for me to prepare myself for it. She remained silent a moment; but soon, unable to restrain the expression of her desire she said to me again: "I am famished." I then consented to yield to her request, and repaired to the chapel in her house, which had been permitted her by the Holy Father; I confessed her; I clothed myself in my sacerdotal vestments, and celebrated the Mass of the day; I consecrated one small Host for her, and when I had communicated, I turned to give her the ordinary absolution. Her countenance was angelic and beaming with light; so changed was she, that I hesitated in recognizing her, and I said interiorly: "Is the Lord truly thy faithful and beloved Spouse?" and on turning again to the Altar, I added mentally: "Come Lord to thy Spouse." At the same instant the sacred Host, before I touched it *moved*, and came at more than three fingers' distance to the paten, which I was holding in my hand, I was so much occupied with the light that I had seen beaming from Catharine's countenance, and of the motion of the consecrated Host, which I distinctly saw, that I do not perfectly remember whether it placed itself alone on the paten, or whether I laid it there; I dare not affirm it, but I think it deposited itself thereon.

God is my witness that I tell the truth; but should any one be unwilling to credit my assertion, because of my defects and the imperfect life he observes in me, let him remember that the bounty of the Saviour assists men, and even animals destitute of reason; (P. xxxv. 7.) and that God's secrets are revealed not alone to the great, but to the insignificant; let them also recal the portion of inspired Truth, *Non enim veni vocare justos, sed peccatores.* (Matt. ix. 13.) "I came not to call the just, but sinners to repentance." As to such as despise sinners, inspiration again says: *Euntes autem discite quid est: misericordiam volo et non sacrificium.* "Learn that I desire mercy and not sacrifice." I limit myself to the defence that belongs to sinners; let the just and God's servants pardon me, as I am sure they will, for the servants of God are full of mercy. If others judge me, their judgment is naught; if I am firm, or if I fall, God alone is my Judge: he sees when I pause, and when I go forward; he is my master and he knows that I declare the truth. I cannot suppose that I was deluded by Satan, in the midst of so august a sacrifice; I am positive that I beheld the Sacred Host, without the least exterior agency, move and advance towards me, at the moment in which I was saying interiorly: "Come Lord to thy Spouse." Let those who believe, praise the Lord; as to others, I am sure that the day will come in which they will discern their error.

I began by describing what occurred to myself alone; I will now relate a prodigy, which I think not less worthy of attention : those who confide in my words, will discover how agreeable it was to the Saviour to find our " Blessed " so ardently desiring to receive him in the divine Eucharist. If my memory does not deceive, this circumstance is antecedent to the one that I have just recounted; but the date is not so essential as a truthful relation of it.

By order of my Superiors, I was in Sienna, and fulfilled the charge of Lector, when I was acquainted with St. Catharine, and I exerted my best efforts to procure her the privilege of receiving the Holy Communion : consequently when she desired to approach the Holy Table, she addressed herself more confidently to me than to other Religious belonging to the Monastery. One morning she experienced an ardent desire of Holy Communion, although her pain in the side and other sufferings were more than usually oppressive; but this obstacle only stimulated her desire; and as she hoped that her pains would subside a little, she sent one of her companions to me as I entered the church to say Mass, requesting me to defer the Holy Sacrifice a short time, as she experienced an invincible desire of receiving Holy Communion. I cheerfully consented, went to the Choir, and after reciting my Office continued to wait. Catharine had entered the church without my knowledge, at the hour of Tierce, hoping to satisfy her pious desire : but her associates seeing the lateness of the hour, and knowing that after Communion she would remain several hours in ecstasy, and cause murmurs at leaving the church open, engaged her to deprive herself of Communion for that day. *She*, ever humble and discreet, did not presume to contradict them, but took refuge in prayer; she knelt beside a bench placed at the very extremity of the Church, and entreated her Divine Spouse, since men could not accomplish it, to deign himself to satisfy the holy desires that he had condescended to excite in her heart. Almighty God who never despises the desires of his servants, heard the prayer of his Spouse in a wonderful manner. I was ignorant of these occurrences, and believed that Catharine was at home,—when it had been decided that she should not Communicate one of her Sisters came to the place where I was still waiting, and told me that Catharine begged me to say Mass whenever it was convenient to me, because she could not receive on that day.

I went without delay to vest in the Sacristy, and offered Mass at an Altar in the upper end of the Church, and which is dedicated to Saint Paul. Catharine was therefore remote from me the whole length of the edifice, and I was completely ignorant of her presence. After the consecration and the *Pater Noster*, I intended, in accordance with the sacred rites, to divide the Host. At the first fraction, the Host instead of separating in two divided into three portions, two larger and one small, which it seemed to me was as long as a common bean, but not so wide. This particle, whilst I was attentively looking at it, appeared to me to fall on the corporal, by the side of the chalice above which I made the fraction; I saw it clearly descend towards the Altar; but I could not distinguish it on the corporal.

Presuming that the whiteness of the corporal hindered me from discerning this particle, I broke another, and after saying *Agnus Dei*, I consumed the sacred Host. As soon as my right hand was at liberty, I used it to seek on the corporal, beside the chalice at the side on which it seemed to me the particle fell: but I found nothing. Extremely troubled at the circumstance, I continued the ceremonies of the Mass, and after having finished the Communion, I renewed my search by examining the corporal in every way; but neither sight nor touch could discover anything. I was so much afflicted that I wept; I determined to conclude the Mass on account of the persons present and afterwards carefully visit the Altar. In effect when all had withdrawn, I examined minutely not alone the corporal, but every portion of the Altar—I could discover nothing. As I stood before a large picture, I could not believe that the particle had fallen behind the Altar, although I perceived it taking that direction when it escaped from my hands. For greater certainty, I searched on the two sides and even looked on the floor; but always with the same result. Then I thought of going to take counsel from the Convent Prior. I carefully covered the Altar, and recommended the Sacristan not to allow any one to approach until my return.

I retired to the Sacristy; but scarcely had I laid aside my vestments, than Father Christopher, Prior of the Carthusians, arrived. I knew him well, and felt a deep affection for him; his object in visiting me was to obtain, through my influence, an interview with Catharine. I asked him to please to wait a short time, because I was obliged to go and speak with the Prior; but he replied: "This is a day of solemn fasting, and I must absolutely return immediately to the Monastery; you know that it is very remote from the city—in the name of God do not keep me waiting, for in conscience I am obliged to speak with Catharine." I bade the Sacristan remain and guard the Altar, until my return, and I went with the Religious as far as Catharine's residence, where they told me she was at the Friars' Church. I was greatly astonished—I turned back with my companion, and in effect, found Catharine, with her associates, in the lower part of the Church. I enquired of them where she was; they answered that she was kneeling on one of the benches in an ecstasy; and as I was still annoyed at the accident that had occurred to me, I besought them to use every means of making her return to herself, because we were in great haste.

They obeyed, and when we were seated with the Prior, I told him in a low voice and in a few words, my anxiety; she smiled gently and said to me, just as though she knew all the particulars : " Did you not search diligently?" on my answering, "*yes*," she added, "*why*, then, should you be troubled so much ; " and again she could not avoid smiling. I observed it, and kept silence, during her conversation with the Prior, who went away as soon as he had obtained the desired response. I was already more tranquillized, and said : " Mother, I really believe that *you* took the particle of my consecrated Host." She meekly answered : " Do not accuse me of that, Father, it was not I, but another; I can merely inform you that you will not find that particle again." Then I *obliged* her to explain. " Father," said she, " be no wise troubled in reference to that particle ; I will tell you the truth as to my Confessor and my spiritual father ; that particle was brought me, and presented for my reception by our Lord Jesus Christ himself. My companions engaged me not to communicate this morning, in order to avoid certain murmurs. I was unwilling to be troublesome to them, but I had recourse to my divine Spouse : he condescendingly appeared to me and gave me, with his sacred hands, that particle which you had consecrated—I received it from his own sacred hands. Rejoice, therefore, in him; because I have this day from him a grace for which I can never sufficiently thank my Saviour!" This explanation changed my sadness into joy; and I was so encouraged by these words, that I no longer experienced the slightest anxiety.

I relate these miracles in order that God and man may not charge me with ingratitude and negligence. We will now pass to other wonders which have been narrated to me by other witnesses.

Several individuals, worthy of credit, assured me that when they assisted at the Mass at which Catharine received holy communion, they saw distinctly the sacred Host escaping from the hands of the priest and flying to her mouth; they told me that this prodigy happened even when I gave her the sacred Host; I own that I never remarked it very clearly, only I always perceived a certain trembling in the consecrated host, when I presented it to her lips: it entered her mouth like a little stone thrown from a distance with force. Friar Bartholomew of St. Dominic, professor of Sacred Scripture (*Ecriture Sainte*) and now Prior Provincial, of my Order for the Roman province, told me also, that when he gave Catharine the holy Communion he felt the Sacred Host escaping notwithstanding his efforts to hold it. I dare neither affirm nor deny it, and I leave it to the reader's piety to decide what he should believe.

I conclude this recital of miracles which refer to the Holy Eucharist, to say a word of those which refer to the relics of the Saints.

It was revealed to Catharine, that in the kingdom of heaven, she would enjoy the same rank as the blessed Sister Agnes of Montepulciano, and that she would enjoy with her celestial bliss; hence she ardently desired to visit her relics, in order to enjoy even in this life, a foretaste of the happiness of being her companion in eternity. But that the reader may know who Sister Agnes of Montepulciano was, and that he may comprehend the prodigies I purpose relating, I must inform him that by order of my superiors, I was during more than three years, director of the monastery in which reposes the body of that holy uirgin. From the manuscripts that I have found there, and the relation of four sisters who had been under her direction and who are still living, I found materials for writing her history, and I intend recapitulating in a few words that work of my early youth, to give an idea of the virtues and the sanctity of the Blessed Agnes, who has not yet been inscribed in the catalogue of the Saints. Divine Goodness had so anticipated her with benedictions that at the moment of her entrance into the world, a great supernatural light filled her mother's house, and did not cease until after her birth, to notify with how many merits God had adorned the little girl that just entered life. Indeed each successive year of her existence adorned her with virtues always greater and more beautiful; she founded two convents of Nuns, and in the second where she reposes, she performed during her lifetime, numerous and brilliant miracles which she multiplied and surpassed after her death.

Among these prodigies, there is one ever subsisting; her virginal body has never been interred and is miraculously and entirely preserved. It was intended to embalm her body an account of the admirable deeds she had accomplished during her life, but from the extremities of her feet and hands, a precious liquor issued drop by drop and the Convent sisterhood collected it in a vase of crystal and still preserve it: this liquor is similar to balm in color, but it is without doubt more precious. God designed thereby to show that her pure flesh that distilled the balm of Grace had no need of earthly embalmment. At the moment of her decease which took place during the night, little infants reposing in their cradles cried out to their parents: " Sister Agnes is leaving her body and becoming a Saint in heaven." In the morning, a great number of young girls assembled under an inspiration from God, unwilling to admit any married woman among them; they went processionally and bearing lighted tapers, to the monastery, to offer that pure soul a homage worthy of her merits. God manifested the sanctity of his servant by a multitude of other prodigies; hence all the inhabitants of the country honor her memory every successive year, and offer her through devotion a considerable quantity of wax candles. Catharine to whom I had narrated these circumstances, had the greatest desire to behold and venerate the body of Blessed Agnes; but always obedient, she asked permission of me and of her other Confessor; we granted it and intended following her, to see whether God would not perform some miracle at the approximation of his two chosen Spouses. We arrived after Catharine; she had entered the cloister and approached the body of St. Agnes, with almost all the nuns of the Convent and the Sisters of Penance of St. Dominic who had accompanied her: she knelt at her feet and prostrated to embrace them piously; but the holy body that she intended honoring, unwilling that she should stoop to kiss it, raised its foot, in presence of the whole assembly. At this sight, Catharine much troubled, prostrated profoundly and gradually restored the foot of Agnes to its usual position.

I call attention here to the following remark: it was not without motive that the Blessed Agnes raised only one foot; she did this on account of the incredulous: had she raised both feet, it might have been believed that her body was capable, by a motion communicated to the superior part of raising the legs without the help of the marvelous; but as only one foot raised, it is evident that divine power acted without regard to natural laws, and that there could not be any illusion.

I have a motive in presenting this remark; for, on the morrow when we arrived in turn at our own monastery, there was much conversation in reference to the miracle that the SPOUSE of virgins had performed in favor of those holy souls; some nuns who had been witnesses of it, calumniated the work of God, like the Pharisees of old who said: "It is by Beelzebub the prince of the devils that he casteth out demons." (St. Luke, xi. 15.,) In consequence, as I had received from the Prior Provincial authority over that monastery, I assembled all the Sisters in conference according to the Rule of the Order, and made a minute examination of this miracle under a precept of holy obedience. All present declared positively that they had seen it perfectly: I therefore called before me one of those who had offered the most opposition and asked her whether the affair had passed as we said: she acknowledged it in the presence of all, but she desired to explain that the intention of Blessed Agnes was not such as we believed it; I replied: "My very dear Sister, we do not interrogate you concerning the intentions of Blessed Agnes; we are well aware that you are neither her secretary, nor her confidant; we merely ask you, whether you saw the foot rise all alone." She said "*yes*." I imposed a penance on her for the discourses in which she had indulged: and this I did for God's glory and the example of others; and I report it here, in order to give a greater proof of the truth.

Some time after, Catharine returned to the convent of the Blessed Agnes, to consecrate two of her nieces, to the service of the Altar. As soon as she arrived, she repaired, as at the first time, to the body of the saintly foundress with her companions and some nuns from the Convent; but she did not place herself at the feet but joyfully approached the head; she designed, by humility we presume, to avoid what had happened, when she attempted to kiss the feet: or perhaps she remembered that Mary Magdalen at first poured her perfumes over the Saviour's feet and afterwards shed them over his head. She placed her face on the ornaments of gold and silk which cover the countenance of Agnes, and there remained a long time: then she turned sweetly to Lysa, the mother of her two nieces, and inquired smiling: "What, do you not observe the present that heaven sends us: do not be ungrateful!" At these words, Lysa and the others lifted their eyes and saw a very fine and very white manna falling like heavenly dews, and covering not only Agnes and Catharine, but also all the persons present, and with such abundance that Lysa filled her hand with it. To comprehend this miracle, it is necessary to know that it was often repeated during the life-time of Agnes, especially when she was in prayer: so that virgins whom she directed, not suspecting a prodigy, and seeing her mantle always white, wished to shake it off: but she prevented them in order to conceal the heavenly favor.

Blessed Agnes knew that Blessed Catharine would be one day her companion in heaven; she therefore amiably desired to share on earth her graces and her favors. The manna in its snowy whiteness and the fineness of its grain, signified purity and humility; and these two virtues shine in a very particular manner in those two virgins, as may be seen in their Memoirs which God in his mercy has permitted me to write. This miracle had for witnesses Catharine's companions, Lysa among others, who is still living : several nuns belonging to the convent have equally affirmed before me and before the Friars who were with me, that thus the occurrences took place. Many are now dead; but myself and my Brethren recal perfectly their depositions : further, Lysa collected the manna which fell, showed it frequently, and gave it to several persons.

God accomplished also for his faithful Spouse during his life, many admirable things which are not written in this book : what I have related above, I have said for the honor and glory of God's holy NAME, for the salvation of souls, and to acquit my conscience; I was unwilling to despise the grace from above, and fold up the talent entrusted to me ; I have placed it according to the best of my ability, so that it might be referred to its divine MASTER.

I here terminate the second part of this biography; the third will contain Catharine's death with the miracles that preceded and followed it. May these three books render immortal praise, honor and glory to the ever blessed Trinity. AMEN.

END OF SECOND PART.

THIRD PART.

CHAPTER I.

CONCERNING THE WITNESSES PRESENT AT CATHARINE'S DEATH, AND WHO RELATED THE ATTENDANT CIRCUMSTANCES TO THE AUTHOR.

THE ancient synagogue, when contemplating the elevation of the holy Church, and the flight of the soul that God had selected for Spouse, exclaims in admiration: *Quæ est ista quæ ascendit de deserto, de deliciis affluens, innixa super dilectum suum?* (Cant. viii. 5.) This passage may be aptly applied to the conclusion of this Memoir. The happy death and the last actions of Catharine, worthily crown all that preceded. The perfection of her virtues leads us to say, with astonishment: Who is this? that abounding in good works mounts to heaven with accelerated flight; who is this, coming up from the desert leaning on "her beloved," united to God by love, for all eternity."

As she approached the term of her mortal career, she made increased efforts to merit the crown she solicited. Her soul, as it were, naturally ravished in ecstasy, rushed onward to heaven. This impetus arose from the fire which acted and continually mounted upward, I mean that fire which the Saviour of the world came to bring on earth, and which he desired to see enkindled. She will be seen in the last days of her life, becoming likened to her Spouse by suffering, uniting her soul to his, and reclining on him as a support for quitting the earth victoriously and soaring to heaven joyously and triumphantly; she appeared to die, because the gross sense of mankind did not descry her glory, but she rests peacefully with the cherished Spouse of her soul and brilliant prodigies have manifested the honors bestowed on her in heaven.

When the blessed Catharine, in accordance with the command of the Supreme Pontiff, Gregory XI., repaired to Florence, [1373] her mission was to establish peace between the shepherd and his flock; she was subjected there to several unjust persecutions. A satellite of the demon precipitated himself upon her, sword in hand, intending to kill her, and God alone prevented him from it. Notwithstanding all kinds of menaces and dangers, she did not retire until the successor of Gregory XI., Urban VI., had concluded peace with the Florentines; as soon as it was signed, she returned to her home and occupied herself actively with the composition of a book which she dictated under the inspiration of the Holy Ghost. She had recommended her Secretaries to be present during her ecstasies, and carefully commit to writing whatever she might then dictate; they did this with fidelity, and collected a whole volume of great and useful truths. She dictated this work whilst her soul was detached from her senses, and her body in complete insensibility. God designed to prove to us that this work does not resemble that of men, but emanated from the Holy Ghost himself.

The Sovereign Pontiff, Urban VI., [1378] who had seen Catharine at Avignon, when he was Archbishop of Acerenza, and who entertained a high esteem for her lights and virtues, commanded me to write to her to repair to Rome. I obeyed, but she, with her usual prudence answered me thus: "Father, several persons of

Sienna, and some of the Sisters of my Order find that I journey too frequently, hence they are greatly scandalized, and say that a Religious ought not to be thus ever on the wing. I do not think that these reproaches should give me any trouble, for I have never journied in any direction, except by order of God and of his Vicar, and to promote the salvation of souls; but to avoid as far as I can an occasion of scandal to my neighbor, I do not think of removing hence; nevertheless, if the Vicar of Christ wills me to go, his intentions must be accomplished not mine. In that case, be so obliging as to make known his order to that effect by a written document, so that those who are scandalized may know that I do not undertake the journey from my own impulse."

Having received this reply, I went to the Sovereign Pontiff, and humbly communicated it to him. He charged me to bid Catharine come in the name of holy obedience; and Catharine, like a submissive daughter, speedily arrived at Rome with a numerous suite; she would have had many more followers had she not opposed it. Those who accompanied her assumed the livery of poverty, by voluntarily relying on Divine Providence, preferring a mendicant life with the Saint, than abundance in their own houses and the deprivation of her pious and captivating conversations.

The Sovereign Pontiff was most happy to see her, and requested that, in presence of the Cardinals, she would give them an instruction, and that she should especially speak concerning the incipient Schism. She did so, learnedly and at some length, exhorting every one to fortitude and constancy. She showed that Divine Providence watches over all, but in a particular manner over those who suffer with the Church, and concluded there from that the threatened Schism ought not 〈 ⁁ighten any one, but that they should do God's work and dread nothing. When she had finished, the Sovereign Pontiff, quite encouraged, resumed her discourse, and said to the Cardinals: "Behold, Brethren, when we yield to timidity how we become guilty before God. This humble woman confounds us; I call her humble, not in contempt, but on account of the weakness of her sex: *she* should naturally fear, even though *we* were of good heart; and yet where *we* are fearful, *she* is tranquil, and inspires us with courage. Is not this a motive for confusion to us all?" And he continued: "What should the VICAR OF JESUS CHRIST dread, though the whole world were to oppose him; is not Christ, the all-powerful, stronger than the world? He can never forsake the Church." The Sovereign Pontiff, encouraged himself and his Brethren; he praised the Saint in God, and accorded her many spiritual favors for herself and her companions.

Jeanne, Queen of Sicily, at the instigation of the devil, declared herself openly against the Church and favored the Schism to the extent of her power. Urban VI thought of sending to her Catharine and another Virgin called Catharine, daughter of St. Bridget of Sweden, who was recently inscribed in the catalogue of the Saints, by Pope Boniface IX. He hoped that these two persons with whom the Queen was acquainted might induce her to forsake he. evil ways. When our Blessed Catharine knew it, she did not shrink from the charge it was intended to impose on her, and she even offered to go, directly. But Catharine of Sweden did not like to undertake the voyage, and refused in my very presence, the mission that was proposed to her. I acknowledge that through imperfection and want of faith I also did not approve the project of the Sovereign Pontiff. I thought that the reputation of persons consecrated to God, is so precious, that we must beware of tarnishing it by the appearance of evil or by the least breath of suspicion. She to whom the Virgins were to be sent, might follow the counsels of Satan's agents by whom she was surrounded, and cause these two devout women to be insulted on their route and prevent them from arriving. I presented these observations to the Sovereign Pontiff who reflected some time and concluded by saying : " Your views are correct, it is more prudent for them not to go." I communicated this conversation to Catharine who was at the time quite ill. She turned to me and said : " Had Agnes, Margaret, and a multitude of other Virgins indulged all these reflections, they would never have obtained the crown of martyrdom ! Have we not a Spouse who can deliver us from the hands of the impious and preserve our honor amidst a throng of debauchees ? All these reasonings are vain ; they spring from a want of faith rather than from genuine prudence." I then blushed interiorly at being so remote from her lofty perfection, and in my heart I admired her constancy and her faith. But, as the Sovereign Pontiff had decided that she would not go, I did not dare to converse longer on the subject.

In the mean time, it appeared advantageous to the Sovereign Pontiff to send me into France, because he had been informed that it would be possible to detach the King of France, Charles V. from the schism excited by himself. The instant that I became acquainted with this project, I went to take counsel from Catharine :—notwithstanding the affliction that my absence would occasion her, she advised me to obey the orders of the Sovereign Pontiff without delay. She said to me : " Hold it as certain, father; that he is truly the Vicar of Jesus Christ; I desire that you would expose yourself to sustain him as you ought for the Catholic Faith itself." I entertained no doubt on this subject; but, that saying from Catharine encouraged me so to combat the schism, that I consecrated myself from that moment, to the defence of the rights of the Sovereign Pontiff: and I continually recalled it to mind, in order to fortify myself amid my difficulties and trials. I acted therefore in accordance with her counsels, and bowed my head beneath the yoke of obedience.

Some days previous to my departure, being acquainted with what would happen, she wished to converse with me concerning the revelations and consolations that she had received from God, and she did not allow the persons present to join in the conversation. After having spoken to me during several hours: she said to me, "Now go, whither God calls you. I think that in this life we shall never again discourse together as we have just now done." Her prediction was accomplished. I departed and she remained. Before my return she went to her heavenly home, and I had no more the privilege of relishing and profiting by, her salutary instructions. It was for this reason, no doubt, that desiring to bid me a last farewell, she went to the place where I was to embark, and when we were setting out, she knelt and after praying, made over us with tearful eyes, the sacred sign of the Cross, as if she would say; "Go, my son, in safety, shielded by the protection of this blessed sign; but in this life thou shalt ne'er again behold thy MOTHER." Although the sea was infested by pirates, we arrived happily at Pisa, and then had an equally prosperous voyage to Gênes; notwithstanding the numerous galleys of schismatics pursuing their route to Avignon. We afterwards continued our journey by land as far as a town called Ventimiglia. Had we gone farther we should have inevitably fallen into the ambuscades of those especially who had designs on my life; but by the permission of God, we stopped there a day and a Religious of my Order, who was a native of that place, forwarded me a letter in which he said: "Beware of passing Ventimiglia, for ambushes are prepared for you, and were you to fall into any one of them, no human aid could save you from death."

On this advice, after having taken counsel of the companion whom the Sovereign Pontiff had given me, I returned to Gênes; I sent word to the Holy Father of what had happened, and asked what step I should take. He commanded me to remain at this place and preach a Crusade against the schismatics. This mission delayed my return, and it was at that moment the Blessed Catharine concluded her pilgrimage and crowned it by an admirable martyrdom. Therefore, from this date, I can no longer describe events as having seen them personally; but all that I shall commit to writing, I know by the letters which she then addressed me and very frequently too; and from persons who assisted her in her latest moments, and who witnessed the prodigies which the Almighty effected by the intercession of his servant. But lest in indicating these witnesses in general, I may appear to suppose them, I intend naming them in order, that others may credit them more thoroughly than they do myself; they are assuredly more worthy, for they imitated better than I, the examples offered by Catharine: they consequently comprehended them more clearly.

I will begin by the females who were her faithful **companions.** Alessia of Sienna, Sister of Penance **of St.**

Dominic, appears to me to be entitled to the highest rank among the disciples of Catharine, not by her seniority, but by the perfection of her virtues. After losing in her youth, a husband equally noted for his nobility and learning she despised all worldly pleasures, and became so wedded to our Saint, that in the end she had not courage to leave her: she renounced her wealth and according to our Redeemer's counsel distributed it to the poor. In the full imitation of her whom she had chosen for Mistress, she afflicted her body by fasts, vigils, and every variety of mortification: prayer and contemplation occupied her continually; she persevered with so much constancy and perfection that Catharine, in the latter portion of her life, made her, I think, depositary of all her secrets, and wished, that after her own death, Alessia should become the superior and model of her companions. I found *her* also at Rome, when I returned there and she gave me many pieces of information; but a short time after she went to rejoin in heaven her whom she had so tenderly cherished in our Lord. *She*, is my first witness of what happened during my absence.

My second witness is Françoise of Sienna. Her soul was always tenderly united to God, and to the Blessed Catharine. As soon as she became a widow, she clothed herself with the holy habit of the Sisters of Penance: she consecrated her three remaining sons to God in the Order of Preaching Friars; and before dying, she had the consolation of seeing them depart for the home of the just— for they piously terminated their career at the period of the Plague, and God assisted them in a special manner, by the intercessory prayers of Catharine. Françoise survived Alessia a short time; but she also recounted to me a number of circumstances. The third companion of Catharine that I shall cite, is Lysa who still lives; she is well known in Rome, especially by the citizens who reside in the district In which she dwells. I abstain from giving her eulogium because she is yet alive: her relation of sister-in-law to Catharine might render her testimony suspected; but *I* know that she always spoke the truth.

After the demise of Catharine, I found several holy men who had been witnesses of her last moments: I will only name *four* among them, all commendable by their merits and their virtues. Two have already followed Catharine to heaven; two yet live, and these I have selected for the conviction of the incredulous.

The first of the four is he, whom we styled Brother Saint, both on account of his name and his life; he was from Téramo; he forsook his parents and his country and fixed his residence at Sienna, where he led during more than thirty years, a very solitary life, never inciting others to speak of him, and obeying the direction of some devout and learned Religious. He found in his old age the precious pearl of the Gospel, in Blessed Catharine. For her, he quitted his peaceful cell and his style of living, in order to labor not solely for himself but for the *good* of *others*; he affirmed that he found greater tranquillity, and more profit to his soul in following Catharine and listening to her, than he ever enjoyed in his solitude; above all he made great progress in patience. He suffered much from a disease of the heart and our Saint taught him to support his continual anguish, not only with resignation, but with joy: he related to me several circumstances which transpired during my absence; but a short time after having quitted her he went again to join in celestial mansions her whose disciple he became.

The *second* witness is a Florentine who had enriched his early years by the wisdom of old age, and had adorned them with all the virtues: this was Barduccio. He left parents, brothers and country to follow Catharine to Rome, and he remained there until his death. I have since learned that our Saint particularly esteemed him, and, I suppose it was on account of his angelical purity. What is there to exite surprise in one Virgin cherishing another! In her last moments, Catharine enjoined him to attach himself to me and place himself under my direction; she did it without doubt because she was aware that he would not live long: in effect, a short time after, he was attacked with a phthisic, and although he appeared at first to be convalescent, it soon became evident that he was beyond hope. Fearing that the air of Rome was hurtful to him, I sent him to Sienna where he slept peacefully in the Lord. Those who witnessed his death, declare that at his last moments, he looked up to heaven smiling, and rendered up his soul with such lively tokens of joy, that death itself could not obliterate their impression from his countenance: he probably saw her whom he had loved during life, with the greatest purity of heart, come forth to meet him, in the glory of triumph. Barduccio told me many things which happened during my absence, and I credit his informations because I knew the solid virtues that adorned his soul.

My *third* witness is a young man of Sienna, Etienne Maconi, of whom I have already written. I will not dilate in words of praise concerning him, because he is yet on the road in which praise is perilous; I will simply say, that he was one of the secretaries of Catharine, and that he wrote the greater portion of her letters and the book that she composed: he was so attached to our Saint, that, in order to follow her everywhere, he quitted his family and his native land. At the moment of dying, Catharine called him, and said to him: "My son, the will of God is that you renounce the world and become a Carthusian." The son pursued religiously the order of the mother, and everything proved that the command came from God himself, for I do not remember having seen any one advance so rapidly in the religious life. Scarcely did he make his profession when he was named Prior, and he acquitted himself so perfectly of that charge, that he has ever since preserved it. He is now Prior of Milan, and Visitor of a great number of Convents of his Order. He committed to writing what happened at Catharine's death, and related to me all the particulars with which he was acquainted. He perused also, nearly all that I have written in this history, and I can say with the Evangelist, St. John: *Ille seit quia vera dicit.* (St. John xix. 35.)

The last witness that I name, among those who have given me hints, documents, or other means of information, is Neri, or Ranieri, son of Landoccio of Sienna. After Catharine's death, he embraced the solitary life which he is still leading. He wrote (with Etienne Maconi and Barduccio) the letters and the book of the Saint; but he was the first that followed the Spouse of Christ—quitting his father, who still lived, and all that he possessed of earthly riches—as he was longer than any other a witness of the admirable actions of Catharine, I invoke his testimony relative to this biography, with that of Etienne the Carthusian.

The several Religious and Sisters whom I have named above, have acquainted me, either in manuscript, or by the living voice, with all that occurred during my absence, before and after the death of Catharine. Hence, dear reader, you are in possession of **my reasons** for believing **them** confidently.

CHAPTER II.

OF CIRCUMSTANCES WHICH HAPPENED A YEAR AND A HALF BEFORE THE DEATH OF THE BLESSED CATHARINE, AND OF THE MARTYRDOM THAT SATAN CAUSED HER TO UNDERGO.

As I have said above, after that, (in accordance with the order of the Sovereign Pontiff,) I had quitted the Spouse of Christ, who remained at Rome, several circumstances occurred which merit narration. I have only cited some of them; but now, with the grace of God, I will declare facts which display the splendid sanctity of her happy death, and which were so many preludes to her entrance into eternal bliss. The Blessed Catharine saw the Church of God, that she so ardently loved, rent by the miseries of schism, and the Vicar of Jesus Christ surrounded by difficulties and persecutions; tears had become her bread by night and by day, and she never ceased crying to God, supplicating him to restore peace to the Church. God gave her some consolations: thus, a year previous to her death, the very day on which she was to quit the earth, he granted a double victory to the Church and to the Sovereign Pontiff. The Schismatics, hitherto masters of the Castle of St. Angelo, disturbed the peace of the city, and ravaged the entire country: they were completely vanquished, the chiefs were taken, and many perished. The Pope could not reside near the Church of the Holy Apostles, on account of the vicinity of the Castle of St. Angelo. Catharine advised him to go, barefooted, to the august Basilica. All the people followed him in great-devotion, and rendered to Almighty

God, solemn thanksgiving for all his benefits. The holy Church and her Pontiff began to breathe a little, and our Saint enjoyed, at last, some consolation in their relief.

But her anguish was soon renewed. The old serpent, who could not succeed by this method, attacked her by others more dangerous and more rude. What he could not effect by foreigners and schismatics, he attempted by means of those who had remained faithful to the HOLY SEE; he created a division between the people of Rome and the Sovereign Pontiff, and things attained such a point, that the populace openly threatened the life of the Supreme Pontiff. When Catharine was informed of it, she was deeply affected; she had recourse as usual to prayer, and ardently implored her divine Spouse never to permit such a crime. At that time Catharine wrote me a letter, in which she told me, that she had seen, in spirit, the city of Rome filled with demons, who excited the people to PARRICIDE; they uttered horrible cries against the Saint, and said to her: "Cursed be thou that wouldst arrest us; but we will put thee to death in a frightful manner." She answered naught, but she continually prayed with fervor, and implored God, that for the honor of his NAME and the salvation of the Church, then rocked by rude storms, that he would deign to subvert the schemes of hell, in order to save the Sovereign Pontiff, and not allow the people to commit such an abominable offence. The Lord once answered her: "Suffer that nation which daily blasphemes my name, to fall into that crime, and when it will be committed, I will execute vengeance and destroy it, because my justice demands that I no longer support its iniquities." But she prayed with still increased fervor: "O most clement God, thou knowest how deeply the Spouse that thou hast redeemed by thy precious blood, is outraged throughout the broad universe; thou knowest how few defenders she has, and thou canst not be ignorant how ardently its enemies desire the humiliation and death of thy Vicar. If that misfortune happen, not only people of Rome, but also all Christians and the Holy Church will suffer deeply from it. Therefore let thine anger be appeased, and despise not thy people for whom thou hast paid so heavy a ransom."

This contest with God endured several days and nights and her feeble body had much to endure. God opposed his justice to her prayers, and the demons continued their vociferations against her. Her fervor was then so great that if God, to use an expression familiar with her, had not encircled her members, she must have sunk back, weighed down upon herself. But at length, in this obstinate combat in which her body was perishing through protracted sufferings, Catharine triumphed and obtained her petition. When God alleged his justice, she replied: "Lord because thy justice must be satisfied, despise not I entreat thee the prayers of thy servant; inflict the chastisement that this people merit on *my body:* yes, for the honor of thy Name and that of thy holy Church, I will cheerfully drain that chalice of suffering and death; thy TRUTH knows, that I have ever ardently desired it, and that thy grace has continually inflamed my soul with that desire." At these words which she pronounced in the intensity of her heart, the interior voice of God was no longer heard and she understood by this divine silence that her prayer had prevailed. In effect from that moment, the popular sedition gradually calmed and at last was completely appeased; but the Blessed like a pure victim supported its expiation. The powers of hell had permission to torment her virginal body, and exert their rage on it with such cruelty, that those who witnessed it, declared to me that it would be impossible to conceive an idea of it without having seen its evidences.

Those cruel sufferings increased daily; her skin adhered to her bones and her body appeared like one issuing from the tomb; she walked, prayed and worked without intermission; but those who saw her, would have believed her to be a phantom rather than a living soul: her tortures multiplied and visibly consumed her body. Far from interrupting her prayers, Catharine increased their length and their fervor; her spiritual family who were surrounding her at that time, saw very distinctly the exterior signs of the tortures heaped upon her by hell; but no one could apply a remedy. The will of God opposed it, and besides, notwithstanding the wasting of her corporeal frame, her soul rose joyfully and courageously above trouble: the more she prayed, the more she suffered: I was informed by the spectators, and indeed she wrote to me herself, that in the midst of her martyrdom, she heard the devils shriek: "Cursed, thou hast always pursued us, and thou continuest thy pursuit: now we intend satiating our vengeance: thou designest to force us to go hence, but we will take thy life." And whilst saying that, they redoubled their blows.

Catharine suffered thus, from Sunday of Sexagesima until the last day of April on which she died, and her sufferings continually increased until her spirit winged its heavenward flight. She wrote me a very remarkable circumstance which took place about that time. Hitherto on account of pain in her side, and other infirmities which never forsook her, she deferred hearing Mass until the hour of Tierce; thus she continued during the entire season of Lent, and went every morning to the church at St. Peter's.

She heard Mass, prayed longer than formerly and returned home at the hour of Vespers: those who then saw her extended on her bed could not have believed her capable of rising; on the morrow however, at the dawn of day, she arose, set out from her house, via del Papa, entered the Minerva and the Campo di Fiore, and went with a hasty step to St. Peter's; this course was capable of fatiguing any one in good health. Some days before she was called to Heaven, she found herself unable to rise; finally, on Sunday April 29, 1380, on the festival of St. Peter, martyr of the Order of Preaching Friars, about the hour of Tierce, she yielded her beautiful soul to its loving Spouse and Redeemer.

Many remarkable events transpired then, which I will narrate in the following chapters.

CHAPTER III

HOW ARDENTLY BLESSED CATHARINE SIGHED TO BE DELIVERED FROM THE BODY AND UNITED TO CHRIST.

CATHERINE's mortal life approached its term, and the Lord manifested by various prodigies, how proportionate the glory with which he would recompense his Spouse in Heaven, was to the treasures with which his grace had favored her on earth. She invoked the blessed moment which was to unite her to Jesus Christ, when she would contemplate face to face in the land of unending felicity, the Truth which she had seen gently reflected during her terrestial pilgrimage ; that desire swelled in her heart in proportion as supernatural light beamed more clearly upon her understanding. Two years antecedent to her death, TRUTH overspread her soul with such lights, that she was obliged to allow them to radiate exteriorly, and therefore she requested her Secretaries to hear and commit to writing what she would say during her ecstacies ; thus in a short space of time a book was composed containing a Dialogue between a soul and God. At the end of that volume, there are two things that I deem very useful to place here, for the reader's edification : these two things form an epitome of all that is said in detail in the work, and a prayer is annexed, by which the Blessed Catharine terminates and shows how fervently she desires to be delivered from her body, in order to be united to Jesus Christ.

Catharine therein relates that God the Father, said to

the soul, after having discoursed at length concerning the obedience of the perfect: "Now, dear and well-beloved daughter, I have satisfied thy desire from the beginning to the end, on the subject of obedience; thou hast requested of me four things: the first for thyself; I granted it to thee, by enlightening thee with my TRUTH, proving to thee how, by the light of faith, by knowing me and knowing thyself, thou wilt attain to an acquaintance with truth. Thy second petition implored mercy for the world; the third was in favor of the mystical body of the Church, supplicating me to deliver it from obscurity and persecutions, and desiring that I should punish the iniquities of others on thyself. I then explained to thee that no trouble endured in time could in itself alone satisfy, for an offence committed against *Me*, the eternal GOOD; such pain can alone satisfy, if it be united to desire of soul and contrition of heart: I explained to thee how. I also replied to thee, that it was my intention to grant mercy to the world, by showing to thee that Mercy is my darling attribute, and to that end, and for the incomprehensible love I felt towards man, I sent the Word, my only SON; and I illustrated his mediation to thee by the representation of a Bridge reaching from heaven to earth; that is, uniting the human and divine natures. I also showed thee, that this bridge is mounted by three degrees, viz: the three powers of the soul. After offering thee the Word, under the form of a bridge, I presented thee another figure and showed thee three degrees on his body; the first at his feet; the second at the wound of the side; the third at its mouth. These degrees indicate three states or conditions of the soul: the imperfect, the perfect, and the superior state, or that in which the souls attain to the excellence of unitive love.

I have pointed out to thee what destroys imperfection, and what conducts to perfection; the way that must be followed, the secret snares of Satan, and the illusions of self-love. I have made known to thee the three methods of punishment employed by my clemency in these states. The first is the pains and trials that I inflict on man during this life. The second is the chastisement that falls at the hour of death upon those who die without hope, being in mortal sin; *they* pass beneath the bridge and enter the road to hell, and I have exhibited to thee their future torments. The third means is the general Judgment, and I have shown thee somewhat of the pain of the condemned, and the glory of the Blessed, when each soul will be endued with properties of its body. I have already promised thee, and I do promise thee to reform the Church my Spouse, by the sufferings of my servants whom I invite to expiate, in union with thee, by sorrows and weeping the iniquity of her ministers. I have clearly shown thee the dignity to which I have exalted them, and the respect which they owe to seculars, and having revealed to thee their defects, I have also declared to thee that these should in no wise diminish respect for their sublime authority, and how hateful to me is any contrary way of acting. I spoke to thee of the virtue of such as live like the Angels and discoursed with thee concerning the excellence of the Sacrament of the Altar. When conversing with thee on the three states of the soul, I designed showing thee the various kinds of tears. I told thee whence they came, and what reference they have to the various conditions of the soul—that all tears emanate from the heart. I explained successively four kinds of tears, and have manifested to thee a fifth whose consequence is death.

"In answer to thy fourth petition: I have given thee

explanations concerning my general and particular Providence: all has been and will be accomplished by my supreme and divine Providence, originating and permitting whatever occurs to you, tribulations or consolations spiritual and temporal, the whole for your welfare, that you may be sanctfied in me and my truth may be accomplished in you: for the Blood of the eternal SON revealed to thee that thou wast created for eternal life. I have shown thee the perfection of obedience and the imperfection of disobedience and the sources of each; I have spoken particularly of the imperfect and perfect Religious; obedience produces peace, disobedience strife; he who obeys not deceives himself, and by Adam's disobedience death entered the world."

"Now, I, God the Father, supreme and eternal TRUTH, I declare to thee that it is only by obedience to my only SON that thou canst have life; I have created a bridge for thee, after the road to heaven was broken, in order that thou mightst pass by that inviting and correct way—which is Truth, *one and distinct*,—by means of obedience. Now, I invite all my faithful servants *to mourn*, by tears and humble, constant prayer, I *may* grant mercy to the world. Run in the path of truth, by dying to thyself, and above all never relent, because I shall require of thee more than I did formerly, having manifested myself to thee in *my truth*. Beware of forsaking the knowledge of thyself, but augment and preserve the treasure of it that I gave thee. That treasure is a doctrine of truth, founded on the immoveable living corner-stone, which is Christ, the meek and lowly JESUS. This doctrine is clad in light by which it may be distinguished from darkness: beloved Daughter clothe thyself with it in truth."

After that soul had seen with the **eye of the under-**

standing and known by the light of Faith, the perfection of Obedience; after hearing with her reason, and relishing by the ardent desire of her heart, she contemplated herself in the divine Majesty, and gave him thanks, saying: "O Father! I thank thee that thou didst not despise the work of thy hands; Thou hast not turned aside thy countenance nor repulsed my desires; Thou Light Eternal, had not spurned my darkness; Thou *Life*, hast not abandoned me to *death*; supreme *Physician*, thou hast had mercy on my infirmity; Eternal Purity thou hast not neglected my iniquities, stains and miseries; Thou unspeakable Wisdom, I folly, Thou Infinite, while I am insignificant; yes, in thy light I have found light, in thy prudence, truth; in thy clemency, Charity and fraternal love. Whence arose thy mercies? Not from any virtue dwelling in me, but from thy charity alone. Grant Lord that my memory may retain thy benefits; that my will may burn with the fire of thy Charity, and that with the key of obedience I may open Heaven. I implore this grace for every rational creature, individually and collectively, and for the mystical body of the Church; I confess and deny not that thou didst love me before I was; and that thou dost love thy creature with an excessive love.

"O Eternal Trinity! O Deity! that by union with the divine nature, hast given such value to the blood of thy Son; O Eternal Trinity! deep sea in which the more I search, the more I find; and the more I find the more I search; in satisfying the soul thou art never satiated; it is always eager, always famished for thee Eternal Trinity, because it desires to see thy light, in thy light; as the thirsty hind pants for the fountains of living waters, so my soul desires to escape from its obscure prison to con template Thee as thou art in the reality of thy existence How long will thou conceal thy countenance from me O Eternal Trinity! fire and abyss of charity, dissipate the mist of my material nature; for the knowledge thou hast given me of thyself, fills me with thy truth and forces me to wish deliverance from my terrestrial bonds; I thirst to give this life for the honor and glory of thy Name, having tasted and witnessed with the eyes of my understanding the depths of thy greatness and the beauty of thy creature. When beholding myself in thee, I saw that I had been created to thy image, because thou didst allow me to participate in thy power. O Eternal Father! thou hast communicated to my understanding the wisdom that appertains to thy only Son; and the Holy Ghost which proceeds from thee and from thy only Son, bestowed on me the will that renders me capable of loving thee; for Thou! O eternal Trinity! Thou art my Creator and I am thy creature; and thou hast revealed to me, by the new creation given to me by the blood of thy only Son, how impassioned thou art for the beauty of the creature.

"O Abyss! O Eternal Deity! O unfathomable sea! couldst thou give me more than thyself. Thou art an ever burning fire, consuming yet never consumed: dissipating by thy ardors all the love the soul bears to itself: thou art a fire that annihilates all colds; a light that illumines souls, and by that light thou hast manifested to me thy truth. By the light of Faith I acquire wisdom, fortitude, courage and perseverance; by the light of faith I also learn hope, and the path of rectitude, and without it I should grope in thick darkness Hence I implore thee, O Eternal Father! to enlighten my soul with the torch of Faith. That light is an ocean, nourishing the soul that dwells in thee. O adorable Trinity!

pacific sea, whose waters never agitated and far from awakening dread, give the correct knowledge of truth; that water in its transparency manifests hidden things. When the soul abounds with the light of faith, it is resplendent, so to speak, with what it believes. That sea is like a mirror held by the hand of thy Love before the eyes of my soul; and in 't I perceive that thou art the supreme and infinite GOOD, incomprehensible and inestimable. Beauty above all beauty, Wisdom superior to all wisdom, for thou art WISDOM herself. Thou, the food of Angelic choirs by the fire of thy Charity, hast given thyself to man: Thou art a garment that covers all nudity: thy sweetness is devoid of bitterness and appeases the longing soul!

"O! ever-living Trinity! I know thee by the light of Faith; and thou hast taught me by numerous and admirable lessons, the way of exalted perfection. Therefore, in that light and not in darkness will I serve thee! Let me become a mirror of a good and perfect life, coming forth from my hitherto miserable way of living wherein I served thee in obscurity: for I knew not thy Truth and therefore could not love it? But why did I not know thee?—because the mists of self-love darkened my understanding. Who can mount to thee, and thank thee worthily for the ineffable treasure and superabundant favors thou hast granted me, and the doctrine of truth that thou hast revealed to me This doctrine is a very particular favor, *above* the general grace accorded to mankind. Thou hast deigned to condescend to my necessities and to those of other beings, that they may henceforth contemplate themselves therein as in a mirror. Lord, answer for thyself. Thou hast given to me largely and thou canst recognize thy benefits and return thanks to thyself for them, by spreading abroad in my soul the light of thy grace, so that with that light I may testify to thee my gratitude. Clothe me, clothe me with thyself, O eternal TRUTH, that I may run through this mortal career in the verity of Obedience, and in the light of holy Faith, with which thou hast inebriated my soul."

May these words induce you reader, to admire this holy woman, not only in the sanctity of her life, but also in the sublimity of her doctrine. By reflecting on the preceding, you will discover that she desired to die and be united to Jesus Christ, because she knew and understood, above all at that period, that it was "*far better to be with Christ,*" the end and the perfection of all good. She at last obtained the object of her ever increasing desire ; the promises made to her by our Redeemer during her youth when choosing her for his Spouse were accomplished, and her soul quitted its mortal tenement to celebrate with him an eternal marriage.

CHAPTER IV.

OF THE DEATH OF ST. CATHARINE, AND OF THE RECOMMENDATIONS PROPOSED TO HER SPIRITUAL SONS AND DAUGHTERS IN HER DYING MOMENTS.

THE Blessed Catharine, perceiving her last hour approach, summoned around her her followers and such as the Lord had made members of her household; she addressed to them first a general discourse, exhorting all to advance in the path of virtue; she developed therein several important points, which I found in the Manuscripts of the witnesses above mentioned.

The first and fundamental obligation that she laid down was this: He who gives himself to God, if he desires to possess HIM in return must divest his heart from all sensible love; not only towards persons, but creatures, in order to tend to God, his Creator, in entire simplicity and sincerity of soul; for, said she, the heart cannot give itself unreservedly to God if it be not liberated, disentangled and disfranchised from every bond. A soul cannot give its heart to God without prayer, founded on humility, which acknowledges itself nothing, and devoid of all personal confidence. A generous application to mental prayer is also requisite, because it increases and fortifies virtues which without that aliment would become weak and then vanish. She taught all her followers to devote *stated hours* to vocal prayer, and to give themselves *continually* to mental prayer either by acts or with the heart.

She said, besides, that by the aid of a strong faith,

she saw and perfectly understood in her mind, that whatever happened to herself or others, came from God, and proceeded from his immense love to his creatures; which excited and developed in her a love for, and a promptitude in obeying the orders of God, and of her superiors, believing always that their orders came from God himself, either for the necessities of salvation, or for the increasing of virtues in her soul. She declared that in order to acquire purity of mind, it was necessary for man to beware of judging unfavorably of his neighbor, and to abstain from all idle words concerning his conduct; for in all creatures we must behold the will of God. She particularly recommended never to despise or condemn any one under form of judgment, even though we should see them commit a fault; if sometimes the evil is evident, we should take compassion on him who committed it, and pray for him without despising or condemning him. She ever entertained a strong confidence in divine Providence, because she knew by experience, how graciously his bounty extends over all. Catharine and her followers had always experienced that God provided for all their necessities. She added, that those who trust in Divine Providence, shall not only never be abandoned, but shall experience a special help.

The Blessed Catharine also gave her followers other counsels; then she terminated by the last recommendation of the Saviour to his disciples, conjuring them humbly and earnestly to love one another. By their mutual affection, they would prove themselves her spiritual children, and she would believe herself their Mother, by so doing they would prove her glory and her crown; and she would intercede with the divine Goodness in their behalf that he would bless them as copiously as he had blessed herself. She commanded them, in the name of charity, to address continual and fervent prayers for the reformation and prosperity of the holy Church, and for the Vicar of Jesus Christ. These had been her ever-present thoughts during seven years: and to obtain an answer to her prayers she had constantly endured in her body, very great pains and infirmities in the latter years. She added that, as Satan had obtained from God permission to overwhelm Job with every variety of ill, it seemed to her that hell had also obtained permission to afflict and harass her body by every species of torments, so that from her head to her feet it appeared " that there was no health in her." She then said in conclusion : " My dear friends, it appears evident to me that my beloved Spouse nas disposed and designed all, so that, according to my hearts earnest desire, after the trials that his goodness has deigned to accord me, my soul shall be liberated from its obscure prison, and return to its true source."

The witnesses whom I have cited have written that the anguish and deep distress of Catharine appeared so terrible, that no one could have supported them without the grace of God; she endured them calmly without demonstrating any sign of sadness. As they were in amazement and wept at beholding her in that condition she thus addressed them : "Beloved sons, you ought not to be afflicted at my death ; you should rather rejoice with me and congratulate me, because I am about to quit this land of exile, and repose in the unending peace of God. I give you the positive assurance that I shall be more useful to you after my decease, than I would, or could have been by remaining with you in this life so obscured by grief and so filled with miseries. Nevertheless I commend my existence, its termination and **my whole being** into the hands of my ever Blessed Spouse; and if he perceives that I can be useful to any living creature, if he will that I yet remain amid anguish and torture, I am ready for the honor of his Name and the salvation of the neighbor, to suffer a hundred times a day, were it possible, death and all other imaginable torments. But if it be agreeable to him that I depart, be certain, dear children, that *I have given my life for the Church:* I have a certain knowledge that *God has permitted it by a peculiar grace."* After that, she called her disciples, one after another, and prescribed to each one the kind of life that he ought to embrace after her death; she desired that all should submit to my direction, as the one who held her place, indicating to some the Religious, and to others a Solitary life. For the women, and particularly the Sisters of Penance, she designated Alessia as Superior. She regulated all, according to the inspiration of the Holy Ghost; the event proved it thus, for her directions proved beneficial to every one.

After that she asked pardon of all. "My beloved," said she, "I have hungered and thirsted for your salvation, I dare not say the reverse; nevertheless I may have been wanting to you in many things; not only I have not given you an example of good works and of virtue as I should and might have done, had I been a true Spouse of our Lord and a perfect Religious, but also, in your temporal wants I have not been zealous and attentive as I should have been. I therefore implore of all, in general and in particular, pardon and indulgence; I entreat you, and I conjure you humbly and earnestly, to pursue to the end the path of virtue, that you may be, as I have foretold you, my joy and my crown." After these words she kept silent: she then made, as she did

daily her general confession, and humbly asked for the
Holy Eucharist and the last Sacraments. Her requests
were granted; she also implored the plenary Indulgence
which had been granted to her by the Sovereign Pontiffs
Gregory XI. and Urban VI., who had already given it to
her. She then began to enter upon her agony and contend against Satan; the assistants perceived it by her
words and gestures. Sometimes she maintained silence,
sometimes she replied, sometimes she smiled, occasionally
she appeared to despise what she heard, and again to
feel indignant.

Those who related to me the events that then transpired,
remarked one peculiar circumstance, and I believe it happened for the greater glory of God. After observing
silence, as though she were listening to an accusation,
she replied with a joyful countenance: *"No, never,
vain-glory, but the real honor and glory of God."*
There was a motive for Divine Providence permitting
these words to be heard; for several persons, on account
of the meekness of her charity and the abudant graces
that were granted to her, believe that she courted praise
or at least enjoyed it, and that on this account she took
delight in appearing before the public. Some said, when
speaking of her: "Why run from all sides to her; it is
only a woman; she ought to remain in her cell, if she
desires to serve God." The response to these reproaches
was complete; *"No, never vain-glory:"* said she, *"but
the true glory of God and his honor;"* that is; no, it
it was not vain-glory that induced me to go on all sides
and perform good works, but I acted continually for the
glory of the Saviour and the honor of his Name. I likewise can give testimony with certitude, having so often
heard her general confessions and her particular ones, and

who have carefully examined all her acts; she always obeyed the direct order of God and his inspirations; not only she sought not praise, but she did not even think of men, except when she was praying for their salvation and laboring to promote it. One who had not been witness of her life, could never know to what a degree, she was a stranger to those human passions which are even usual in persons consecrated in religion. The words of the Apostle may most suitably be applied to her: *Nostra autem conversatio in cœlis est.* (Phil. iii. 20.) "Our conversation is in heaven." Nothing could for one moment distract her desires, and weaken the ardor of her charity.

After this prolonged contest and her victory, Catharine came to herself, renewed the public confession she was accustomed to make and for greater security asked to receive again the absolution and indulgence that had already been given; she followed in that, the doctrine and the example of St. Martin, St. Jerome, and St. Augustine, who wish that no Christian, whatever be his state of perfection, leave this world, without accusing himself of his defects, and exciting in his heart regret for having committed them. St. Augustine, in his last malady, caused the seven Penitential Psalms to be inscribed on the wall, near to his bed; he read them constantly and with an abundance of tears. St. Jerome, when dying, confessed his sins and defects publicly. St. Martin, in his last moments, taught his disciples, by word and example, that a Christian ought to die on sackcloth and ashes, to testify his humility and heartfelt repentance. In imitation of those great Saints, Catharine showed her contrition, by all possible means—and twice humbly petitioned absolution for her sins, and satisfaction of pains which are attached to the indulgence.

When all was terminated, the attendants observed that her physical strength diminished rapidly. She never desisted, however, from giving pious recommendations to her spiritual sons and daughters, to those present and to those who were absent; for, in her last agony she said to the individuals who were present: "Apply to Friar Raymoud in all your doubts and difficulties, and tell him never to become remiss and to fear not, in whatever may befall him. I will be with him continually and will protect him in all his dangers; when he does wrong I will warn him, so that he may correct himself." I was assured that she repeated these words often, and pronounced them as long as she had strength to do it. Seeing that the moment of her exit had arrived, she said: "Lord, into thy hands I commend my spirit;" *Domine, in manus tuas commendo spiritum meum.* And as she had so long desired, that devout soul was freed from its captivity and united in an indissoluble, eternal union, to the Spouse whom she had so ardently loved, in the year of our Lord, 1380, on Sunday, the 29th of April, at the hour of Tierce. I was at that instant in Gênes, and her soul communicated to mine, in some way, what I have recounted above, and which she enjoined me to repeat. I call to witness Him who can neither deceive nor be deceived; but then my darkened understanding did not comprehend whence came the words, the sense of which I was completely seized. I was at the time fulfilling at Gênes my functions of Provincial; it was the moment of the Chapter which was to be held at Bologna for the election of a GENERAL, and I was making arragements to set out with some Religious. We were to go by sea as far as Pisa, and thence repair to Bologna, as we did in effect. We had hired a vessel and were awaiting a favorable wind.

The same morning in which the Blessed Catharine expired, I had gone to the Church, to celebrate the festival of St. Peter, the martyr. After saying Mass, I went again up to the dormitory to prepare my little bundle for my prospective journey; when passing before an image of the Blessed Virgin, I said in an undertone, according to the custom of the Religious, the *Ave Maria*, and I remained there kneeling for a few moments. I then heard a *voice* which was not in the air, and which pronounced words which seized me mentally but not orally; and nevertheless I perceived them more distinctly within me than if they had come to me exteriorly. I know not by what other title to designate this method of communication, if we may call *voice* that which is destitute of sound. This voice uttered these words or presented them to my mind: "Fear not, I am here for your sake; I am in heaven for you: I will protect and defend you; be tranquil, and fear naught, I am here *for you*." These interior words threw me into great trouble, and I endeavored to ascertain what this promised assistance could mean. I could not, at that moment, attribute them to any other than to the Blessed Virgin whom I was saluting; but I dared not think so, because of my unworthiness. I imagined that some terrible calamity was about to befal me, and that I as was imploring the Mother of mercy the constant comforter of the afflicted, she designed by this consoling promise to warn and prepare me to support courageously the coming event. I suspected that as I had preached at Gênes a crusade against the schismatics, there might be some among them awaiting an opportunity to injure me and mine. I endeavored thus to comprehend that prodigy which God mercifully granted me by the soul of his Spouse, to support my weakness; and in relating these circumstance, I discover more reason for experiencing a sentiment of shame than of vanity.

The following vision was presented to a Roman lady, at the instant in which Catharine expired; she related it to me herself, and I do not lightly give credit to her recital, having been acquainted with her conscience and her life, during more than twenty years.

There dwelt in Rome a Lady, the mother of two sons, and whose name was Semia. Previous to her husband's death, and still more perfectly after it, she consecrated herself to the service of God and devoted herself wholly to prayer and the visiting of Churches. She had a habit of rising during the night for MATINS but yielded to a sort of half-sleep after, so as to be more capable of accomplishing the pious pilgrimages of the day. When Catharine arrived at Rome, the Lady was informed of her virtues by myself and others; she visited her and became so captivated with the charms of her society, that she determined to enjoy them continually, but on account of her exercise of piety and her sons who were entitled to her care, several days sometimes intervened between her opportunities of seeing Catharine; and besides, she was not aware of her being *seriously* ill at that time.

In the night preceding the morning of our Saint's death, Semia arose, to pray as usual; and when her prayer was concluded, she reflected that as it was Sunday she ought to rise earlier than ordinary, so as to attend the solemn High Mass, and see to the preparation of the morning repast of her children. She therefore laid down, intending to catch a few moments of repose and then get up, and in consequence of thus charging her mind, even while dozing she was thinking of rising. Whilst in her partial sleep as she was saying to herself, "I must leave my bed in order to be in time for the service in the Church," she saw a very beautiful child apparently eight or ten years of age. This child said to her: "I do not wish you to rise until you have seen what I intend showing you." Ravished with the charms of the child, but yet intent upon hearing Mass, Semia answered: "Suffer me, dear one, to get up, because to-day we must not neglect High Mass." The child said: "I cannot positively suffer you to arise before you see the wonders that I have to exhibit to you, being commissioned by Almighty God." And it seemed to her that the child drew her from the bed and conducted her into a spacious place which was shaped like a Church; at one extremity of it there was a tabernacle of exquisitely burnished silver, but it was closed. "Wait a little," said the infant, "and you shall behold what is within the tabernacle;" and directly another little child, similar to the first, brought a ladder to the silver tabernacle which occupied a lofty elevation and opened the door of it with a golden key. As soon as it was unclosed, Semia who was looking, perceived a young girl very magnificently and richly adorned: her robe was of dazzling whiteness and plentifully ornamented with precious stones. She wore three superb crowns on her head so well arranged that the three could each be clearly discerned. The inferior crown was of silver, white as driven snow; the second was of silver mingled with gold and shone like red materials woven with golden threads; the third was of purest, finest gold bestrown with pearls and precious stones. At this spectacle; Semia wondered who this richly dressed child could be, and on considering her very attentively, she recognized distinctly *Catharine* of *Sienna*; but knowing her to be much older than the figure represented in this vision, she suspected it might mean some other. The child that first appeared to her, inquired whether she recognized her that she saw. "It is indeed," said Semia, "the countenance of Catharine of Sienna, but it is not her age." As she continued earnestly gazing on her, the person in the tabernacle smiled and said to the two children: "You see that she does not recognize me." Then advanced four more children similar to the two first, they bore a species of bier formed like a bed, and draperied around with rich purple, precious cloths, and when they had deposited it near the tabernacle, they mounted with speed and took in their arms the little crowned maiden, and laid her on the bed that they had brought. Then the youthful maiden said, "Allow me to go to that lady who is looking at me and does not recognize with certainty who I am." And directly she appeared to approach her as if by flying, and said, "I am Catharine of Sienna, Semia." She rejoined "What, are *you* mother Catharine?" "Yes," answered she; "but consider well what you now see and what you are about to see."

At these words, she was conducted by the six children to the bed, and was raised on it towards heaven. Whilst Semia saw her thus gradually mounting, she suddenly beheld a throne in Heaven; and on that throne a King crowned and covered with jewels, holding in his right hand an opened book; the children who bore the lovely Virgin elevated her to the very steps of the throne and to the feet of the King; and instantaneously the virgin cast herself at the feet of the King and adored him. Then the King said: "Welcome dear Spouse and cherished daughter, Catharine." At the order of the King, she raised her head and read in the open book, during sufficient time to say devoutly the "Lord's Prayer;" then, on a new signal from the King, she arose and took a position near to the throne, awaiting the Queen who was advancing at the head of a numerous group of virgins. At her approach, our Saint, hastened to descend the steps and prostrate before her: after which the Queen of Heaven taking her by the hand said: "Welcome Catharine, my daughter;" and raising her up gave her the kiss of peace. She offered a second act of homage to the Queen by his command, and then she moved towards the other virgins, and all joyfully received her, giving her the "kiss of peace."

Whilst all this was transacting, Semia cried out: "O my Sovereign Lady, Mother of our Lord Jesus Christ, intercede for me! St. Mary Magdalen, St. Catharine, St. Agnes, St. Margaret, pray for us!" She informed me that, although this vision seemed to be in heaven, she distinguished all the actors perfectly, and recognized not only the Blessed Mother of God, but also the other Virgins, each in her turn. She called each one by her name, for they severally bore the tokens of their martyrdom: St. Catharine her wheel; St. Margaret, a dragon beneath her feet, and St. Agatha her scarred bosom, and in like manner the others. In fine, amid the felicitations of all those virgins, the youthful Catharine was placed, and crowned with glory.

When Semia awoke and opened her eyes, she saw that the sun already indicated on the horizon the hour of Tierce; she was grieved on account of the Mass she de sired to hear, and the repast which was to be prepared for her children; but yet she could not refrain from mentally inquiring what this vision could signify? She did not know, and could not persuade herself to believe that Catharine was deceased, although she knew her to be feeble. Her occupations had prevented her from seeing her during several days, and she had often known her to recover from even alarming sufferings; she concluded therefore that Catharine might have been favored with some extraordinary ecstacy. She also feared on account of the lateness of the hour, she had lost the opportunity of hearing Mass that day, and suspected Satan of intending to cause her to violate the precept of the Church in reference to the sanctification of the Sabbath; she hurriedly placed her repast on the fire and hastened to the parish church, saying within herself; "If I lose Mass, it will be a proof that this vision comes from Satan; but if I can obtain the hearing of Mass, I shall believe that I owe it to the pious Mother Catharine." On arriving at the Church they were singing the Offertory; she became sad; and said "Ah! unhappy me, the demon has deceived me." She returned home instantly, attended quickly to her domestic affairs and prepared to go to other churches, so as to be present at the entire Mass.

Whilst thus occupied at home, she heard a bell that announced Mass in a neighboring monastery of NUNS; she joyfully hastened there, leaving the vegetables as she had prepared them, and without putting them into the soup. She *locked* the door, leaving no one in the house, found the Mass which was just commencing, and joyfully said to herself—Satan did not deceive me as I feared. Only she regretted the vexation of her sons, who had attained a certain age, knowing certainly that their dinner would not be ready and that there would be no more time for her to prepare it. She heard the whole high Mass. When it was ended, she returned home and met her sons who said: "Mother it is very late, please arrange it, so that we can have our dinner." She replied: "Dear children, wait a short time, and all will be ready." She ran home, found the door shut as she left it, and opened it so as to finish very quickly what remained to be done: the meat and vegetables were all prepared and served, and naught remained but for them to take their seats at the table. Semia was filled with amazement, and determined to go directly after dinner and see Catharine whom she believed yet living, in order to give her a full account. She called her two sons who were near, and whilst they were dining, she was absorbed with the idea of her vision. The youths who were not aware of what had happened found their repast better than common; but she could only say interiorly: "O beloved Mother! you came, even though the doors were closed, to dress and prepare my dinner. I see that you are holy, and an acceptable servant before God."

On this very account, she had not the slightest suspicion of Catharine's death, and as soon as her sons had withdrawn, she ran to the house of our Saint and knocked at the door as usual; but no one answered. The neigbors informed her that Catharine had been visiting the churches and that there was no one there; she believed it, and went away. The truth was, that all those who were within mourned their mother and concealed her death, because they desired to avoid the rumor getting abroad as they would be distracted in their sorrow and might not tranquilly discuss what ought to be done. In fine, it was decided that on the morrow the body of

Catharine should be transferred to the church of Preaching Friars, called *Ste. Marie-de-la-Minerve* and that there her funeral should be celebrated.

As soon as the corpse of Catharine was borne to the church the whole city of Rome became aware of it, and a multitude collected from every side; they moved forward like turbulent waves to touch her garments and her feet, her spiritual sons and daughters feared that they would divide her body on the spot, and they consequently placed it behind the grate of the chapel of St. Dominic. Semia, by accident went also to the church, and beholding such an agitation, asked its cause. Directly she heard that Catharine was dead, and that it was she that attracted the crowd, she advanced sobbing to the place where the body of Catharine was exposed, and said to Catharine's spiritual daughters: "How cruel to have concealed from me the decease of my beloved Mother! Why did you not summon me to assist at her last moments?" And as they were offering their excuses she inquired at what time she expired. They replied yesterday about the hour of Tierce she gave up her soul to her Creator. Semia immediately cried: "I saw her; I saw my beloved Mother quitting her body: the angels bore her to Heaven in my presence; she had three precious crowns, and her raiment was resplendently white. I know now that God sent me an angel and showed me the death of mother Catharine. O mother! mother! how is it that I did not comprehend, during that vision, that you were quitting the earth." And Semia then gave a full description of her vision to the disciples of Catharine who were shielding her corpse by their presence.

CHAPTER V.

SOME PRODIGIES AND MIRACLES WHICH THE LORD ACCOMPLISHED AFTER CATHARINE'S DEATH, BY HER INTERCESSION.

CATHARINE's mortal pilgrimage was terminated; but the divine energy that had accompanied her during life, manifested the greatest of her merits, after her decease. Almost all the people of Rome collected spontaneously at the Church in which her corpse was exposed, desirous of venerating her remains and of recommending themselves to her prayers. Many persons brought their sick who requested to be cured by the intercession of Catharine; and God did not deceive their expectations. I intend relating what I know on this subject from the informations of others and by my own observations.

A Sister of the Third Order of St. Francis, called Dominica, was so infirm in one arm that during six months previous to Catharine's demise she could not use it; she came to the church, and being unable to approach her body on account of the crowd, she untied her veil, and requested that it might touch the Saint's remains; when they returned it to her, she put the veil under her arm, and it was promptly cured. She instantly exclaimed; "See! by the merits of the Saint I am freed from a malady pronounced incurable and which was destroying my arms." In consequence the eagerness of the multitude increased; they brought her the sick from all quarters, in hopes that they might succeed in touching the "*hem of her garments.*"

Among others they brought, a little child of four years of age, the nerves of whose neck were so drawn, that his head rested on his shoulder, without his being able to raise it; they carried him near the body, and as soon as Catharine's virginal hand was applied to the diseased portion, and they had put around his neck a veil which she had worn, favorable symptoms commenced, and very soon his head was straitened and the restoration perfect. During three days it was found impossible to conclude the Interment on account of the miracles which were performed; and during those three days, there was such an affluence of people that a Doctor in Theology who had ascended the pulpit, intending to preach her funeral discourse, could never obtain sufficient calm to allow him to proceed; he said merely to those who were listening to him: "this privileged Virgin has no need of our preaching and eulogy; she speaks, and declares it convincingly herself." And he came down, without having even begun his sermon.

A Roman named Lucius of Connarola, had an infirmity where medicine was powerless to effect a cure. His thigh and his leg were in such a condition, that even with the aid of a crutch he could not succeed in walking more than a few steps. Having heard of all the miracles that God performed through Catharine's intercession, he dragged himself with much difficulty as far as the Church and caused himself to be conducted near the holy body; he with deep devotion placed Catharine's hand on the leg hitherto so weak and feeble, and instantly he felt his strength and energy revive; before retiring he was perfectly cured.

A young girl named Ratozzola had her face so attacked by a horrible leprosy that her nose and upper lip offered one shocking wound, she, also, was attracted to the church by the reports. As she endeavored to approach the body she was repulsed several times; at length by repeated instances she succeeded in entering, and in her ardent desire to be relieved, she not only applied her diseased face to Catharine's hands and feet, but also to her face: she instantly perceived her leprosy diminish, and she was soon so perfectly restored that her countenance did not even retain one scar.

A Roman named Cyprius and his wife Lelia had a daughter who from infancy had suffered with asthma, and the physicians had pronounced her case incurable. The parents having learned the miracles which were performed applied with fervor to Catharine and put a veil and a *Pater Noster* that had touched her body on their child; wonderful to relate, scarcely had she, that was despaired of, touched these objects, than she was restored to her primitive health.

An inhabitant of Rome, named Antoine Sello, who was attached to the church of the Prince of the Apostles, heard the prodigies worked by Catharine much talked about: he was sick from excess of labor, and walked with great difficulty: the remedies of physicians had proved inadequate, but he had procured himself a little relief. Inspired by all that he heard, he devoutly recommended himself to the Saint and promised to accomplish a vow, if he were cured through her merits. Scarcely had he drawn up the formula of the Vow than he was completely delivered from his sufferings; he was no longer conscious of them, walked with ease, and went to visit the remains of his benefactress; he accomplished the promise or vow which he had taken, and gives an account to all that are curious to hear the particulars of the grace which he obtained.

There was a pious lady, Paula by name who had been very intimate with Catharine; she was not only her friend, but had offered her hospitality together with her followers. At the moment of Catharine's death, she was cruelly tormented by the gout and also with an acute pain in the side. As these two maladies demanded different kinds of treatment, the unfortunate patient suffered greatly and was in danger of death. After the death of Catharine she earnestly implored the favor of having something that had touched her body; it was given to her in the evening and on the following morning, she was able to rise from the bed on which she had been extended during four months; she walked with as much facility as before the commencement of her illness: I received this account from herself at Rome.

When Catharine's body was interred, the divine power it possessed of curing diseases was in no wise weakened, it rather augmented. A Roman named Veri or Neri, had a little child who could not stand erect upon his legs; he conducted him to Catharine's tomb, and hardly had he placed him on it, than his feet and legs grew strong, and the little fellow walked as though he had always enjoyed good health.

Jean de Tozo, had a disgusting and horrible disease in the eyes: worms crawled out of one of them; he took a vow to the Virgin of Sienna and was instantly relieved. He went to her tomb, narrated a description of the cure he had obtained, and deposited an ex-voto in wax as is customary. A German lady who came on a pilgrimage, and whose name they neglected retaining, suffered so much and so long with her eyes, that she had almost lost her sight and entertained no hope of cure. She recommended herself piously to Catharine, and gradually recovered her sight without the help of any remedy.

A lady of Rome named Maria, endured such excruciating pains in the head that she lost an eye, notwithstanding all the efforts of her attendant physicians: she became so sad on this account and felt such shame that she remained at home and declined seeing any one. Having been informed of Catharine's miracles, she devoutly recommended herself to her intercession. The succeeding night the Saint appeared to the domestic of that lady, saying: "Let your mistress Maria adopt no more remedies, but go every morning and hear the Divine Office and she will be healed." The servant gave her commission, and her mistress obeyed Catharine's injunction; the pain ceased directly; she began to use the eye that had lost its sight, and persevering in the pious exercise that had been indicated, she was restored to sight and general corporal health. The Reader should here remark what the Blessed Catharine did: she might have cured her who invoked help immediately, but she was desirous of granting more than was asked in imitation of our Saviour who never healed the body without curing the soul. To him who came to implore health, he first remitted his sins, by saying: *Confide, fili: remittuntur tibi peccata tua.* (Matth. ix. 2.)

A youth called Jacques, son of the Roman citizen Pierre de Niccolo, was grievously ill: all remedies had failed and the physicians thought that, according to the laws of nature, his end was near; he recommended himself devoutly to the Blessed Catharine; he became better at the very moment, and a few days after, was in perfect health.

The noble and pious Lady Jeanne Ilperini was particularly acquainted with Catharine during her life-time; the miracles she saw inspired her with an exalted idea of her sanctity, and she counseled all the sick to have recourse to her intercession. One day this lady's son, was running imprudently on the terrace (or flat-roof) of the house and fell without any one being able to offer him any assistance; his mother seeing him fall cried with all her strength: "*St. Catharine protect my son!*" The child who was exposed either to be killed or have his limbs broken, had not the slightest bruise, or wound. The mother descended to him promptly, thanked God and Catharine also, whose holy influence she proclaimed to every one.

There was another female who gained a livelihood by serving others; her name was Buona Giovanni. One time as she was washing a counterpane on the shore of the Tiber, it escaped from her hands and was drawn off rapidly by the current of water; as Buona was poor, and unable to reimburse its value, she attempted to get it back, and reaching too far in an effort to catch it, she was herself drawn into the river; there was no one near to assist her; but she recollected the miracles daily accomplished in the city, by Catharine's intercession. She invoked Catharine at once; and her prayer was heard, for she felt herself elevated above the water, and as though waves had ceased flowing, she quitted the stream with the coverlid, and attained the shore without difficulty.

Almighty God glorified by these miracles and by others, his favored Spouse, previous to my return to Rome; later, I was recalled there, when I received the, for (*me*, too heavy) charge of General Master of the Order of Preaching Friars. Then my Brethren and Sisters who had been Catharine's spiritual children related to me all that I have written. There was, however, one miracle which took place after my arrival; I was a partial witness of it, and I do not like to pass it in silence.

I was at Rome, and had the sacred remains of Catharine transferred on the very day on which she had foretold it, several years beforehand. One of my friends, a physician, styled M. Jacques de-Sainte-Mariê-de-la-Rotonde, informed me that a young man of the city, named Nicholas, a son-in-law of Cintio Yancancini, was so alarmingly ill of the quinsy, that he saw no remedy; other persons told me that the youth was at the point of death; but Alessia, Catharine's associate, having heard it, and being aware that Cintio, and all her household, had been very devoted to, and much cherished by Catharine, repaired without delay to the young man, carrying with her one of the teeth of Catharine, which she regarded as a precious relic. She found the patient in extremities; the inflammation impeded respiration. She applied the tooth to the throat, and instantly there was heard a noise similar to the detaching of a stone; the abscess opened, the invalid raised his head and ejected from his mouth a great quantity of corrupted matter; in a short time he was perfectly restored, returning thanks to God and to the saint, whose tooth had delivered him from the teeth of the grim messenger DEATH. This prodigy surprised people in general and above all the physicians who understood more clearly than the others, the imminent danger in which he was placed. The young Nicholas relates publicly what happened to him, so much so, that once while preaching and telling some miracles performed by the

Saint, and among others this one, he arose in the midst of the assemby and said: "Father what you advance is correct; I am the subject of that miracle."

To the above wonders, I could add many others of which no note has been taken; the proof is in the numbers of waxen *ex-voto* offered at her tomb. But these offerings of homage, or of pious gratitude, have been gradually removed. I know not whether to accuse the inhabitants of Rome, or foreigners, of which the city is continually full, but the purloiners are either already punished or will soon be. For myself, I confess in the presence of God, of Angels and of all the Faithful, that many persons have sought me, in order to unfold to me the wonderful favors that they have received through Blessed Catharine's intercession, and it is my fault if these circumstances have remained buried in forgetfulness—I neglected to write them. I had designated a notary to do it, but he did not fulfill my intentions; but I remember one event that I cannot well conceal. At the time in which Queen Jeanne (Joan) sent against Rome Rinaldo des Ursins, at the head of armed men, to arrest the Sovereign Pontiff, Urban VI., several inhabitants were taken by the enemy. Some were fastened to trees, and thus abandoned to a cruel death; others were led to the camp loaded with irons, hoping to procure a ransom. I have learned from those who were delivered, that as soon as they invoked Catharine, they felt their chains drop, without human help. One among others informed me that after praying he found himself disencumbered from the bonds by which the enemy had attached him to a tree, and that he had returned to Rome, supplicating Catharine, without meeting any one to arrest him.

I remember to have heard many miracles of this kind

related; but my memory fades with years, and the peculiar details escape me. I beseech the reader to collect, notwithstanding the lengthened and imperfect details of this work, both flowers and fruit from this holy life, and to shun as they would a pestilence, the indifference of the lukewarm, and the malice of calumniators. I desire before concluding, to speak of Catharine's patience. The Church militant admires this virtue in her Saints more than she does miracles; I therefore consecrate a chapter to this subject. Catharine will obtain for me in return a grace from her heavenly Spouse, who lives and reigns with the Father and the Holy Ghost, world without end. Amen.

CHAPTER VI.

OF THE GREAT PATIENCE THAT CATHARINE MANIFESTED IN ALL HER ACTIONS, FROM HER INFANCY UNTIL HER DEATH. THIS CHAPTER WILL BE A SORT OF CONDENSED STATEMENT OF HER WHOLE LIFE.

THE ETERNAL TRUTH, incarnate for our salvation says: *Qui in corde bono et optimo audientes verbum retinent, et fructum afferunt in patientia.* (St. Luke. viii. 15.) "Who in a good and very good heart, hearing the word with patience, keep it, and bring forth fruit in patience." In his Book of Dialogues, St. Gregory said: "I think that the virtue of patience, is above prodigies and miracles: *Ego virtutem patientiæ signis et miraculis puto majorem.* The Apostle St. James says in his canonical Epistle (St. J. i. 4,) *Patientia opus perfectum.* Patience hath a perfect work. She is not the chief and the queen of virtues; but according to the testimony of the Apostle, she is the inseparable companion of that virtue which is the greatest, and shall never fail. When speaking of Charity, St. Paul said: "Charity is patient, is kind; charity envieth not, dealeth not perversely; is not puffed up." (I. Cor. xiii. 4.) Hence, when the Church examines the lives of her Saints, she does not apply her principal attention to the prodigies they have performed, for two reasons: 1. The wicked have accomplished and still effect prodigies which resemble miracles, which are not such, as those of the Magicians of Pharaoh: Anti-Christ and his followers will do the same in their time 2 Some have actually performed miracles by the help of divine power, but have afterwards been reprobate like Judas, and to those who, according to the Gospel shall at the last judgment say: *Lord have we not performed miracles in thy* NAME; it will be answered "*Withdraw from me, ye workers of iniquity.*" Consequently, in accordance with the doctrine of Divines, prodigies and miracles cannot of themselves, assure to the church militant, the eternal glory of those who performed them, though they are nevertheless a strong indication of their sanctity, especially when they happen after their decease; but even those do not give a definite certitude, because God in his compassion, may recompense the faith of those who pray, without intending to manifest the glory of those whom they supplicate.

When the Church wishes to ascertain the merits of the Saints, she informs herself of their lives, and actions on earth. Her Divine Spouse taught her this, when he said "*By their fruits you will know them, for a bad tree cannot produce good fruit, nor a good tree evil fruit.*" (St. Matth. vii. 18.) Good fruits are the works of charity towards God and towards the neighbour. Those works are agreeable to God, and consequently insupportable to Satan, who makes untiring efforts to hinder them, either in himself, or by men who belong to him in the world. The Saints who are faithful and who persevere, have necessarily practiced patience which preserved them in the love of God and of the neighbor, notwithstanding all imaginable persecutions. Our Lord said to his disciples; *in patientia vestra possidebitis animas vestras*, "in your patience you shall preserve your souls." (St. Luke xxi. 19.) And that is, according to the Apostle, the first condition of Charity. *Charity is patient; charitas patiens est.* (1. Cor. xiii. 4.) Therefore this point is greatly insisted upon in the canonization of the Saints;

their *deeds* are more exactly scrutinized than their *miracles*: and among their actions, their fruits of patience are particularly sought, because they prove charity and sanctity more than all others.

My intention in writing this volume, being to make known Catharine's sanctity to the Catholic Church and those who govern it, I thought that I would complete my work by adding a chapter on the PATIENCE of Catharine, it having been the glory of her life. I will recapitulate her entire annals, and I shall thus prove useful to a class of readers who find an hour longer than a day, when pious subjects are in question, while a day seems to them to fly more rapidly than an hour when they are occupied in perusing fables.

Patience is exercised in enduring things opposite; its very name indicates it, since it is derived from *patir*, to suffer. The things contrary to man may be divided into two classes, according to their double nature; those which affect the mind, and those which affect the body.

The good possessed by man is separated by philosophers into three classes: the *agreeable, useful* and *honorable*, and it is by the continued privation of these blessings that patience is exercised. The *agreeable* comprehends health, the pleasures of the table, of the toilette, with whatever flatters nature, and in particular sensuality. The *useful* comprehends riches, houses, lands, money, animals, luxury, parentage and kindred, with domestics and whatever serves to the material existence. The *honorable* embraces whatever gives man consideration among his equals: as a good, or a renowned name, a great reputation, distinguished friends, recognized abilities, and the means of doing good.

Among the things that I have enumerated, some are

culpable and must be renounced; some are hindrances to perfection, and must be avoided and despised; others are allowed and are even necessary sometimes, and their privation must be supported patiently. We shall consider Catharine's conduct in all these, pursuing the order that we have selected. The Saint understood that patience is not serviceable when we do not first shun what is forbidden, as all sensual pleasures; hence, at a tender age, she avoided them with fortitude and prudence. It was in consequence of a remarkable vision with which she was favored at six years of age, when the Lord appeared to her with his chief Apostles, and blessed her with his kingly hand, and gave her a look of tender affection. Her soul was then filled with such perfect love, that she abandoned the habits of infancy, and consecrated herself, notwithstanding the weakness of her years to penance and to meditation. So rapid was her progress that the following year, namely, her seventh, she made a Vow of perpetual chastity, in presence of the Blessed Virgin, after having maturely reflected and prayed much.

As the pious child had understood that there was nothing more necessary for preserving her virginity than sobriety and mortification in her diet, she applied to that at a tender age, and finished by practising it with a marvelous perfection. She began by depriving herself of meat and then renounced it wholly; the wine which she drank was mingled with so much water that it lost its taste; at fifteen she abstained from it completely, and refused all food except bread and vegetables; in fine, at the age of twenty, she retrenched bread, and supported her body with uncooked herbs; she did so, until God granted her the favor of living without taking any food; and this took place, if I am not deceived, at the age of twenty-five or twenty-six. I have declared the murmurs that were excited against this extraordinary state, which she then endured and with admirable patience.

Having thus retrenched, by abstinence and purity, against the pleasures of sense, Catharine was deprived by others of many things permitted and even desirable. Some trials gave her a veritable joy, but there were others that afflicted her profoundly. Among her relatives and friends, many were an occasion of pain from her infancy until her death. Her mother and brothers in order to force her to marry, took away her room, and obliged her to perform the vilest employments of the kitchen, so as to prevent her from praying and meditating. She remained fixed and immovable in her resolutions; not only the privation of her cell, and the services of the house did not induce her to neglect ordinary prayers, but she daily increased them, until she triumphed. The demon was intent upon hindering her austerities, the length of her vigils and the hardness of her bed; he excited her mother Lapa against her, we may say, even to rage; but *she*, armed with invincible patience, and wonderful discretion, softened her mother's anger, while continuing her vigorous penances.

The enemy of salvation sought by all possible means to deprive that holy soul of the consolations and favors of her divine Spouse, or at least to distract her from them for a time; but she triumphed over her attacks by fervor; she disconcerted his snares and projects by her wisdom, and confounded him by her perseverance. The evil spirit endeavored to induce her to forget her Vow, by means of her sister-in-law, who succeeded in inspiring her with a kind of particularity in the arrangement of her hair and in her toilette. God permitted this for her good, as

I have shown in the fourth Chapter of the First Part. He afterwards tormented her by temptations and even by false visions.

One day when she was praying before a Crucifix the demon presented himself holding a robe of rich silk with which he desired to clothe her. She repulsed it with contempt, and armed herself with the sign of the Cross; the devil disappeared, but left in her mind a temptation to vanity, in adorning her person, and she was extremely troubled by it; but she remembered the vow of virginity that she had contracted, and said to our Saviour: "Beloved Spouse, thou knowest that I never desired any other spouse than thee; assist me to triumph over these temptations; I do not ask thee to remove them, but only deign in thy mercy never to permit me to yield." She had scarcely terminated this prayer, than the Mother of God, the Queen of Heaven, appeared to her, and it seemed to her that she drew from the side of her crucified Son, a magnificent robe, which she embroidered with her own hand, setting it with dazzling and priceless gems; she clothed her with this robe, saying: "Know, my daughter, that the garments which come from the side of my Son surpass all other garments in brightness and beauty." The temptation vanished immediately, and the Saint was filled with heavenly consolation.

The devil, seeing that he could not lead her to be less fervent in keeping her resolutions, strove to render them useless during a period of time, and aided himself by several individuals. He employed her mother, who conducted her to the Baths, so as to oblige her to suspend her austerities; but Catharine contrived to find ruder mortifications than she practiced in her cell, by exposing her body to boiling water. . . . . Deficiency of light in her directors, and in the Prioresses of the "Third Order," also caused her much suffering. They hindered her from confessing as much as she desired to do, and constrained her in the exercises of piety which she loved the most. Their understanding was incapable of comprehending them; they condemned light because they were in darkness, and they wished to take measure of the mountain peaks, without leaving the shades of their humble valleys.

The following fact will show the extent of her patience. It will redound to the shame of a few Religious, but it is better to publish it than to be silent concerning the gifts that the Holy Ghost lavished on that faithful soul.

Catharine could scarcely perform any public exercise of piety, without exciting a calumny, and drawing upon nerself the persecutions of those same individuals who ought to have defended and encouraged her; and let us not be astonished: Religious who have not perfectly overcome their self-love, allow their jealousy to carry them farther than persons in the world. As the Sisters of Penance saw Catharine, yet so young, surpassing all the others by the austerity of her life, the severity of morals, and the fervor of her prayer and a sublime contemplation, some among them were seduced by Satan, and began through envy to censure her conduct, and denounce her to some Religious of the Order. If *some* extolled her virtue, and proved it by things evident to all, *others*, maintained that she was instigated by an evil spirit. Those females, genuine descendants of Eve, acted so adroitly that they seduced Adam himself, that is to say, the Superiors of the Convent of St. Dominic, who would not receive her, refused her holy Communion, and even went so far as to deprive her of her Confessor. She supported the whole with patience and without murmuring, as though she were not the injured one, and no one ever heard her utter the smallest complaint.

If they allowed her to approach Communion, they exacted that she should terminate her prayers directly and quit the church, which was wholly impossible; for, she received holy Communion with so much fervor, that she lost the use of her senses; her body became completely insensible, and she remained in that state for several hours. Those whom the Sisters had misled, became furious at this; they would take her during her ecstacies, carry her away in a rough, even brutal manner, and throw her down at the Church door as though she were the most contemptible of human beings. Her companions bathed in tears, remained around her to protect her, exposed to the burning rays of the noonday sun, and awaiting the moment in which she would return to herself. Some individuals gave her furious blows with the foot, whilst she was in ecstasy, and nevertheless she never uttered a word of reproach: she never even mentioned that ill-treatment except to excuse those who made her suffer! But the more she remained patient, amid these injuries, the more her divine Spouse, who is justice itself, was provoked against her persecutors, and punished them with severity. I know this by the Confessor who preceded me and from several persons worthy of confidence.

A woman who gave her a blow with the foot, during an ecstasy, was taken, just as she entered her house, with agonizing pains, and expired directly, without being able to receive the last Sacraments. Another wretch also struck her with the foot, and carried her to the door of the Church, offering her the grossest injuries; his punishment was awful; that man (whom I knew perfectly well) not only behaved odiously towards Catharine, but he even designed to kill her. A few days after, the unhappy individual, without any apparent cause, became enraged as though he was possessed by the devil; he shrieked continually: "In mercy help me! see, here comes the executioner to cut off my head!" The occupants of the house were anxious to encourage and comfort him, but they soon perceived by his words and gestures that he had entirely lost his reason; they therefore watched him closely, because they discovered that he was tempted to commit suicide. Some time after, as he appeared more calm, the care diminished; he found means of escape, and went like Judas to hang himself! I have this fact from the very person that found his corpse; he was not buried in consecrated ground, but in a ditch, as he well merited.

Catharine had much to suffer in her reputation, and in this especially appeared her admirable patience. What more precious than the reputation of a Maiden, and what more delicate than the honor of a consecrated Virgin! It was in consideration of this that God would have his Mother, the Queen of Virgins protected by a husband in the eyes of the world; and on the Cross, he confided the virginity of his Mother to the virginity of St. John. Three facts which I have narrated, show Catharine's patience and her continual progress in virtue. The first was the story of Tecca, the leper whom Catharine nursed when she was slighted by everybody. I also mentioned Palmerina who wore the same religious habit as Catharine and who indulged an unjust and implacable hatred against her. Perfect charity triumphed in this case; persevering prayer destroyed all the evil that the devil had created in that poor soul, and grace diffused in the heart and on the lips of Catharine was so potent, as to save Palmerina from the flames of perdition. Although in those two circumstances, and particularly in the second, Catharine's patience is displayed in an admirable manner it shone even more brightly in the case of Andrea the cancerous woman.

After having recalled the prodigies of patience of the Blessed Catharine, it appears to me beneficial to give some details of which I have not yet spoken. Almost all the persons who approached her to follow her counsels and her examples, afflicted her in some way; the demon thus endeavored to torment her by means of those who were dearest to her. Catharine suffered more vexations from those whom she directed than from strangers: she however triumphed over them by patience. Like an immovable column which the power of the Holy Spirit had fixed in Charity, the most violent persecutions could not weaken her stability; the words of the wise man might be aptly applied to her: "She has her everlasting foundations on the solid rock, and God's commandments are in the heart of the devout woman:" *Fundamenta aeterna super petram solidam et mandata Dei in corde mulieris sanctæ* (Eccl. xxvi. 24.) yes, the soul of Catharine was so established by indissoluble bonds with the foundation stone Jesus Christ, that she preserved piously within her heart the precepts of God.

A Religious (man) had been so misled by the devil, that he insulted Catharine in the coarsest manner in the very presence of her companions. She was so patient that she would not allow any exterior sign of trouble to appear; she uttered not a word, and expressly recommended not to offer the slightest reproach to the culpable individual, and not to give him any pain. He therefore, emboldened by Catharine's meekness, went so far as to take the money that had been remitted to her for giving alms. The Saint did not swerve from her charity; she would not allow any one of those who were aware of the theft to say or do any thing; but she remained steadfast in silence and hope. She finished by vanquishing, and thus teaches us, by her words and her example, to overcome ourselves.

It is quite impossible to describe the patience that Catharine exhibited in corporeal infirmities; she suffered a continual and very violent pain in the side, and it was this that delivered her father's soul from the anguish of purgatorial flames. She had likewise an unintermitting pain in the head, and an acute pain in the breast; this last named torture, commenced on the day that our Lord permitted her to take the sufferings of his sacred Passion; it remained with her ever after, and she affirmed that it surpassed all the others. To these dolors were frequently added violent fevers, and yet she never breathed a plaint or showed that she was ill. Her countenance bore no impress of sadness, and with a gentle and engaging smile, she received and consoled those who approached her for consultation or conversation. When words would not suffice, and fatigue and labor were requisite to promote the salvation of souls,—all her infirmities seemed to vanish; she arose and walked as though she were not subject to any infirmity.

What persecutions did not that holy soul endure from Satan! I recount an incident that I witnessed. We were returning to Sienna, one day, when she was suddenly precipitated from the ass on which she was riding into a deep ravine; I ran, invoking the Blessed Virgin, and found her on the ground, laughing and saying "that it was a blow from the '*evil beast*'"—meaning Satan. She seated herself anew; but scarcely had she advanced a few steps than the malign spirit again threw her into the dust, and in such manner that she found herself directly underneath the animal. She said to us laughingly; "This good mule warms the side in which I suffer pain." She thus mocked Satan who could not succeed in doing her any injury. We drew her from the ground, but, we were unwilling to allow her to mount the animal anew, and as we were near the city, we wished her to walk in the midst of us. Her enemy was not yet deterred, he dragged her every way, and if we had not sustained her, she would certainly have been overthrown; but she continued to rally the evil spirit on his impotence. It was at this time that Catharine effected so much good in souls, and the devil showed by his persecutions, the rage which embittered him.

The incredible sufferings that charity led Catharine to undergo, a short time before her death, entitle her (it appears to me) to the dignity of martyr. The Blessed Anthony thirsted for martyrdom and petitioned it from our Lord, who heard him by allowing the demons to beat him cruelly, without however taking away his life. Catharine was frequently beaten, and even found death in the last torments which hell obliged her to suffer. It alone would be a sufficient proof of her holiness, and for the conviction of those who may doubt it, I will cite a fact which will show how similar Catharine was to her Spouse, at least as to the cause of her sufferings.—I will thus terminate this chapter to the glory of the Incarnate Truth, to the honor of the virgin Catharine, his Spouse, and in opposition to what may be said by the devotees of falsehood.

Towards the year 1375, either by the malice of the great Sower of tares, or through defect of those in charge of the Holy See, or by the pecuniary aid of certain Florentines, or by reciprocal arts, the City of Florence, which hitherto had ranked among the most devoted daughters of the Catholic Church, assembled the enemies of the Church and used great efforts to destroy in union with them its temporal power; the Sovereign Pontiff of Rome, who commanded in Italy sixty Episcopal Cities and a thousand fortified places, was reduced to a few meagre, paltry strips of land. Pope Gregory XI fulminated against the Florentines terrible decrees which caused all their goods to be seized by the Proprietors of the countries with which they carried on commerce. The consequences accruing from this chastisement, forced them to sue for peace to the Supreme Pontiff, by the intermediation of persons whom they knew to be agreeable to him. It was made known to them, that the Blessed Catharine, on account of her reputation of sanctity, would be perfectly well received by his Holiness; they therefore decided that I should be commissioned by Catharine to go to the Holy Father; then they caused her to be conducted to Florence. The chief citizens went forth to meet her, and supplicated her to go in person to Avignon, and treat with the Holy See. Catharine, abounding with love for God and her neighbor, and very desirous of promoting the welfare of the church, undertook this journey and came to Avignon, where I was at the moment. I acted as interpreter between her and the Pope, because the Sovereign Pontiff spoke Latin, and she employed the dialect of Tuscany. I can affirm, before God and before man, that the Holy Father, in my presence and by my mouth committed the treaty of peace to the decision of Catharine, saying to her, "*In order to prove to you that I desire peace, I commit the entire negotiation into your hands: only be careful of the honor of the Church.*"

But some among the individuals who then governed Florence, at the same time that they publicly asked for peace, secretly plotted against her, and endeavored to destroy the temporal power of the Church, and place it in an impossibility of obtaining the smallest satisfaction; they owned it to me themselves, when they could fearlessly say aloud what they then carefully concealed. They acted as genuine hypocrites, and exhibited these dispositions by their conduct towards Catharine.

When that Saint undertook the long and painful journey, they promised to send after her deputies who would have orders not to attempt, or do anything absolutely, without her counsel. As they delayed long in sending those whom they had announced, the Sovereign Pontiff was surprised, and said to Catharine: "Believe me, they have deceived and will deceive you: those ambasadors will never come, or if they do come, their mandate will be useless." In effect when the ambassdors arrived at Avignon, Catharine caused them to come, and told them in my presence, the powers that the magistrates of Florence had bestowed on her; she announced to them that the Sovereign Pontiff entrusted the peace into her hands, and that thus they could if they would, obtain favourable conditions. But, they far from responding to these advances, pretended that they had no orders to treat with her. Catharine then discovered their dishonesty and perceived that the Holy Father had predicted correctly; she did not however discontinue her solicitations to Gregory XI. to ask him for them, the clemency of a father, rather than the severity of a Judge.

When the Vicar of Jesus Christ, in conformity with Catharine's advice, returned to establish himself at Rome, we went back to Italy. Catharine sent me to him with several projects, which would have proved very useful to the church, had they been carried out. During my sojourn there, I was compelled by my Order, to accept the charge of Prior of a Roman Convent, which I had formerly governed under the pontificate of Urban V., and it became impossible for me to go back to Catharine. Before quitting Tuscany, I held an interview with Nicholas Soderini, a citizen of Florence, a man most faithful to God and the church, and strongly attached to Catharine; we had spoken of the affairs of the Republic, and in particular of the ill-will of those who pretended to desire reconciliation with the church, and who did all they could to prevent peace. As I complained of this course of conduct, that excellent man answered me thus: "Be convinced that the people of Florence and every honest man in the town desire peace: but some obstinate hearts that govern us, offer an obstacle." I said: "Could there be no remedy applied to this evil?" He rejoined: "Yes, if some respectable citizens took to heart the cause of God, and had an understanding with the Guelphs, in order to deprive those intermeddlers of their power, for they are enemies of the public good, it would be sufficient to remove four or five of them." When I went to fulfill my commission to the Sovereign Pontiff, I related to him the conversation which I had held with Nicholas Soderini

I had been occupied several months in fulfilling my charge of Prior, and announcing the word of God, when one Sunday morning an envoy of the Pope came to inform me that His Holiness awaited my presence at dinner-time. I obeyed this command, and after the repast the Holy Father sent for me, and said, "I am told that if Catharine of Sienna repairs to Florence, peace will be concluded." I replied, "Not only Catharine, but we all are ready to obey your Holiness and to suffer, if necessary, martyrdom." The Holy Father said to me: "I do not desire *you* should go to Florence, because they would maltreat you, but for *her*, she is a woman and they venerate her, I do not think she will incur any danger. Consider what powers it would be suitable to grant her; present them to-morrow morning for my signature, so that this business may be promptly concluded." I obeyed, and forwarded the letters to the Saint, who submitted and set out directly. Arrived at Florence, she was received with much honor by those who had remained faithful to God and the Church, and with the aid of Nicholas Soderini, she held conferences with the well-disposed citizens, whom she persuaded not to offer longer opposition to the Shepherd of their souls, and to be reconciled directly with the Vicar of Christ. She was also able to confer with the Guelphs, and lead them to understand that those who entertained division between the Father and the Children, ought to be deprived of their functions; that they were rather the destroyers than the governors of the public weal; that not only peace was necessary to the preservation of their goods and of their lives, but that it was indispensable to their souls' salvation. They had actively contributed to stripping the Roman Church of her incontestable rights; and even though there were merely questions of private interests, **they ought** before God, and for conscience' sake, to make restitution of what they had taken, or caused to be taken by others. The chief of the party and a great number of good citizens surrendered to these considerations, and asked the Governors of the city to labor for peace not merely in word, but by prompt and energetic action.

The opposition was violent, especially among those who had been chosen to war against the Church; they were eight in number; the chiefs of the Guelphs deprived one of them of his charge, and succeeded in discarding from affairs a few other citizens. But soon serious troubles declared themselves: they had exiled those who were opposed to the peace, many others were so, but only to satisfy their private revenge. The number of the banished became so considerable that the whole city murmured: minds were irritated against Catharine, who was however a stranger to what was passing; she even complained of these proceedings bitterly, saying and causing to be said everywhere, that it was very ill to strike so many citizens, and that they ought not, under pretext of procuring peace, satisfy their personal and individual hatred.

These excesses increased continually, and disorder soon reached its height; those who had been formerly named for commanding the soldiery, collected troops and excited the lower classes of the population against the authors of all these banishments, and set the whole city in revolution; they succeeded in chasing out those who had banished others, they confiscated their goods, burned their houses, and even massacred, as I was informed a very great number.

Many innocent persons suffered, and almost all those who desired peace were obligated to become voluntary exiles. Catharine who came to labor to arrange a peace, and who had given from the outset merely an advice to deprive some few persons who offered an obstacle, was consequently seriously compromised; the leaders designated her to the people, and the cry was everywhere heard: "*Take that wicked woman and burn her alive; let us cut her in pieces.*" Those who had received her in their houses were frightened, and sent her away with all those who accompanied her. Catharine, quite sure of her innocence, suffered the whole joyfully for the sake of the Holy Catholic Church, and lost nothing of her ordinary tranquillity; she continued cheerful and encouraged her companions. After giving them an exhortation, she withdrew, in imitation of her Spouse, into a place where there was a garden and gave herself to prayer.

While she was praying in that garden with our Lord, the satellites of Satan came also in tumult, armed with swords and clubs. They cried out: *Where is that cursed woman—where is she?*" Catharine heard them and prepared herself for martyrdom, as for a delicious banquet. She went out before one of those furies who was armed with a sword, and who shrieked louder than the others: "*Where is Catharine?*" She knelt joyously and said to him: "I am Catharine, do whatever God suffers you to do to me; but in the name of the Almighty, I command you not to touch any of mine." At these words the man who threatened her so lost his strength, that it was impossible for him to endure her presence. He ordered her to go away; but she, in her ardor for martyrdom, answered: "I am well *here;* where would you have me go? I am ready to suffer for God and his Church; this is the object of all my wishes. Why flee since I have found the object of my search? I offer myself a living holocaust to my divine Spouse; if you are charged to kill me, act fearlessly; I will make no effort to escape; but do not harm those who are with me." God visibly protected his servant, and the man who had menaced her departed, quite confused, with his iniquitous associates. Then Catharine's spiritual children surrounded her and congratulated her on her fortunate escape; but she, on the contrary, was quite sad and said weeping: "Ah! how unhappy I am! I thought this day the Almighty was about to crown my desire; he has deigned to bestow on me the white Rose of Virginity, and I hoped that he would join to it the crimson Rose of Martyrdom. But alas! I am deceived in my expectations; my innumerable sins have deprived me of that great blessing. O! how happy for my soul had I poured out my blood for the love of HIM who redeemed me at the price of his own."

Although this tumult was appeased, the Saint and those who accompanied her, risked many dangers. So great was the terror, that no one was willing to receive her into her house. Her friends advised her to return to Sienna, but she answered that she could not quit the territory of Florence before peace had been restored between the father and the children, because she had received an order from God. Those who surrounded her dared not contradict her, and at last found a "*good man fearing God*," who concealed her in his house.

Some days after the popular effervescence was calmed, Catharine was conducted outside of the city, but not out of the territory; and that holy Virgin departed with those whom she had cherished as her children in the Lord, into a solitary place inhabited by Hermits.

Divine Providence put an end to this tempest; those who excited it were punished by justice and obliged to flee on all sides. Catharine then came back to Florence; she remained there in secret at first, on account of the hatred existing towards her: but she remained there afterwards publicly until the death of Gregory XI., and the election of Urban VI. Peace was then concluded between the Holy See and the Florentines, and Blessed Catharine said to her spiritual children: "We can now quit the city of Florence, because, with the grace of God, I have followed his commandments and those of his Vicar; those whom I found in revolt against the Holy Church, I have left subject to that kind and tender Mother. Return therefore to Sienna."

Catharine thus escaped the hands of the wicked; she obtained the peace that she desired, and that, by the power of the Saviour Jesus, whose Angels accomplished what the malice of men obedient to Satan, intended to prevent. How can we fail to admire Catharine in the perfection of her patience, the uprightness of her prudence, and that settled confidence which led her to knock at the door of the pacific King, until she obtained for the Church and for Florence, that peace which she so earnestly desired!

Let us now speak of that supreme patience of Catharine, displayed in the long and cruel death that she suffered for the love of our Lord Jesus Christ and of his holy Church. Not only she equalled the merits of the Saints, but it also appears to me that she surpassed several among them. The martyrs were tortured by *men* who sometimes ameliorated their sufferings, or yielded at least to their own weariness; but Catharine was tormented by *devils*, whose cruelty was insatiable, and who never reposed. Some martyrs fought a short time and died in excessive sufferings; Catharine suffered thirteen weeks, from Sexagesima till the last day of April; her torments were incredible, and her anguish increased daily; she supported all these with patience and with holy joy; she thanked God for them, and offered her life to appease his anger, and preserve his Church from scandal. Hence, neither cause, nor suffering was wanting to the perfection of her martyrdom, and in the canonization the process might have been as short and as certain as in the procedures that the Church employs in the canonization of Confessors of the Faith. The witnesses of whom I have spoken in the first Chapter of the the Third Part, may also be invoked for the second and the following Chapters.

All that I have written proves that Catharine, Virgin and Martyr, is worthy of being inscribed by the Church militant in the catalogue of the Saints. . . . . . May the happiness of eternal life be granted to me and her other spiritual children, by the Eternal Bounty who lives and reigns in his Unity and Trinity, world without end. Amen.

THE END.

APPENDIX

TO THE

Life of St. Catharine of Sienna.

Our Lord Jesus Christ, for the glory of his faithful Spouse Catharine, designed that her memory should remain intact and incorruptible in the Church, like those sacred bodies which, venerated by the people, and respected by successive ages, await in their integrity, beneath the shade of her Altars, the day of final resurrection. Not only did Friar Raymond of Capua write the life of our Saint, but her other disciples were providentially called upon to render testimony to her virtues, and by their depositions we will conclude this volume.

The miracles performed by Catharine, during her lifetime, and after her decease, had given such proofs of her sanctity, that the devotion of the faithful was manifested by public honors. The Preaching Friars of Venice and other Italian cities celebrated the anniversary of her death, on the Sunday following the feast of St. Peter, martyr. The preacher of the day pronounced her eulogium, and exhorted his auditors to imitate her virtues; this usage was followed in 1411, in the Convents of St. John and St. Paul, at Venice. Public opinion was displeased; the Religious were accused of rendering public homage to a person whom the Church had not yet canonized

The affair was deferred to Francois Bembo, Bishop of Venice, and legate of the Holy See, who assigned the 26th, of May following, to the originators of the Feast, Father Bartholomew de Ferarre, Inquisitor, and Father Thomas of Sienna, Prior of the Convent, that they might explain themselves concerning this accusation. They appeared before him and declared that they had not paid devotion to Catharine; that they had celebrated the Office of the Day, and had simply proposed to the imitation of the faithful, the virtues with which Heaven had enriched that holy soul; that these virtues were well known, and the general belief was that Catharine deserved to be inscribed in the number of the Saints; that they were ready to give testimony of the truth,, but they preferred doing it by writing rather than viva voce. The Bishop's Vicar consented to this; the two Religious wrote their testimony concerning the sanctity and the doctrine of Catharine. They also invoked the testimony of other persons of distinguished merit, such as Dom, Etienne Maconi, General of the Carthusians, Dom Bartholomew de Ravenne, Prior of Gorgon Isle and Friar Angelo of Sienna, of the Order of Friar Minors.

The Collection of those important documents, uselessly sought for by the continuators of Bollandus, has since been published by Dom Martène, from a manuscript of the Grande Chartreuse, copied from a manuscript of the Dominicans of Sienna, by Dom Piere Masotti, Prior of the Chartreuse of Pontigniane.*

---

* Procussus contestationum super sanctitate et doctrina Beatæ Catharinæ de Senis, de mandato Reverendi in Christo Patris ac D. D. Francisci Bembo, Dei gratia Episcopi Castellani, per Franciscum de Viviano, Notarium dictæ Curiæ positus. . . . Dom Martine. *Veterum Scriptorum et Monumentorum amiplissima Collectio.* Tom. 6. p. 1238.

The acts of the Process were committed to writing by the Notary François de Viviano, and all the proceedings may be examined. The Preaching Friars having been accused of celebrating Catharine's feast, Friar Bartholomew of Ferrara was cited on the 24th of May 1411, before François Bembo Bishop of Venice. The plaintiffs whose names and address are given, expose their plaint, and require that in future such an abuse may be prohibited.

On May 26, Friar Bartholomew of Ferrara, and Friar Thomas of Sienna made their appearance before the Bishop, assisted by his vicar, Dominique *de Esculo*, in the Episcopal Chapel of the Palace. The affair was discussed, and the Bishop decided that it should be exposed in written memorials. Friar Bartholomew being obliged to set out that same evening, the Vicar General wrote on the following day to the Bishop of Ferrara, praying him to hear Friar Bartholomew, and send him his deposition, invested with his Episcopal seal.

Friar Bartholomew having had information of this letter, wrote to Friar Thomas of Sienna, that it was not suitable, on account of his title of Inquisitor of Ferrara, that he should be examined on this affair by the Bishop of that city; that it was better for the Vicar of the Bishop of Venice to write to him directly, and that then he could publicly satisfy his demands. Father Thomas of Sienna therefore went to the Bishop of Venice and his vicar, who acceded to the proposition which was made to them, and the day preceding the last day of June, the Vicar addressed to Father Bartholomew, a letter in which he requested him to expose to him what he really said in the discourse delivered at the Convent of St. John and St. Paul. As soon as Father Bartholomew had received this letter from **Ferrara**, he occupied himself with its response; but serious obstacles hindered him from terminating it immediately; it was not ready until the 27th April 1412, and it was remitted with the other depositions before the Episcopal audience, in presence of three Religious, and the undersigned Notary. The Vicar General adjourned to the fifteenth, the decision of this affair, in order to give the manuscripts a full examination.

A decision was rendered to the glory of the Blessed Catharine: it was declared that the Preaching Friars had done nothing reprehensible in honoring her memory: the Plaintiffs withdrew their expostulations, and the Notary François de Viviano drew up a digest of the verbal process and of all that had passed. This instrument was signed by him and the witnesses, on January 5th, 1413.

We intend analysing carefully these depositions of St. Catharine's cotemporaries, and we will quote all the passages which may complete the biography written by Blessed Raymond of Capua. We shall terminate by giving the Bull of canonization,—the summary and conclusion of all these testimonies.

FRIAR BARTHOLOMEW OF FERRARA.

THE DEPOSITION OF FRIAR BARTHOLOMEW OF FERRARA, IS DATED THE LAST DAY OF SEPTEMBER, 1411. IT WAS PUT INTO AUTHENTIC FORM BY THE NOTARY OF THE INQUISITION, URBAIN OF RUSSETIS, THE TWENTY-SEVENTH OF APRIL, 1412, FOLDED AND SEALED THE SEVENTH OF MAY FOLLOWING, AND PRESENTED THE SIXTEENTH OF THE SAME MONTH, IN PUBLIC AUDIENCE, BEFORE THE VICAR GENERAL OF THE BISHOP OF VENICE.

FRIAR BARTHOLOMEW was not personally acquainted with St. Catharine. He applies particularly to the justifying of the festivals celebrated in her honor, and explains the causes that retarded her canonization. He admits that during several years, they had celebrated a feast on the Sunday following St. Peter martyr, in honor of her who was generally styled Blessed Catharine of Sienna, *quæ comminiter appellatue beata Catharina de Senis:* for more than ten years, he had seen this anniversary celebrated with much edification, and nothing had transpired that was not conformable to the doctrine of the Church, since no honors were paid to Catharine which are reserved to canonized Saints. On the 3rd of May 1411, the feast of the Finding of the Holy Cross, they honored the memory of the Blessed, and he himself preached. To avoid any possible error, he had declared to his auditory that the "Order of St. Dominic, so zealous for the laws of the Church, *did not* pretend to celebrate the festival of Catharine, as though she was canonized. The title of 'Saint' could not be given to her, but that her life might well entitle her to the style of Blessed." Our Lord had called Peter, Blessed, because he confessed his Divinity, those who hear the Word of God are denominated

Blessed, and in the Sermon on the Mount, it is declared: Blessed are the poor in spirit. If this title be given to those who have not yet concluded their mortal pilgrimage can it be justly refused to those who have led a perfect life, and died with all the tokens of the most exalted piety? Yes, Catharine may be called *Blessed*, and it is allowable to celebrate her holy life, since in sermons, we mention, in order to excite the devotion of the faithful, the virtues of pagans, and of heathen philosophers. We may, in presence of the holy Altars, speak of either a secular or a religious, who was a sinner during life, and who gave at death signs of repentance; much more then may we speak of a person who exhibited such admirable virtues."

Friar Bartholomew afterwards exposes the power of the Cross over souls, and makes the application of it to the blessed Catharine. His text is: *Ergo evacuatum est scandalum crucis*, (Gal. chap. v.;) and after establishing the division of his discourse, and reciting the *Ave Maria* according to custom, *juxta morem*, he enters into his subject. Dom Martene does not give Friar Bartholomew's sermon, he only quotes from it what refers to St. Catharine. (Page 1247.)

Saint Catharine loved the Cross so tenderly, that she obtained the grace of participating in the torments which our Lord endured thereon for us, and she suffered so largely that her heart broke, *literally*, and her soul separated from her body during several hours. Our Lord imprinted on her the sacred stigmata but in an invisible manner, and he frequently appeared to her crucified, for thus she loved him most. Catharine was passionately devoted to the Holy Eucharist, because it represents the sacrifice of Calvary; to recall it, thirty times the august sign is made during Mass.

Catharine was morally crucified by the four cardinal virtues. 1. *By temperance.* At six years of age she practices abstinence, and urges it to incredible limits during her life; she contents herself with one dress, refuses the simplest style of bed, deprives herself of food; a little infusion of herbs and water suffices for her. At seven years of age she takes a vow of virginity and keeps it with perfection until death. 2. *By prudence.* Her proceedings are all marked with heavenly prudence, she clothes herself enthusiastically with the religious habit; she lives in retirement, practices frightful austerities and appears in public only on receiving a formal order from Almighty God. She never uttered a frivolous or useless word. 3. *By justice.* She renders to every one his due, to God, herself, and her neighbor; she was compassionate towards all, and no necessity escaped her charity. 4. *By fortitude.* She was equally patient, courageous and constant in sufferings, persecutions and injuries, and notwithstanding all the obstacles that she encountered she persevered in her holy enterprises, at the peril even of her life.

After recalling some traits of heroic virtue in the life of Catharine, Friar Bartholomew terminates his discourse by saying that the Blessed arrived at perfection, by loving the Cross of the Saviour, and we must walk in her footsteps on earth, if we would share her glory in heaven. He then exhorts persons who are desirous of knowing more of Catharine's history, to go and hear Father Thomas of Sienna, who would preach on that very day, in the Church of St. Mark, not alone on the subject of the

Redeemer's Cross, but concerning the virtues of his devoted hand-maid.

Friar Bartholomew knew Catharine by the reputation of sanctity that she enjoyed throughout all Italy, and by her memoirs composed by Father Raymond of Capua, her last Confessor. He had also became acquainted with the contents of a collection of her letters, written to Sovereign Pontiffs, Cardinals, Kings and persons of every condition. He had seen those letters in that same year, in the apartment of the General Master of the Order of Preaching Friars, who, during an attack of illness, caused them to be read to him for his consolation. He also knew her by the admirable book which she composed during her ecstasies, in the last two years of her life. This book has been translated into Latin by a man of merit, who entertained a great esteem for Catharine!*

He likewise knew her from informations received from a respectable man named Dino, from Lucca, who was at his side in the refectory as they were one day celebrating the feast of the Blessed Catharine.

He also had received testimonies from another inhabitant of Lucca, called Leopardo, and from the nobleman Jacques des Guerriero de Montepulciano, who composed a little work in her honor. But his most elaborate informations were obtained from Friar Thomas of Sienna, who held relations with her during a long course of years More than fifteen years that he had spent at the convent of SS. John and Paul, he had been laboring indefatigably in honor of the Blessed: if she is not yet enrolled

---

* Qui liber postea latinizatus est per quendam valentem vrum, virginis devotum, et tunc est in uno volumine in libraria Conventus, S.S. Joannis et Pauli: Ord. Præd.—Page, 1251.

among canonized saints, it must be attributed solely to the troubles that have agitated the Church. Petitions for her canonization were addressed to Boniface IX., and to Gregory XII. when he was at Sienna. The life and doctrine of Catharine have been examined, and all in it has been found capable of edifying the faithful, and strengthening their faith. Although her veneration is not yet approved, it is already permitted to honor her memory, and persons who are frightened at the feast we celebrate, will be re-assured by those explanations. In reference to whatever he has said or written, Friar Bartholomew submits entirely to the decisions of the Holy Catholic Church.

After that declaration, and previous to the examination of the affair, the day for the feast of Blessed Catharine arrived. Friar Bartholomew, then Prior of the Convent of St. John and St. Paul, collected the Fathers and Brethren who composed the council, and it was unanimously decided that that year (1412,) and the succeeding years, the memory of Blessed Catharine should be celebrated, because in the observance of that feast, nothing could occasion complaints, but that on the contrary every thing in it was calculated to excite the devotion of the Faithful. Therefore the feast took place, as usual, in the Convent of SS. John and Paul, and in the other churches of the Preaching Friars, and no more reclamations were made on the subject.

FRIAR THOMAS OF SIENNA

FRIAR THOMAS OF SIENNA HAD BEEN SUMMONED WITH FRIAR BARTHOLOMEW OF FERRARE, BEFORE THE BISHOP OF VENICE. HIS DEPOSITION IS DIVIDED INTO TWENTY ARTICLES. HIS TESTIMONY IS EXTREMELY INTERESTING, BECAUSE HE WAS PARTICULARLY ACQUAINTED WITH SAINT CATHARINE AND VERY INTIMATE WITH HER FAMILY. HE WAS SIXTY-TWO YEARS OLD AT THE PERIOD OF THE ECCLESIASTICAL SUIT.

1. It is long since the festival of Blessed Catharine has been celebrated throughout all Italy. The day selected, is the Sunday after the feast of St. Peter, martyr. No particular Office was instituted for her; in the sermon her doctrine, her virtues and her miracles were alluded to. Her portrait with its history are represented in a great number of churches, and Friar Thomas had it painted, but always with the head encircled with luminous rays, like personages who have not yet been canonized. On the 3rd of May, 1411, day of the "*Finding of the Holy Cross,*" Friar Bartholomew of Ferrare spoke of the Blessed Catharine on the occasion of the festival, and her Confession. Friar Thomas, did the same in the church of St. Mark, in the presence of the Inquisitor. He had been a long time Prior of the Convent of Preaching Friars, and had always seen Catharine's memory celebrated in the same manner. She is also feasted in the Convents of Rome, at "*Ste. Mary-sur-Minerva,*" where her virginal body reposes; at the Convent of the Sisters of Penance of St. Dominic of Rome, where resides her sister-in-law Lysa. The same happens at Lucca at the Roman Convent; at Pisa in the Convent of St. Catharine; in Germany at the Convent

of Nuremberg, her history and her writings are generally known and are retained in the library of the Convent, or in the Church. Friar Thomas sent faithful copies of them.

Friar Thomas declares that at Gênes, at Venice, Pisa, Sienna, and Civita Vecchia, and in several other cities of Italy, he had seen and heard the memory of persons not yet canonized celebrated in this manner. He had sometimes preached concerning their virtues, and the people always derived particular benefit. He had himself preached several times at Venice, in the Church of St. John Chrysostom, on the life of the Blessed Zithe of Lucca. He had done the same for the Blessed Catharine in 1396: during the Lent, he explained the Gospel every day, and illustrated it by examples drawn from her history. For sixteen consecutive years he had preached on her festival, which fell sometimes on the day of " *St. Philip and St. James,*" sometimes on the day of the Holy " *Crown of Thorns,*" and often on the day of the " *Finding of the Cross* " or of " *St. John at the Latin gate.*" He had even preached in *two* churches, and always before an auditory which listened to him with avidity.

2. Friar Thomas declares that he knew particularly all the Confessors of the Saint who are mentioned in her life. 1. Friar Thomas de Fonte, dead many years ago. 2. The Father Bartholomew de Dominici of Sienna, Professor of Theology who is yet alive. 3. The Father Raymond of Capua, who shortly after the death of Catharine in the Chapter held in Bologna in 1380, was named General Master of the Order of Preaching Friars. It is he who wrote the memoir of the Saint. Those Religious were her ordinary Confessors: in their absence, she addressed herself to Father John, Doctor in Theology, of the Order

of Hermits of St. Augustine, or to an Abbe de Saint Authime, both of exemplary life and high reputation. The original manuscript of the annals of the Blessed Catharine composed by Friar Raymond, were written for the greater part with his own hand—the remainder under his dictation by Friar Thomas himself. This copy is in possession of Father Nicholas, Professor of Theology, who assisted the General Master in his last moments at Wimberg, in the month of October 1399. It was from Friar Thomas' copy that all the others were made.

3. Friar Thomas was very young when he became particularly acquainted with the Saint, and her father, mother and whole family. She had already taken the Habit of the Sisters of Penance of St. Dominic, when he himself entered the Order of Preaching Friars, and he had the means of admiring her holiness and her great austerities. Her first Confessor showed him a discipline used by Catharine; it was composed of several cords at the extremity of which were iron points which were intended to rend her body. That dicipline seemed to have been steeped a long time in a vase full of blood and then dried. He had also seen an iron circle that she wore during a whole year, and at Venice, an iron chain garnished with crosses which served her as a belt. After her death, that precious relic was given to the Chaplain of the monastery of Saint André who left it as a legacy to the Prior de la Misericorde of Venice. Friar Thomas afterwards renders testimony to the other austerities of Catharine, of the planks that served for her bed, of her miraculous fasts and of the sufferings caused by even the small portion of food she attempted to take.

4. Her ecstasies and her conversations with our Lord were continual. Once Friar Thomas was witness of her

holy intimacy. He heard the burning words of her soul, and felt escaping from her an ineffable perfume, the impression of which threw him, during several days into a delicious intoxication. Catharine dwelt near the Church of the Preaching Friars and passed a great part of the night in prayer. When she heard the Bell that announced Matins, she allowed herself a short repose. Ah! how zealously did she excite the Religious to imitate our Lord, and to take with him, on the table of the Cross the nourishment of salvation, to enclose themselves in the "*cell* of *their souls*," that is to say, in the knowledge of themselves, to pray therein efficaciously for such as have lost the life of grace! She said continually: "Ah! let us stay in our *cell* and mourn, yes, let us mourn over those dead." It is impossible to tell the good that her exhortations and her examples produced among the Religious of the Order of Preaching Friars.

5. Catharine of Sienna was devotedly fond of flowers Often before her appearance in public, divine love would throw her into a holy languor, and she found delight in singing hymns amid the flowers of earth, which represented to her the flowers of her celestial Spouse. She formed of them bouquets, with admirable skill arranging them into Crosses which she afterwards distributed, in order to excite in the souls of others the love of our divine Lord. Friar Thomas often partook of her bounty; these flowers typified the life of St. Catharine and her charity towards God and her neighbor. The Cross of Jesus Christ was to her the flowery couch of her love: she was destined to collect like a nosegay of odorous flowers a multitude of souls to offer them to God; her words and works were so many bouquets which embalmed the earth. She bloomed for heaven in the season of

flowers, (April) and ever since, her memory has been particularly honored by flowers. Annually, in the Church of St. John and of St. Paul, at the chapel of St. John the Baptist, where there is a portrait of Catharine, a great number of persons inspired by her divine Spouse, come and offer flowers in profusion. They arrange them into Crosses, Bouquets, Crowns, Wreaths, and Garlands, and during the whole year, these testimonies of homage embellish and perfume the altar. This custom is equally prevalent in the other churches of Venice, *they* also feast Catharine of Sienna with nature's fairest buds and herbs of delicate fragrance.

6. The union of Catharine's heart with God was uninterrupted, even by the painful functions which her parents imposed on her. At the head of her bed was written this verse of the Psalms of David: "Lord enlighten my eyes that I may never sleep in death." *Illumina, Domine, oculos meos, ne unquam obdormiam in morte.* She feared nothing so much as to offend her Creator, and she expiated the least faults that she thought she had committed, by torrents of tears, and by frightful austerities. All who knew her, especially her Confessors, are convinced that she not only preserved her virginal purity, but also her baptismal innocence.

7. Catharine effected such an amount of good in souls, that even during her life-time she was generally known by the title of 'saint.' Her activity was prodigious. When she was not in prayer or in ecstasy, she instructed the neighbors or dictated letters to her secretaries; she was never idle. She attracted to the path of perfection a great number of Religious, Preaching Friars, Friars Minor, Hermits of St Augustine, young and old.

ignorant and learned, men and woman, noble and ignoble.

She influenced a great number of persons to enter the Third Order, of St. Dominic; Friar Thomas knew among others two Sisters of the name of Tholomei. They had been extremely occupied with their personal adornment and were strongly attached to the world. They employed a quantity of essences and perfumes when making their toilette, and when the Saint had made them acquainted with the Spouse of Virgins, they broke all their vials and threw them away in contempt. They afterwards led an angelical life in the bosom of their family.

Among those who were indebted to Catharine as the instrument of their conversion, we may cite Gabriel Piccolomini of Sienna. Neri of Landoccio who became one of her secretaries, Christopher Ghanni who translated into Latin the book she composed, collected a portion of her letters and wrote a poem in her honor; Etienne Macconi; Nanni, who gave her a chateau for the establisment of a monastery; François Malevolti, etc.

8. Her charity towards the sick was admirable; it shone especially during the Plague which ravaged Sienna in 1372 and 1373. She was constantly near those who were attacked by the epidemic; she prepared them for death and buried them with her own hands. She also visited prisoners and succeeded in bringing back to better sentiments, condemned criminals that the most skillful could not convert. Friar Thomas was witness of a miraculous change which she effected in the soul of a young man who was detained in the prison of that city: it is the same circumstance that the Saint describes in one of her letters in a style so poetic and so sublime.

That young man belonged to one of the first families

of Perugia, and was called Nicholas Toldo. In an affair with which he was charged he spoke ill of the Senator of Sienna who had him condemned to death. This cruel sentence threw him into despair. Catharine heard of it, and in her love for the salvation of souls, she went to visit him, and succeeded so well by conversing with him, that he who hitherto paced to and fro in his prison like an enraged lion, became as a meek lamb, ready to be offered on the Altar of immolation. He went with holy joy and a devout spirit to the place of expiation, and presented without one regret, his youth and his life to the axe of the executioner. Catharine was present and received his head in her hands; his eyes were fixed on heaven with a gaze so deliberate and firm that his eyelids were motionless. The spectators wept and fancied they saw a martyr rather than a guilty man under capital punishment, and his obsequies presented the aspect of a solemn religious festival.

9. One of Catharine's great thoughts was the organization of a Crusade; she spared nothing to promote it, letters, prayers, nor discourse. She solicited in particular Gregory XI. to this expedition, and a great number of individuals pledged themselves to take an active part in it. She hoped thereby to possess the means of visiting our Saviour's tomb. Nothing was comparable to her zeal for the souls whom God had especially entrusted to her. She exhorted them vocally or by letters to tend to perfection; and when she was near the Sovereign Pontiff, she obtained for them continually, particular favors and indulgences. She assumed the expiation of the sins of those whom the justice of God affrighted. She said to such, in order to inspire them with confidence: " Do not think about your transgres-

sions, *I* will take them on myself, I will answer for *them* before God; *I* will cancel your debts towards him.'

10. Friar Thomas never heard Catharine utter a frivolous, useless, or reprehensible word; all her conversations exhaled sanctity. One sole thing could trouble her, that was, to see God offended. She was ever affable, benevolent and gladsome, above all amid sufferings and in the persecutions which her parents caused her to undergo; trials appeared to render her happy, and when fresh sorrows came she gaily called them her Roses and her Flowers. One day when suffering a great deal she said: "Did we but know how sweet are the pains that are suffered for the love of God, they would be accepted with more joy and gratitude than all his other benefits." Once a servant of God came from Florence to examine personally what had been made known to him concerning our Saint. He was accompanied by two Religious, and after some gracious words from Catharine he commenced giving her the most humiliating and harsh reproofs. Catharine was extended, (on account of illness) on the planks that served as her bed; she bowed her head, crossed her arms on her breast and listened submissively to the whole, without any change of countenance. She avowed to her Confessor who interrogated her on this subject, that she was very privileged and felt very grateful on hearing the verities that her divine Spouse had caused to be said to her for the interest of souls. The servant of God, who had thus tried her, was greatly edified and proclaimed openly that Catharine was "fine gold without alloy."

11. It is impossible to describe the sentiments that inspired Catharine when she was receiving the Holy Eucharist. Her radiant countenance was bathed in tears, and quite covered with pearl-like drops of perspiration.

At her return to Avignon, when she received the Holy Communion in the Chapel that the Sovereign Pontiff had permitted her to have in her house, she was so inebriated with the blood of our Lord, that she could not detach her lips from the rim of the chalice, in which was offered (in accordance with the usage of the Church at that time) the wine of ablution. Her teeth left their impress on the border of the two chalices which were employed in her chapel.

In reference to Catharine's Communions the Bollandists give the following details, extracted from the manuscript of Friar Thomas, her first Confessor. The Saint received the Holy Eucharist from our Blessed Lord Himself, not merely once, but several times, and in various ways; often, instead of Sacramental Communion, he applied Catharine's lips to the wound of his sacred side. Sometimes when she communicated, she saw angels holding a golden veil and burning torches in their hands around the Altar. The Sacred Host would be transformed into an infant of ravishing beauty; sometimes three figures appeared there, and then blended into one. Sometimes the priest, our Lord and herself appeared to be inflamed, and a bright light issued from the Altar and illuminated the whole Church. Often, when the priest divided the Consecrated Host, it was shown to her how our divine Lord is found in each particle; occasionally the Holy Trinity manifested himself under different forms. She also distinguished perfectly a Consecrated Host from a Host that is not consecrated.

She dictated her letters and her book during her ecstasies. She would then walk in her room, with her arms crossed on her breast; sometimes she knelt or took some other devout posture but always turned her face to

Heaven. What was most marvelous was, that when obliged during several days to interrupt her dictation, she unhesitatingly resumed it at the place in which she left off, without a re-perusal.

12. The Supreme Pontiffs Gregory XI. and Urban VI. granted to St. Catharine a great number of particular favors. Friar Thomas has seen the authentic bulls of them, and exhibited them publicly in the Convent of St. John and St. Paul. One of those Bulls permitted Catharine, to have (always) a portable Altar, to be able to hear Mass whenever she desired it. Another granted to three Confessors who accompanied her, powers for absolving all sins, except such as are reserved to the Holy See. Another, authorizes Catharine to establish a Convent of Nuns, in a chateau, given to her by a converted citizen of Sienna, and to receive for that foundation the sum of 2000 florins. Other Bulls mention special indulgences and graces, obtained by Catharine for her disciples, and for other individuals, particularly for the Sisters of the "Third Order" whose number she had greatly increased. There were more than a hundred in Sienna during her life-time.

13. Friar Thomas had seen a great number of letters addressed by the Blessed to persons of every condition. He had a collection of them in his own hands, in 1398, that he brought himself to the Sisters of Penance of St. Dominic at Venice. He has seen at the house of Nicholas de Guaderoni of Lucca, (actually in Venice), several volumes enclosed in a coffer: 1. one volume, containing the book composed in the vulgar tongue by the Blessed. 2. The Latin translation of that book. 3. A collection of 155 letters addressed to the Supreme Pontiffs, to Cardinals, Archbishops, Bishops, Laymen, to Religious of

all Orders, to the Members of the Third Order of St Dominic and St. Francis. 4. Another collection of 139 letters addressed to seculars. 5. The memoir of F. Raymond of Capua. 6. The same memoir translated into Italian. Nicholas de Guaderoni offered to give these volumes to the Court of Rome, or to deposit them in the library of the Preaching Friars of Sienna, so that they may serve in the process of her canonization.

14. The relics of the Blessed Catharine are venerated throughout all Italy. Her head being brought from Rome, was solemnly received at Sienna, and deposited in the Convent of Preaching Friars; it is in the Sacristy, in a beautiful gilded reliquary, with the relics of other Saints. At Venice, there are relics of the arm and of the hand of the Blessed; in compliance with an order from the General, Friar Thomas presented them to the veneration of the faithful in 1396. They have since been carried back to Rome, and are venerated in the Convent of la Minerva. They were purloined from the Sacristy or from the Altar; but it is said that they have been restored. A Sister of the Third Order, coming from Rome, and going to the tomb of Saint Dominic, gave Brother Thomas a fragment of a bone of the Blessed, a piece of it was placed in a silver Reliquary which contains some relics of St. Christopher, and is found at Venice, at the house of the Sisters of the Third Order. Those same Sisters have, in a silver reliquary, a finger of the Blessed sent by Lysa, her kinswoman. Friar Thomas saw another finger of Catharine in the possession of Etienne Maconi. This finger is perfectly strait, and according to the testimony of Etienne Maconi it was so, previous to its separation from the others. When that disciple of Catharine carried her body, and exposed it in

the church of the Minerva, her arms were crossed on her breast and all her fingers were bent, except that one which remained erect, until the moment that Catharine's kinswoman detached it from her hand. This was intended to indicate the finger that received the nuptial ring of the Spouse.

A tooth belonging to Catharine, taken by Etienne Maconi, was given by him to Angelo Corario of Venice, Patriarch of Constantinople, become Pope under the title of Gregory XII. When the Sovereign Pontiff set out for Rome, he gave that precious relic to a venerable Father, Antoine David of Venice, who had been his Professor. It passed then into the hands of Friar Thomas who had it set in a Reliquary, and was given at last to Duke Albert of Austria, who had a great devotion to the Blessed Catharine. Some Religious Olivetaines are said to have in the sacristy of their Convent another tooth which was given to them by Neri Landoccio, of Sienna, one of the secretaries of the Blessed. Friar Thomas has seen and had in his possession several days a chain of iron trimmed with crosses, which Catharine of Sienna wore a long time. It belongs to the Father Prior of the church De la Misericordia at Venice, where it is preciously preserved, and who says that after his death, it must pass to the monastery of St. André at Venice.

The Blessed Catharine learned to write miraculously; one day on coming from mental prayer; she wrote to Etienne Maconi a letter which concluded thus "you must know, my beloved son, that this is the first letter I ever wrote myself." Etienne Maconi certifies that she wrote many after, and that several pages of the book that she composed, are written with her own hand. At the Chartreuse de Fontigniano near Sienna, there are preserved many autographs of Catharine, Friar Thomas had solicited some of them from Etienne Maconi, who had not yet sent them. Father Raymond also received two letters written by the Blessed; one among them concludes thus: "I wrote this letter myself and the one that I already sent you. For God gave me the facility to write, so that when coming forth from ecstasy, I might discharge my heart; and as the Master who instructed the pupil shows him the model which he must copy, so he placed before my mental vision, the things that I should write you." At Venice is preserved a sheet of paper on which is written by her with cinnabar, this prayer in Italian. "Come Holy Spirit, into my heart, let thy power draw it to God, grant me charity and holy fear. O Christ preserve me from every guilty thought, warm me, inflame me with thy sweetest love, and every pain will become easy to me. O holy Father, O sweet and gentle Master, aid me in every necessity, O loving Christ, O loving Redeemer." This piece of writing was given to Father Jerome of Sienna of the *Order of Hermits of St. Augustine;* it then passed to the celebrated Preacher, Leonard de Pise, who made a present of it to Friar Thomas, and it is now with the other relics of the Sisters of Penance of St. Dominic of Venice.

In 1398, Friar Thomas brought from Sienna to Venice the mantle with which the Blessed was clothed on the day in which she was received into the Order of the Sisters of Penance of St. Dominic. Her disciple Neri Landoccio said that she valued this mantle very highly, undoubtedly because in it she was solemnly consecrated to her Spouse. She said: "I will never part with this mantle, and I wish that it may last longer than my life." Therefore as soon as the precious cloak became worn or had a rent in it, she mended it with great care. The numerous pieces in it were inserted by her. Many persons through devotion desired to be received in the Third Order with that cloak, which has therefore received several blessings. The Blessed left it to her first Confessor Friar Thomas de Fonte, who gave it as a legacy when dying to his niece Catharine Cothi, Sister of the Third Order; she gave it to Friar Thomas. It is now in a case of gilded wood, among the Sisters of the Third Order, and it has performed, by the merits of the Saint many spiritual and corporeal cures.

15. Catharine's cononization has been petitioned for frequently. Albert, Duke of Austria, sent two Carthusians to Master Thomas de Firino, General of the Preaching Friars, to have Boniface IX. solicited on the subject. Some letters were also addressed to the Sovereign Pontiff, by the Bishop of Poitiers, by the King of Hungary, and by the Duke of Austria. The same instances were renewed with Innocent VII. and Gregory XII. Gregory XII. commenced the process, and heard a great many witnesses. He desired to see what the Blessed had written concerning events which were to happen in the Church; and the Archbishop of Ragusa, who loved Catharine as a Mother, and who was disposed to do all in his power for her canonization, presented the letters that she had addressed to Urban VI. at the commencement of the Schism, and translated them *into* *Latin*, that the Sovereign Pontiff might read them with greater facility. Gregory XII. was at that time occupied with restoring peace to the Church, and the moment was not favorable for terminating the informations; they were necessarily suspended.

16. This commencement of procedure caused many letters to be written, and collected a vast number of documents concerning Blessed Catharine. Her reputation spread throughout Europe. Etienne Maconi sent her memoirs to the King of England, who had asked for them. He sent the same to the King of Hungary with the Book composed by her. Other copies were addressed to the King of Naples, of Prague in Bohemia, at Trêves in Germany, in Prusssia on the confines of Poland, and at the Chartreuse in Rome. In all the documents relating to the Saint, they give her titles which prove now worthy they deem her of canonization. They call her *"Mother of a multitude of souls," "most meek and gentle Mother," "blessed Catharine," "privileged Virgin," "servant of God," "most faithful Spouse of Christ," "admiracle in her holiness,"* etc., etc.

17. Father Thomas names persons still living, and who are able to render testimony in favor of Catharine's sanctity: Friar Mathieu of Venice, Religious Camaldule, Nicholas of Prato, Father Securian of Savona, Etienne Maconi, Chartreux, Bartholomew of Ravenna, more than sixty years of age, François Bartholomew Montucci, who sometimes confessed the Blessed, the venerable Thomas, Prothonotary of several Sovereign Pontiffs, Jacques of Montepulciano, who knew Catharine and composed a poem in her honor; the noble Lady Lancina of the house of the Lords of Foligno.

18. Other witnesses are dead, but their testimony remains, and the reputation they have left, gives them singular weight. Among others may be cited the Archbishop of Ragusa, Father Raymond of Capua, Father Thomas Fonte, Father John of the Convent of Vallombrosa and Barduccio of Florence, who was particularly

dear to the Blessed. He was her secretary, accompanied her to Rome and assisted her in her dying moments. He afterwards returned to Sienna, *sick*, and having languished there a short time, slept peacefully in the Lord, with a smile on his countenance after death, caused it was generally believed by the presence of that favored virgin, Catharine, who came to console him in his last moments.

19. Friar Thomas gives the name and address of the writers who have contributed the most to propagate the life and portraits of the Blessed. A considerable number of copies of her life and works were sent into the surrounding countries, *except* in Spain, in Catalonia and in France, which were all desolated by the Schism. Catharine was however well known in France, on account of her voyage to Avignon.

Her picture is greatly multiplied. Catharine is represented like those holy souls whom the Church has 'beatified' but not canonized. These likenesses are found in Poland, Hungary, Dalmatia, Tuscany, Lombardy, above all in Venice, at Rome and in the kingdom of Naples. She is painted on wood, on plaster, cloth, and in books, among christians and among infidels; for some of her pictures have been sent from Venice to Alexandria. A person who entertains a great devotion to her, has caused her likeness to be painted on cards, so that on the day of her feast, all who take part can procure a picture of her. It is then placed in the churches, amid branches and bouquets offered in her honor, and each one can adorn his own residence with it. Thousands of them are daily made, not alone for the city of Venice, but for other countries whither great quantities are forwarded. It was these pictures of Catharine which suggested the idea of multiplying in the same manner the pictures of the canonized Saints. The faithful procure them on the days of their festivals, and find in them a means of augmenting their devotion.

During 16 years, the feast of Blessed Catharine has been celebrated in the Convent of SS, John and Paul. On that day, from the early morning, there is fine music, the Altar is adorned with its richest ornaments, and the whole church is decorated with garlands and bouquets of flowers. The school of Mercy comes, and sings a solemn high Mass. In the evening, there are Vespers, sermon, and a grand public repast, at which the sweetest joy presides; persons of every age and of all conditions come and mingle with the Friars of the Convent; there are seculars, pupils, Religious, poor, Prelates, Nobles, Doctors in Medicine, Merchants, Artists, youth and infants. The members of the Third Order of St. Dominic serve the table with their Prior Antoine Superantio of Venice. The history of Catharine is read, her praises are sung, and conversations are held concerning her virtues and her miracles.

A young married person conceived such a devotion to Catharine that she renounced the world, assumed the Religious Habit and passed her remaining days, in the exercise of exalted piety. When dying she left by will a certain sum of money to the Convent of SS. John and Paul, for providing the repast that is given on Catharine's festival. Her name was Sister Maria Nicoleii; her Mother who was executrix of her testament not only faithfully paid the legacy, but also secured to perpetuity other sums to the same intention, to the monastery of *Corpus Domini* and to other Convents of the Order of Saint Dominic. The custom was likewise introduced of offering presents to the Church on Catharine's feast; every one brings according to his means and his inspiration, flowers, crowns, garlands, portraits of Catharine, silver and brazen medals, bread, wine, fruits (dry and fresh,) vegetables, and money; others offer their services to adorn the Church or serve at the repast. Among all most worthy of remark were Antoine Superantio and his wife Sister Marina de Contarinis of the Third Order of Penitents of Saint Dominic, and several members of the same Fraternity.

Friar Thomas infers that no woman, if we except St. Bridget, can be compared in these latter times with the Blessed Catharine. She is worthy without doubt of being inscribed in the catalogue of the Saints, and would be so already had not the Great Schism afflicted and agitated Christendom. Her life was admirable, and her death may be considered as a voluntary martyrdom endured for the Church and the Papacy. The venerable Friar Guillaume *de Silvalacus*, was right in saying in a sermon which he preached in honor of Catharine's virtues: "It is with pious *hymns* and not with *tears* we should celebrate the death of Catharine of Sienna. Remember that she died for the Church and is crowned in heaven." God showed her to a devout person in a vision, carrying on her shoulders the vessel of the Church and sinking beneath its weight.

Her death or rather her birth to eternal joys is another shade of reremblance she has with the Saviour. Our Lord Jesus Christ announced his death and gave to his disciples whom he was about to leave, a discourse abounding with admirable instructions; Catharine did the same.

Our Lord was tormented in his passion by the demons who caused him to be crucified, by men; Catharine was tormented by the demons who put her to death for the Church. Our Lord was assisted in his last moments by his mother and a few disciples; the others were absent: the same happened to Catharine. As our Lord, Catharine died far from her native city and had a stranger's sepulchre; her body remained incorruptible during three days, and her tomb became glorious; people hastened to it from all parts of Europe, and great miracles were performed there. Finally, like our Blessed Lord, Catharine has disciples who are faithful to her memory and spread abroad her name and her instructions.

20. Friar Etienne finished his deposition by giving the sermon which he pronounced on the 3rd of May 1411, and which was one of the causes of the Process. His text was these words of the Apostle: *"Mihi absit gloriari nisi in cruce."* Dom. Martina does not give this discourse which is very long and gives no new information. Friar Thomas calls God to witness that he speaks the truth.

FRIAR BARTHOLOMEW OF SIENNA

THE DEPOSITION OF FRIAR BARTHOLOMEW DE DOMINICI OF SIENNA WAS DELAYED; IT IS DATED THE TWENTY-NINTH OF OCTOBER 1412. IT WAS RECEIVED AND WRITTEN BY M. ADAM (NOTARY,) CLOTHED WITH ALL REQUISITE FORMALITIES, AND SENT IN THE COURSE OF NOVEMBER TO FRIAR THOMAS, WHO FORWARDED IT TO THE VICAR GENERAL OF THE BISHOP OF VENICE. AS IT DID NOT APPEAR SUFFICIENTLY COMPLETE AND CONFORMABLE TO THE MEMOIR OF BLESSED RAYMOND, FRIAR BARTHOLOMEW MADE A FEW ADDITIONS DURING THE MONTH OF DECEMBER; HE WAS THEN NEARLY 68 YEARS OF AGE.

Friar Bartholomew was yet in early youth when he became acquainted with Blessed Catharine; she had already worn the habit of the Sisters of Penance many years, and her Confessor at that time was Friar Thomas de Fonte, of Sienna. Friar Bartholomew had made his Novitiate with him; he often accompanied him when he went to visit Catharine, who lived in a room, the door and window of which were continually closed. A lamp burned there day and night, before the Portrait of our Blessed Redeemer, and the likenesses of the Blessed Virgin and other saints, which were there represented. From that period Friar Bartholomew has always had relations with the Blessed, at Sienna, at Pisa, Lucca, Avignon, Gênes, Florence and Rome. He testifies to the austerity of her life, mortifications and abstinence, and to her humility and the painful functions that she selected. As soon as she had any leisure, she washed all the soiled linen that she could find in the house. She was extremely fond of lilies, roses, violets, and all flowers; and composed them into crosses, and superb bouquets, when she had terminated her penances. Her companions were young maidens who wore the same Religious garb, and entertained the same heavenly desires; and they sung together devout hymns.

When I commenced visiting her in her cell, says Friar Bartholomew, she was young, and always wore a cheerful countenance. I was also young; yet not only did I not experience any trouble in her presence, but the longer I conversed with her, the stronger became my love for the religious virtues. I saw in succeeding times many laymen and monks who visited her and who all experienced impresssions similar to mine. The sight of her, and all her conversations breathed and communicated angelical purity.

Friar Bartholomew cites her charity towards the individuals who persecuted her. When Andrea accused her to the Prioress of the Fraternity, she who had so long consecrated the virginity of her body and of her soul, to God, to Holy Mary and St Dominic,—knelt down and replied with virginal bashfulness and dove-like simplicity: "O mother, forgive me, but I do not know how I could commit the faults of which you speak to me, for by God's grace, I had rather die than offend God, above all in the way you say." The Prioress seeing her humility and simplicity sent her away in peace.

In respect to the alms which she distributed in secret, Friar Bartholomew thus narrates the story of the Cask which yielded good wine so long. It was observed that the cask was empty, thence arose a great tumult in the house: Catharine saw that her Father was troubled, and she sympathized in his annoyance, but put her trust in God. She succeeded in appeasing the disturbance: "Father" said she, "what is it that troubles you?" and when Jacomo had explained, she added, "Be calm Father, I will go and draw wine for you." She went to the cask, knelt, and said to God with fervor: "Lord thou knowest that that wine was distributed to the poor for love of thee; suffer not that for this I become an occasion of scandal to my brethren." She then made the sign of the Cross over the Cask, and wine flowed from it in abundance. She thanked Almighty God and did not speak of the miracle to any one.

On coming out of ecstasy, which sometimes lasted more than two hours, she reproved her companions for their idleness, and when they attempted to excuse themselves, presuming that she was ignorant of what had transpired she rebuked them more severely, saying: "Were you not in such a place, and did you not say such a thing." Friar Bartholomew could not believe in that prophetical spirit. Going once to visit her with her Confessor, he asked her, (to give her a trial,) what they were doing at two and three o'clock in the morning. She answered: "Who knows better than yourself." Her Confessor said: "I command you to tell, if you know, what we were doing at that time." She was obliged to obey, and humbly bowing her head, she replied: "You were four in the cell of the Sub-Prior, and there you conversed together a long time." She named all who were present, and the subject on which they had spoken. Friar Bartholomew was amazed, but he thought she might know from some of the persons present, so he determined to try her again. On the morrow he went to her and said: "Then you know, Mother, what we do?" She answered: "My son, know that my divine and sweet Saviour having given me a spiritual family, leaves me in ignorance of nothing that concerns them." "You know, then, what I was doing yesterday evening at such an hour?" She answered "Certainly, you were writing on a certain subject. My son, I watch and pray for you continually, until the Matin Bell of your Convent. I see all that you do, and if you had good eyes, you would behold me as I do you. Often our sweet Saviour deigns to come and walk, repeating psalms with me in my cell; he converses with me on a variety of things, and when he discovers that I am fatigued, he sits down at this place, and bids me sit at his feet, and we hold conference until Matins. Then he gives me permission to sleep, saying: 'Go, my daughter, and take some repose, thy children are rising for Matins, they will praise me in thy place.' I then sleep a few moments."

Friar Bartholomew describes a spiritual aid that he received from Catharine. His superiors had sent him to Florence, and the Blessed remained at Sienna. In a conversation between himself and a Religious of the Convent, he conceived doubts concerning the validity of his ordination, because he had received the priesthood before the age of twenty-five—he thought at once that it would be a great sin for him to continue celebrating Mass, and discontinued offering it. The Prior who asked the reason, could never induce him to surmount his scruples. One day as he was weeping bitterly, he regretted not being at Sienna, thinking that Catharine would be capable of giving him great consolation in this circumstance. He invoked her in the midst of his grief, when Father Raymond, who compassionated his state, called him and conducted him to the Bishop of whom he was the Confessor. When he had manifested to him what tormented him, the Bishop who was very learned, said: "My son, it is a fault to act against the canons; but in this circumstance, I am able to grant you the necessary dispensations, because you acted ignorantly, and not in contempt of the decisions of the Church. Therefore entertain no further anxiety." Friar Bartholomew took courage and returned to his Convent, with his conscience in perfect peace. The very morning in which he invoked Catharine, she was in the church of the Preaching Friars at Sienna, before the Altar of the Blessed Peter Martyr; she was aware of Friar Bartholomew's trouble, and compassionated him with her whole heart. In the midst of her ecstasy, she besought God to deliver him, and in her enthusiastic devotion to God her body was elevated above the ground. When she had returned to herself, her companions asked her what was passing at that moment; she answered: "My son Bartholomew was cruelly tormented in Florence by the Demon."

When Pope Gregory XI. inquired of her her opinion concerning his return to Rome, she humbly excused herself, saying that it did not become a poor, lowly woman like her, to give advice to the Sovereign Pontiff. The Holy Father rejoined: "I do not request you to give me *advice*, but to declare to me *the will of God.*" And as she constantly excused herself, he commanded her in holy Obedience, to tell him whether she was really aware of God's will on the subject. She bowed her head, and said: "*Who knows more perfectly the will of God than your Holiness, who has pledged himself by a Vow?*" At these words the Holy Father was seized with astonishment; for no one knew that he had taken a Vow to return to Rome, and it was at that very moment that he took the resolution to quit Avignon.

A short time after, when the Blessed was returning into Italy, she found herself, on the vigil of St. Francis, at Varragio, near the city of Gên s. She called Father Raymond, her Confessor, and told him that God had just revealed to her that on such a day as that, in a few years, he, (Father Raymond,) would transport her body from one tomb to another. The prophecy was accomplished. Catharine's eloquence was remarkable; the ignorant and the learned said: "Whence comes so much knowledge, since she never studied?" Some thought that the Preaching Friars had taught her, but it was she on the contrary that instructed them! Whatever she knew came to her directly from God, as may be seen in letters, and in the book that she composed during her ecstasies. Frequently she dictated to two or three secretaries at the same time, on different subjects, and that without the least hesitation. Her discourse charmed every one, and her detractors after having listened to her, celebrated her praises every where; so great was the unction which animated her, that a great multitude of men and of women flocked around her to enjoy her teaching.

When speaking of her delicacy of conscience, Friar Bartholomew recalls the fault that she mourned during three days. She had said, that she would willingly go to visit a hermit in the environs of Sienna, although she did not mean to do so. Our Lord said to her: "Daughter, do not weep longer for thy fault; I allowed thee to fall into that sin, that remorse of conscience might recall thee to thy senses, which thou art rejoiced to have quitted. It is a means of self-knowledge, and of shunning pride, when my liberality grants thee spiritual consolations, in order to fortify and encourage thy weakness."

Friar Bartholomew thus relates the distraction that she had on the eve of St. Dominic. The first toll of Vespers having sounded, she hastened to the Church. I called her, and seated myself to converse with her; she knelt down near me and as her countenance was lighted up with joy, I said to her; "We have good news to day, I perceive you are quite joyous." Then she related to me admirable things concerning St. Dominic. "Do you see him," said she to me, "our Blessed St. Dominic?" "how much he resembles our Saviour! he has an oval face, a grave and mild physiognomy, brown hair and a beard of the same hue."

I questioned Catharine concerning the reality of her death; I asked her if her soul were truly separated from her body, she answered that she believed so: and as I asked her how she could be sure of it, when the Apostle Paul was not able to say, whether he had seen God, "*in or out of the body,*" she said that she believed it, because her heart was broken by the violence of her desires. And as I repeated that she could not know what the great Apostle was ignorant of, she surrendered to this argument. Her Confessor commanded her to ask God what had happened to her. She obeyed, and our Lord answered that her soul had been actually separated from her body, and added: "Learn, beloved daughter, that I raised thee to a new life; thou shalt travel, thou shalt go from city to city, as I will indicate to thee, thou shalt live with the multitude and speak in public: I will send some to *thee*, and I will *send thee* to others, according to my good pleasure: be ever ready to do my will."

Catharine suffered with wonderful patience, and she was fastened to the Cross by three kinds of dolers; in the head, breast, and side. Never did these acute pains excite the least shade of melancholy in her countenance, which was ever cheerful and even gay. When the pain in her side tortured her cruelly and hindered her from rising, her disciples pitied her, and said: "Mother, what are you suffering?" She would answer smiling: "I feel a gentle beating in my side." Her sufferings were to her valuable *presents* from her Spouse; they even seemed to her to possess an extreme sweetness, and when they increased she found them sweeter still.

One day Friar Bartholomew asked her what she suffered in her breast; she replied, that she was enduring what our Lord underwent on the Cross, when one of his hands being already nailed, they drew the other with such violence that all his ribs were disjointed; that was her greatest corporeal suffering. Catharine longed for martyrdom, and when she spoke of it, her visage appeared all inflamed. She showed her white robe, saying: "Oh! how lovely it would be, were it stained with blood, fo love of Jesus!"

There reigned such authority in her discourse, and so much grace on her lips, that she attracted the greatest personages to God. This was particularly observed at the court of Gregory XI. Those who had been most opposed to her quickly yielded to her benign influence, and became her friends and benefactors. The Duke d'Anjou, uncle of the King of France, was, among others, so changed in respect to her, that he wished to conduct her to Avignon, to one of his chateaux, that the Duchess, his lady, might enjoy her presence. Three days after, he offered to present her to the King of France; but Catharine humbly declined. He then gave her a hundred francs in gold to defray her returning home into Italy. At her persuasion, he promised the Sovereign Pontiff, Gregory XI., to go to Palestine, when he would tell him to do so, with an army equipped at his own expense. The Holy Father would not allow her to quit Avignon before him, and he provided, until her departure, for her personal expenses and that of those who accompanied her, who numbered twenty-two. He sent her 100 florins to defray the expenses of her journey

There was in Sienna a nobleman named François, whose years numbered more than eighty. He had never been to Communion, and had never confessed but once, and then in his youth, during a serious illness. Alessia, Catharine's beloved companion, was his daughter-in-law, and that devout woman frequently exhorted her father-in-law to obey the precepts of God and of his church. But as she gained nothing, she besought Catharine to come and reside with her, so that during the long evenings of winter she would have an opportunity of conversing with the old gentleman. Catharine consented to it, and undertook this difficult conversion. She combatted a long time against the poor obstinate, who mocked her pious exhortations; but finally he could resist no longer; his heart became softened before the fire of her discourse, and he said: "I am determined to confess! but first of all, I must tell you, that I entertain such a hatred against the Prior of a certain church that I daily seek means of killing him." The Blessed Catharine said such affecting things to him on this subject that he finished by exclaiming; "I am ready to do whatever you order me; you need only speak." Catharine said to him: "I wish that for the love of our Lord Jesus Christ, and that he may pardon you, that you should forgive the Prior, and be reconciled with him." He promised it, and although the wrongs did not proceed from him, on the morrow at dawn of day, he took a falcon which he was very fond of, and went alone to the church at which the Prior remained. The latter immediately fled; but the old man charged a Canon to go and tell him that he did not come to injure him, but on the contrary to bring him good news. The Prior on learning that he was alone and unarmed, caused several persons to come into his apartment and permitted his visitor to be introduced—who bowed to him and said: "The grace of God has touched my heart and I am come to offer to be reconciled with you, and to prove that this step on my part is sincere, I entreat you to accept this falcon, of which I am extremely fond." Peace was concluded, and the aged nobleman returned to Catharine: "I have obeyed your orders," said he, "and I will obey you again." The Blessed told him to go and confess to Friar Bartholomew. His general confession occupied three days, and when he had received absolution, his Confessor was at a loss what penance to assign him, because he was very aged, and was in indigence although he was noble.

He gave him a trifling penance, and bade him—"Return to her who sent you, and the penance that she gives you, I give also." Catharine told him to rise during a certain period, every morning at dawn of day, and go in silence to the Cathedral, reciting each time a hundred *Pater* and a hundred *Ave;* and she gave him a cord on which a hundred knots were to serve him to reckon them. The good old man accomplished the whole with fidelity; and he who formerly, seldom entered a Church and never observed a fast, undertook, notwithstanding his burden of eighty years, to pass daily prolonged hours at the foot of the Altar. He observed Lent scrupulously, and zealously attended all the sermons, and after persevering a year in these pious exercises, he slumbered calmly in God.

Catharine had relations with Friar Bartholomew during several preceding years when she began to confess to him, and receive the holy Eucharist from his hands.

The witness on this subject, certifies "The ardor of her desire and of her love was so great, that, at the moment of giving her Holy Communion, I felt the consecrated Host which I held in my hand move and escape violently. At first I was much troubled, and sometimes feared lest the sacred Host should fall to the ground; but it appeared to fly towards her mouth. Many individuals told me that the same thing had happened to them. When, after Communion, we presented her the wine in the chalice, she imprinted her teeth so forcibly on the margin that we could not withdraw it without great difficulty; two silver Chalices that had been given to her for the use of her Chapel bear the marks of her teeth."

Catharine had no sins to tell in her Confessions; she accused herself only of failing in virtue, and of not being sufficiently grateful for the benefits bestowed on her by Almighty God. She treated herself as unworthy and most miserable, and as one whose guilty conduct was the cause of all the ill that happened in the world. These words so holy and so profound scandalized instead of edifying me; I was incapable of understanding them, and in my gross ignorance of things spiritual, I went so far as to suspect her of not *believing* herself to be such as she said. One day as she was thus humbling herself before me, I interrogated her in order to have an occasion of reproving her: "How" said I, "can you thus speak, when it is evident you have a great horror of sin, which so many others love to commit every day?" She answered me weeping: "O father, I see truly that you do not know my misery. Alas! I have received from my Creator graces so great and so numerous, that in my place, the most contemptible being on earth would be *inflamed* with the love of God. Her examples and her words would have spread, everywhere enthusiasm for the heavenly country and contempt of the present life ; men would *sin no more !* But I who have received so much, *I*, can truly say that I am the most ungrateful of creatures, and that I am a cause of ruin to the world, because I ought to save so many, preaching both by word and example: I have therefore failed in my duty, and I am very guilty before God !"

Among those who blamed the extraordinary life of Catharine, the most remarkable was Father Lazarini, of the Order of Friar Minors, who was then professing Philosophy with eclat, in his convent of Sienna. Not content with openly attacking the reputation of the Blessed, he resolved to come and see her, so as to find in her words and actions, materials for condemning her further : on the eve of "*St. Catharine, Virgin and Martyr,*" he repaired to her house at the hour of Vespers. He had requested me to accompany him and I had consented to it, because I believed that he would repent of his conduct towards her. We entered her pious cell ; Lazarini seated himself on a chest, and Catharine on the floor at his feet ; I remained standing. After a few moments of silence, Friar Lazarini began to speak : "I have heard " said he "many speaking of your sanctity, and of the understanding God has given you of the Holy Scriptures, and I have been eager to visit you, hoping to hear something edifying and consoling to my soul."—Catharine replied : "And I, rejoice at your arrival, because I think that the Lord sent you to allow me an opportunity of profiting by that learning, with which you daily instruct your numerous disciples. I hoped that charity would induce you to comfort my poor soul, and I entreat you to do so through love of our Lord." The conversation continued some time in this tone, and as the night was approaching Friar Lazarini finished by saying: "I see that it is late, and that I must retire, but I will return at a more suitable hour." He arose to depart; Catharine knelt, crossed her arms, and asked his blessing When she had received it, she commended herself to his prayers, and Friar Lazarini, more through politeness than from devotion, asked her also to pray for him which she cheerfully promised to do. He went away, thinking that Catharine might be a good person, but that she was far from meriting her great reputation.

The night following, on rising to study the lesson that he was to explain to his pupils the next day, Friar Lazarini began to *shed tears involuntarily*. The more he wiped them, the more copiously they flowed, and he could not discover the cause! In the morning, they came to call him at the hour of Class; but it was impossible for him to speak to his pupils: he wept without intermission. Returning to his cell, he continued weeping, and was indignant towards himself. "What ails me," said he; "what do I want: is my mother dead suddenly, or has my brother fallen on the battle-field; what can this mean?" The entire day passed in this state, and when evening came on, he slept a few moments, being overcome with fatigue and wearisomeness; but he soon awoke, and his tears began to flow afresh, without his being able to restrain them. He therefore reflected whether he might not have committed some grave fault, and invoked the divine Mercy to recall it to him: whilst he was examining his conscience, he heard an interior voice that exclaimed to him: "Do you forget so quickly that yesterday, you judged my faithful servant Catharine in a spirit of pride, and requested her to pray for you through politeness."

As soon as Friar Lazarini had received this advertisement and discerned his fault, his tears subsided and his heart became inflamed with a desire of again conversing with Catharine. At the first glimmering of day, he hastened to knock at the door of her cell. The Blessed, who was aware of what her Spouse had done, opened the door to Friar Lazarini, who prostrated himself at her feet. Catharine also prostrated, and implored him to rise, after which they had a lengthy interview, and the Religious conjured her to condescend *to direct him in the way of salvation*. Catharine, overcome by his instances answered him: "The way of salvation for you is, to despise the vanities of the world and its smiles, to become humble, poor, and destitute in imitation of Jesus Christ and your holy Father, Saint Francis." At these words the Religious saw that Catharine read his soul; he shed tears profusely and promised to do whatever she might command him. He accomplished his promise, distributed his money, and useless furniture, and even his books. He merely reserved a few notes, which were necessary aids to him when preaching, and became truly poor, and a veritable follower of our Blessed Redeemer.

During Catharine's sojourn at Pisa, a great number of persons visited her, and many knelt down before her, and kissed her hand. Some persons were scandalized at this, and were desirous of putting an end to this devotion. A celebrated Physician among others, Jean Gutalebracia who could not persuade any one against her, resolved to confound Catharine, by proposing to her difficulties in the Sacred Writings. He invited Pierré Albizi, a Counsellor at law of mature age and consummate prudence, to accompany him, and went to pay a visit to her. The Doctor opened the conversation in the following manner: "We have heard your virtues praised, and your intelligence in the Holy Scriptures, and we are come in the hope of receiving from your mouth some spiritual consolation. I am anxious to know how you understand that passage, in which it is said, God spoke in order to create the World: "has God a mouth and a tongue?" He addressed her several other similar questions, and awaited her reply. Catharine then rejoined: "I am astonished that you who teach others, (as you inform me,) should present yourself before a poor woman whose ignorance it would be more suitable to you to enlighten. But as you wish me to reply, I will do so in accordance with what God will inspire me. What benefit will it prove to me to know *how* God who is a pure spirit, *spoke* in order to create the universe? What is necessary for both you and me to know, is, that our Lord Jesus Christ, the only Son of God, has assumed our nature to save us, and that he suffered and died for our redemption. Yes, the essential for me is, to believe this and to meditate on it, so that my heart may be inflamed with love towards him who so loved me."

Catharine continued speaking some time with such unction and fervor, that Dr. Pierrè Albizi, could not refrain from shedding tears, and fell on his knees to obtain her forgiveness for having come to tempt her. Catharine prostrated herself also, conjuring him to arise, and when she had succeeded they held a long and pleasant discourse on spiritual subjects. When departing, Pierrè Albizi implored Catharine to be so condescending as to present his new-born infant at the Baptismal Font—she cheerfully consented, and he who was hitherto bitterly prejudiced against her, became one of her warmest defenders.

In reference to these honors that were paid to Catharine, another person, enjoying a great reputation for piety, wrote her a letter, from excellent motives, and with excellent arguments, reproving her for suffering such attentions. He recalled to her the example of the Saviour and of the Saints, exhorted her to live in retirement, and told her that the real servants of God loved solitude above all things, and that hypocrites only sought renown. This letter was forwarded to Father Raymond who communicated its contents to me. We were indignant and intended without even showing it to Catharine, to respond to the writer, and reproach him with his temerity and his ignorance of the spiritual life. Whilst we were conferring together on that subject, the Blessed perceived our trouble and inquired of us the cause; as soon as she had learned it, she claimed the letter, and as we hesitated to give it to her, she said "If you refuse it to me, I must at least hear what concerns me in it." Father Raymond then read her the letter; she gently rebuked us for indulging indignation. "You ought, to thank with me the author of that letter; do you not perceive that he gives me valuable advice for my salvation? he fears that I may wander in the paths of God, and he is anxious to shield me from the snares of the enemy. Let us be filled with gratitude for his charity, I must have that letter and return thanks to the author of it." She did so in effect, in an admirable manner, and as Father Raymond did not submit to her reasons, and continued to wish to reply to it, she gave him a severe look, and reproached us with discovering evil where there was but good. (*Dom Martene*, p. 1355.)

Father Bartholomew then explains the apparent differences, between his depositions and the writings of Friar Raymond. These differences are not contradictory; they prove like those that are found in the Gospel, the independence and sincerity of the witnesses. He afterwards proceeds to describe his last interview with Catharine:

"When she became sick, I was Prior of the Convent of Sienna, and the Provincial of the Order sent me on some business to Rome. I arrived there on Holy Saturday; I hastened to the residence of Catharine, of whose state I was utterly ignorant. I found her extended on planks, surrounded on every side by other planks, so that she seemed to be in a coffin. I approached her, in the hope of being able to converse with her as usual. Her body was so emaciated, that her bones could be easily counted, it appeared to have been sun-dried, and no longer presented the same beauty. This sight broke my heart, and I said to her amid my tears: "Mother, how do you find yourself." When she descried me she was anxious to testify her joy, but she could not speak, and I was obliged to place my ear close to her mouth, to be able to understand her reply, that "all was going on well, thanks to our beloved Saviour!" I then disclosed to her the motive of my journey, and added: "Mother, to-morrow will be the Passover of our Lord, and I should like to celebrate it here, so as to give the Holy Eucharist to yourself and your spiritual children." She answered: "Oh! would that our sweet Saviour would permit me to communicate!"

I left her, and on the following day, I returned to fulfill my promise. I approached her so as to hear her confession and give her absolution; no one hoped to see her go to holy Communion; for during several days she had been incapable of making any movement. However I gave her for penance, to ask of God, for her consolation and ours, the grace of receiving Communion on so great a Festival; and I then went to the Altar which was quite close to her bed. I prepared the hosts and then commenced Mass. Catharine remained motionless until the holy Communion; as soon as I had terminated and had taken the ablutions, she got up suddenly, to the great astonishment of all present, who shed tears of joy; she advanced unassisted, as far as the Altar, knelt down with her eyes closed, her hands clasped, and remained there until she had received the consecrated Host, and the wine it was customary to present for washing the mouth. She afterwards fell into an ordinary ecstasy, and when she came forth from it, it was impossible for her to return to her bed; her companions carried her there, and she remained on it in a state of perfect immobility as before. God permitted her however to converse with me, during the few days that I still remained in Rome, and it was then that she explained to me the incredible pains and sufferings that the demons forced her to undergo. She prayed with unabated ardor for the peace of the Church; she desired and asked of God to expiate in her person, the sins of those who separated the faithful from the real Sovereign Pontiff, Urban VI. "*Be assured,*" said she, "*that if I die, the sole cause of my death is the zeal which burns and consumes me for the holy Church. I suffer gladly for her deliverance and am ready to die for her, if it be necessary.*"

The affairs that led me to Rome were terminated when my companion pressed me to return, I constantly resisted, and I told this to Catharine. She said that I must go back to him that sent us. "Mother," said I, "how can we go and leave you in such extremity? Were I absent and were informed of your condition, I would quit all and hasten to your side. No, I cannot resolve to depart without seeing you convalescent, or without at least having reasons for hope in your recovery." Catharine said: "My son, you well know how great consolation I experience in beholding those whom God has given me, and whom I love in the Truth. It would give me the greatest pleasure, would our Lord accord me the presence of Father Raymond as well as yours; but it is his intention that I should be deprived of them, and as I desire not my will but his, you must depart. You know that at Cologne a Chapter of your Order will soon be celebrated for the election of a General Master. Friar Raymond will be nominated; I wish you to be there with him, and always be obedient to him. I command you this as far as I have power."

I then told her that I would do whatever she commanded me, as soon as I saw her better in health, and I added: "If it is God's will that I go, ask him to give you health before my departure." She promised me to to do so, and when I returned there on the following day, I found her so calm and contented, that I approached her full of hope. But she, who had hitherto remained immoveable, extended her arms towards me and embraced me so affectionately that I could not refrain from shedding tears of joy; it was to make known to me God's will, and exhort me to depart. "The Lord had deceived me," to speak like the Prophet—*Seduxisti me, Domine, et seductus sum; fortior me fuisti et invaluisti.* (Jer. xx. 7.) I left Rome. A short time after I had returned to Sienna, a letter informed me that the saintly Catharine had quitted this life to be united to the Spouse she so much desired.

Friar Bartholomew, at the conclusion of his second deposition, gives a letter to M. Thomas Petra, Notary of the Sovereign Pontiff, in which he thus describes a vision that he had after Catharine's death; "In the latter period of Catharine's life, Our Lord granted me the grace of being united to her by the bonds of a pure and holy affection. She styled me her Father, and I often saw her. One day, I found her in the garden of a lady in Rome; she was very much enfeebled, and I said to her: "Mother, it appears to me that Christ, your Spouse, wishes to withdraw you from this life in order to unite you to himself. Have you made all your dispositions in consequence?" "What disposition can a poor woman make who owns nothing?" "You would make a fine testament if you were to indicate to each of your disciples what he ought to do after your death. I request it of you, for the love of God, and I am convinced that all will obey you as myself." She answered: "I am very willing, and I will do so with God's grace." She did so in effect, a little while after, and all her recommendations were followed. I added: "Mother I have another favor to ask of you, and I beseech you to grant it to me for the love of our Lord Jesus Christ. Obtain from this moment from your divine Spouse the favor of showing me the state of your soul after your death." "That," said she to me, "does not appear possible; for, either the soul in the other life is saved, and then the perfect happiness which it enjoys, leads it to forget the miseries of this world; or it is lost, and then the infinite torments that it endures prevent it from obtaining that favor. If it be in

Purgatory it must participate in the two states, and the difficulty remains the same." I said: "I am unwilling to dispute with the Holy Ghost, and I do not believe that you would, in such a case, limit his power. I trust in God, and do not refuse me my request." She promised me to grant it, if our Lord would permit. She died a short time after.

Eight days had elapsed since her death, when very early one morning, a man of exalted piety, named Jean de Pise, came and knocked at my door. I opened it directly. "Catharine of Sienna is coming," said he to me. I answered him: "How can she come, for she has been dead some time." He said: "Be sure that you will see her." Then he went away and I could not call him back. The morrow, the day after it, and during nearly thirty days, I received a similar visit from men estimable for their virtues and their saintly lives. I presume they were angels from God, who took their forms to announce to me what was to take place. At last, one Sunday, after having recited my midnight Office, I disposed myself to take a little repose, when, towards day-break, I saw in a cloudless sky, a multitude of Blessed Spirits who advanced in regular procession; they were clothed in white and and marched three by three, bearing ornaments, relics, crosses, silver chandeliers, lighted tapers, and musical instruments, and they sung in several choirs, sacred Hymns, the *Kyrie Eleison*, the *Gloria in Excelsis*, the *Sanctus*, the *Benedictus*, and the *Te Deum*.

The magnificence of this spectacle ravished me completely, nevertheless I remembered the promise that had been given me, I took courage and said to one of the Angels: "What are you doing?" He answered me: "**We are conducting the soul of Catharine of Sienna, in** presence of the divine Majesty." When he had passed on, with those who accompanied him. I addressed another; I said: "Where is she?" Directly he heard me, the whole procession formed an extended circle in the centre of which was CATHARINE: she was clad like the Angels, and resembled the Saviour, (as he is painted in the tribune of Churches.) Her hands were filled with palm-branches,—her head was inclined, and her eyes modestly cast down. I recognized her perfectly well by her exterior. I then asked Almighty God to complete the vision, and to comfort my soul by allowing me to behold Catharine's countenance. I was heard, she raised her head and looked at me with that gracious smile, which always expressed the joy of her soul. The procession then resumed its onward march, continuing the heavenly chants.

BARDUCCIO.

THE LETTER OF BARDUCCIO WAS WRITTEN LONG BEFORE THE PROCESS AT VENICE. IT IS TO BE REGRETTED THAT, THAT HOLY YOUNG MAN WAS UNABLE TO JOIN HIS DEPOSITION TO THOSE OF THE OTHER DISCIPLES OF SAINT CATHARINE. OUR SAINT ESTEEMED HIM PARTICULARLY, AND HE SURVIVED HER BUT A SHORT TIME

LETTER OF SER BARDUCCIO DI. P. CANIGIANI,

To his Sister Maria Petriboni, at the convent of St. Pierre de Monticeli, near Florence.

IN THE NAME OF JESUS CHRIST,

My very dear Mother in our Lord, and Sister in holy affection to the saintly Catharine, I, Barduccio, unworthy and miserable sinner, commend myself to your prayers, as a feeble child, left an Orphan by the death of our glorious Mother.

I received your letter and read its contents with the greatest pleasure, communicating them to my afflicted Religious; they thank you from the depth of their hearts, for your charity, and the tenderness you condescend to bear them. They commend themselves to your prayers and likewise solicit those of the Prioress and the other Sisters, that they may accomplish with zeal the good pleasure of God towards themselves, and in your behalf. Tender and faithful Daughter, you desire to become acquainted with the details of the last moments of our common Mother, and I must satisfy your desire; I feel myself quite incapable of such a recital, however I will write to you what my eyes witnessed and what my poor soul was able to comprehend.

That favoured Virgin, that Mother so useful to the Church, experienced about the feast of the Circumcision, so great disorder in her whole system, soul and body, that she was obliged to change completely her manner of living. The food necessary for her corporeal sustenance exited such horror, that she was obliged to do violence to herself even to touch it, and when she partook of any, it was impossible for her to swallow it. She could not even drink a single drop of water for her refreshment, though she was consumed with a burning thirst, and her throat was so inflamed that she seemed to breathe fire. She however continued to appear active and gay as usual, and thus attained to Sexagesima. On that day, whilst she was praying at Vespers, there occurred an accident so grave that from that moment she was never able to recover her wonted health. On the night of the following Monday, after dictating a letter to me, she had so violent a crisis that we mourned her as dead. She remained a long time without giving the smallest sign of life, then she suddenly arose and appeared as though she had undergone no change whatever.

From that moment, commenced for her new and extraordinary corporeal sufferings. When Lent began, she applied, notwithstanding her infirmities, with so much devotion to meditation, that she astonished us by the abundance of her humble sighs and by the greatness of her moanings. You are aware that her prayer was so fervent that one hour of mental prayer weakened her delicate frame more than two days of uninterrupted spiritual exercises would fatigue any other person. Every morning after Communion, they were obliged to raise her from the floor and carry her to her bed as though she were dead. An hour or two after, she would arise, and we would go to St. Peter's, a mile distant, there she would stay until the Vespers, and then return in an almost lifeless condition.

Such were her exercises until the third Sunday of Lent; she then bowed beneath the weight of sufferings which overwhelmed her exhausted body, and the anguish that rent her soul in view of the sins that were committing against God, and the dangers which more and more sensibly threatened the holy Church. She was one mass of interior and exterior suffering, and thus she continued during eight entire weeks, being unable even to raise her head. In the midst of that martyrdom, she frequently said, "*These dolors are physical, but they are not natural, God allows the demons to torment me thus.*" It was evident that what she advanced was correct, and that those sufferings were unheard of. It is impossible to give an idea of the patience she displayed, I will merely say that at each new torture, she joyously elevated her heart and her eyes to God, saying: "Thanks be to thee, O my ever-living Spouse, who dost continually crown thy hand-maid so poor and wretched with new proofs of thy favor."

Her body was thus consumed until the Sunday preceding the Ascension; it was then reduced to that state in which Painters represent death. Her countenance however was beaming with Angelic devotion, whilst her limbs seemed to be a mere skeleton covered with a transparent skin. Her strength was so annihilated that it was quite impossible for her to turn herself from one side to the other. The night that preceded Sunday, two hours before morning's dawn, she had a strong crisis, and we believed that she was on the verge of her last moments. She then called all her family around her, and gave those who were nearest her to understand by signs that she was desirous of receiving absolution from her faults. Her wish was gratified. She gradually fell into a state in which there was no perceptible sign of life but a gentle sighing. It was therefore deemed expedient to give her Extreme Unction, and the Abbe de-Saint-Anthime hastened to administer it to her, because she appeared to be already destitute of consciousness. This Sacrament accomplished a certain change in her, it seemed by the motion of her countenance and of her arms that she was sustaining assaults from Satan. The combat lasted an hour and a half. After keeping silence some time, she commenced saying: "I have sinned, O Lord, have mercy on me,—*peccavi, Domine, miserere mei.*" I think she repeated these words more than sixty times, and every time she raised her right hand and then let it fall, striking the bed. Then, she also said frequently, but without moving the arm, "Saints of God, have pity on me,—*Sancti Dei, miserere mei.*" She added other words expressive of her humility and her devotion, and made acts of the different virtues. After which her countenance suddenly changed, and became radiant like that of a Seraph. Her eyes obscured by tears, became lighted with joy, she seemed to come forth from a profound abyss, and that sight softened the heavy burden of grief that weighed upon us.

Catharine was at that time reclining on the shoulder of Sister Alessia; she tried to rise, and with a little help remained in a sitting posture, though still supported by Alessia. We had placed before her view a little table on which were some relics and pictures of Saints; but she fastened her gaze upon the Cross which was in the centre, expressing sublime thoughts concerning the goodness of God. Then she accused herself before HIM of all her sins. "Yes, it is my fault," said she, "O Eternal Trinity! if I have so miserably offended Thee by my negligence, my ignorance, my ingratitude and my disobedience. Alas! wretched me, I have not observed the general and particular commandments that thy bounty has given to me. Thou didst tell me to seek Thee in all things and to labor continually for thy honor and the neighbor's good, and I have avoided fatigue even though it were necessary. Didst thou not command me O my God! not to value myself, to think only of the glory of thy NAME, by saving souls, and finding my delight in the nourishment which flows from thy sacred Cross; and I have sought my own consolation! Thou didst continually invite me to unite myself to Thee by the ardor of desires, the humility of tears, and perseverance in prayer for the salvation of the world and the reform of the Church; thou didst promise me to accord thy mercies to men, and new treasures to thy Spouse; and unhappy me, I did not obey thy wishes, I slept in my negligence. Alas! thou didst confide souls to me, thou didst give me children that I was bound to love in a special manner and conduct towards Thee, in the way of life. I have been distinguished for my weakness towards them, I have failed in solicitude for their interests, I have not succored them by addressing Thee an humble and continual prayer, I have neglected giving them good examples and useful advice. Wretched me! with how little respect I have received the innumerable graces and treasures of pain and suffering, that it has pleased Thee to grant me. I did not gather them with that insatiable desire and that burning love which thou didst experience when sending them to me. Alas! my LOVE! thy infinite goodness chose me for thy Spouse, in my tender infancy; but I have not been faithful enough to thee, for my memory has not always remained full of thee and of thy immense benefits; for my understanding has not been solely attached to their comprehension, and my will has not been devoted to loving thee with all my soul and all my strength."

In this manner that pure dove accused herself of her faults; then turning towards the Priest, she said to him: "For the love of Jesus Christ crucified, remit me the sins of which I have accused myself, as well as all those which I cannot recall." She then asked for the plenary Indulgence which had been granted to her by Gregory XII., and Urban VI., and in requesting it, she appeared famished for the Blood of our Lord Jesus Christ. Her petitions were granted. She began her adorations anew, and with such fervor and in uttering such sublime things as my sinfulness rendered me wholly unfit to comprehend. The grief which inundated my soul also hindered me from hearing her, for her voice was so feeble, and her sufferings so keen that she pronounced her words with great difficulty. She afterwards addressed some of her spiritual children who were not present at the admirable discourse which she gave several days previous to her assembled family, pointing out the way of perfection and indicating to each one what he should do after her death. When she had finished, she asked pardon of us all for the little care she had taken of our salvation, and also addressed a few words to Lucio, to another, and to myself, miserable man, after which she resumed her prayer

Oh! had you but seen with what humility and with what respect, she asked repeatedly the benediction of her aged Mother, who was plunged into the deepest affliction. How could one restrain his tears when beholding that tender Mother who recommended herself to the highly privileged nay! blessed Daughter, and implored her to obtain grace for her not to offend God in her grief! But nothing could distract that holy soul from her deeply fervent prayer, and the nearer she approached death, the more she prayed for the Holy Catholic Church for which she offered in sacrifice her life. She also prayed for Pope Urban VI. whom she declared to be the real Sovereign Pontiff, and she exhorted all her children to die, were it necessary, in order to acknowledge him. She also offered prayer for all those whom the Lord had given her to love in a special manner, and she borrowed from our Lord the words she adopted,—when he commended his disciples to his Father. She expressed herself with such devout tenderness that we thought our hearts would cleave asunder.

Finally, she made the sign of the Cross, blessed us all, and hailed that supreme moment of life that she so much desired, pronouncing these words: "Yes, Lord, thou callest me and I go to thee; *I go*, not on account of *my* merits, but merely on account of *thy mercies*, and that mercy I implore in the name of thy precious Blood." She cried out several time: "Oh! Blood, Oh! precious Blood." And then in imitation of the Saviour she said: "Father into thy hands I commend my spirit." And, with a countenance radiant as an Angel's she meekly bowed her head and expired.

Her death occurred, at Sext. We kept her body until Complin on Tuesday, without the least sign of corruption, it was on the contrary cool, and exhaled a pleasant odor. Her arms, neck and legs were flexible during those three days as though she had been alive, An immense crowd visited her precious remains, and those who could succeed in touching them, considered themselves highly favored.

God accomplished many miracles at that time, which I pass over in silence. Her tomb is honored with devotion as are the tombs of other Saints in Rome, and numberless graces have been obtained through the name of that faithful Spouse of the Saviour. I doubt not you have already heard what they were, hence I will not inform you more at length. I commend myself to the Prioress and to all the Sisters, for truly, I never so much needed prayers. May God preserve you and give you an increase of his heavenly grace!

ETIENNE MACONI.

ETIENNE MACONI, WAS ONE OF THE MOST CHERISHED DISCIPLES OF CATHARINE AND ONE OF THE MOST ZEALOUS FOR HER GLORY. WHEN DYING THE SAINT COMMANDED HIM TO ENTER THE ORDER OF THE CARTHUSIANS, WHICH HE ADORNED WITH HIS LIGHTS, AND HIS VIRTUES. (THIRD PART, FIRST CHAPTER, P. 254.) HE DIED IN 1424, AND WAS INTERRED AT THE CHARTREUSE IN PAVIA. HIS LIFE WAS WRITTEN BY A CARTHUSIAN, DOM BARTHOLOMEW OF SIENNA; IT WAS PUBLISHED IN 1626. THE TITLE OF "BLESSED" IS GENERALLY GIVEN TO ETIENNE MACONI, BUT HIS FESTIVAL IS NOT CELEBRATED. THE BOLLANDISTS HAVE EXTRACTED SOME FACTS FROM HIS LIFE, RELATIVE TO THE HISTORY OF ST. CATHARINE, WE SHALL RECAPITULATE THEM BRIEFLY.

THE occasion of the conversion of Etienne Maconi was his reconcilation with the enemies of his family, as he himself relates in his deposition; but through delicacy no doubt, he does not give the following details.

The enemies of the Maconi were the Tholomêi and the Rinaldini. The Saint had fixed a day in which they were to be reconciled in the Church of St. Christopher; but the pride of their nobility and their power unsettled their minds anew. They were unfaithful to their appointment, and avoided meeting Catharine, or any of the Maconi family. Catharine, was informed of it. "They will not listen to me," said she, "but willing, or unwilling they shall be obliged to listen to Almighty God." She went immediately to the Church whither she had convoked Etienne Maconi with his father Conrad and his other relatives. She placed herself before the principal Altar, and offered frequent prayers to Heaven. Whilst she was praying, ravished in ecstacy, those who refused to be reconciled, came to the Church, unknown to one another. *God brought them there!* As soon as they saw the Blessed in prayer and perceived, as they afterwards admitted, the rays of divine light that darted from her countenance, they felt themselves vanquished and ready to renounce their anger; they addressed themselves to Catharine who returned to her ordinary state; they charged her to regulate the conditions, and all soon embraced each other and mutually asked pardon.

Etienne Maconi formed part of the Confraternity of the Blessed Virgin, which assembled in the basement of the hospital of Sienna, for various exercises of piety. He allowed himself on one occasion to be drawn into a conspiracy which was plotting against the government in that place consecrated to prayer. Catharine discovered it supernaturally and said: "O my son Etienne what evil do you contrive in your heart? What are you doing? Is it thus that you change the house of God into a workshop for treason!" Her companions were astonished at hearing these words, and suspected there was question of some great secret. A few days after, Etienne came to visit Catharine as usual; but before he had time to speak to her, Catharine cried out to him; "Is it thus, Etienne, that you risk the loss of both your soul and body? What a stupid project! Return I entreat you, return to yourself, and reject from your heart the venom of conspiracy. You deceive yourself if you imagine that we can with impunity turn the house of God into a den of conspirators. To wash away the fault you have committed, go and in that spot witness to it, shed by scourging yourself, as many drops of blood as you uttered guilty words." Etienne perceiving himself discovered, withdrew and submissively performed what she had commanded him.

Etienne became one of Catharine's secretaries, accompanied her in her journey to Avignon, was present during her agony, and paid the last duties to her remains. He carried her corpse on his shoulders to the church of the Minerva, guarded it piously, so long as it was exposed, and buried it, covering it with kisses and tears. He was afterwards faithful to the worship of his saintly Mother, and zealously collected her relics and whatever could preserve her memory. He assisted Friar Raymond a a great deal in the writing of her life. At the period of the translation of the head of St. Catharine, to Sienna, he was miraculously warned of the feast that would take place on that occasion, and he went out to meet those who came to invite him.

This ceremony took place in 1385, amid a concourse of people and clergy, who carried lighted torches and made the air resound with pious canticles. The kindred and the disciples of Catharine surrounded the precious relic; but every eye was intent upon the aged LAPA, who had seen more than 80 revolving suns, and who walked in procession beside the head of her daughter. "Oh! but thou art happy," said they to her, "to witness the triumph of thy daughter! Catharine is in Heaven and thou art sure of receiving there the recompense of all thy sufferings. How could it be otherwise, than that she who has promoted the salvation of so many souls will procure thy eternal happiness?" In effect the good Lapa died at the age of 89, with such sentiments of piety, that it is evident she went to enjoy in heaven the affectionate embrace of her holy daughter.

Etienne Maconi was miraculously healed of a disease

in the eyes by a relic of St. Catharine. He had obtained the ring-finger of the Blessed and placed it in a beautiful reliquary. When he lost his sight, to such a degree as not to be able to write or to fulfill the duties of his Office, he took the precious relic in his hands, and kneeling down, he thus invoked his protectress in heaven: "O Mother! who didst bring me forth to the life of grace; behold me almost deprived of sight, and unable to accomplish any longer, what I desire to do for the glory of thy heavenly Spouse. I do not refuse to become blind and I will cheerfully accept all the crosses that God may deign to send me; but prove to me that my attachment is agreeable to thee; I implore with confidence an assistance that thou hast so frequently granted to me, and with this motive I touch notwithstanding my unworthiness thy holy relics." So saying, he applied the finger of the beatified Catharine to his diseased eyes. His hope was not deceived; the pain instantly disappeared and he recovered his sight perfectly. To crown his joy, he heard a voice that told him not to fear anything, because she who formerly protected him on earth, would still protect him in heaven.

Etienne Maconi used strenuous efforts to hasten Catharine's canonization. Gregory XII. sent for him to Sienna to labor for it there, but the troubles of the church suspended the informations. Etienne was one of the most active in organizing the anniversary feasts of the the Blessed at Sienna, at Venice, and in other cities; he composed, in order to spread a knowledge of her life and miracles, some dramas that were played on that day in great magnificence. Years only increased his zeal and his affection to Catharine, and he toiled until his last moment to propagate her honor and devotion.

LETTER OF THE BLESSED ETIENNE MACONI,

CONCERNING THE DEEDS AND VIRTUES OF SAINT CATHARINE OF SIENNA.

To THE pious and good Brother d'Antonio, of the Order of Preaching Friars, residing at the Convent of SS. John and Paul in Venice, Friar Etienne of Sienna, notwithstanding his unworthiness, Prior of the Chartreuse de-Sainte-Maria des gracês, near Pavia, health in Him who is the salvation of all.

I received joyfully and read attentively the letters in which you ask of me a faithful deposition, in authentic form, concerning the life, virtues and doctrine of the Virgin, Catharine of Sienna; you remind me of my numerous relations with her during her life-time, and claim my testimony on the occasion of certain complaints which have been made to the Bishop of Venice, in reference to the Feast commemorative of that holy woman, many being unwilling to believe in the virtues that are attributed to her.

I must acknowledge, that, although a citizen of Sienna, neither I nor mine had any acquaintance with Catharine and her relatives previous to the year 1376. At that time I was drawn away by the vortex of the cares of the present life, and had no sort of idea of forming her acquaintance; but the eternal Bounty, who wills the death of none, saved my soul from the abyss of perdition by means of that saintly Virgin. We were then in open contest (without fault on our part) with a family more powerful than ours, and notwithstanding the negotiations and efforts of honorable citizens, it was impossible to obtain from our enemies any hope of adjustment.

Catharine then enjoyed a great reputation in Tuscany, and everybody was celebrating her virtues and relating wonderful things concerning her. I was told that if I asked her to intercede in this affair she would certainly obtain peace as she had already done so many times. I took counsel of a gentleman who having been thus reconciled had become Catharine's friend. As soon as he heard me, he answered me directly :—" Be sure that you will find no one in the city more capable of effecting peace; do not defer, and I will accompany you." We paid her a visit and she received me, not with the bashful timidity of a young maiden as I had fancied, but with the tenderness of a sister who saw once again a brother who had been absent on a long journey. I was perfectly astonished and I gathered eagerly the pious discourse which she held, engaging me to confess and live like a good Christian. I said, the finger of God is there. *Digitus Dei est hic.* When I explained to her the object of my visit, she answered me unhesitatingly : "Go, my Son, trust in the Lord ; I will do all in my power to procure a satisfactory reconciliation : allow me to take charge of this affair." Thanks to her intercession, we obtained the peace in a miraculous manner, notwithstanding my adversaries' great influence.

On account of this reconciliation I visited her often, and every day, by the efficacy of her words and the perfection of her examples, I felt within me a blessed change. At that period she asked me to write some letters under her dictation ; I accepted with joy, and soon I felt my heart inflamed with a new ardor for heavenly things. I despised the world and all that belonged to it, and conceived so much shame for my past life that I could not even think upon it. This change appeared exteriorly, and nearly all the city was in astonishment. The more I examined the life, the examples, the manners, and the conversation of that privileged virgin, the more I felt growing within me the love of God and a contempt for the world.

A little while after, Catharine said to me in secret: "You will see, my dear son, that ere long your highest wish shall be accomplished." That saying amazed me much; I did not know what I could desire in *the world*, I was thinking rather of quitting it entirely. I said to her: "My very dear Mother, what is that greatest desire?" She replied, "Look into your heart" I said "Beloved Mother, I do not find any greater desire than that of remaining near you." She answered instantly, "It shall be satisfied." For myself, I could not understand how that could be done without violating the rules of propriety; but He to whom nothing is impossible, by a marvelous act of his will, arranged that she should be sent to Avignon to Gregory XI. and then, notwithstanding my unworthiness, I was chosen to travel in her holy company. I quitted with joy my father, my mother, my brothers and sisters, and all my kindred; so glad was I to enjoy the intimacy of Catharine and her virginal presence!

In consequence of this voyage, the Sovereign Pontiff returned to Rome, encouraged and fortified by Catharine who had received that special mission. The Holy Father sent her to Florence, on affairs of the Church. That city had revolted against his power, and God performed many extraordinary things there by means of his servant, as may be seen in her memoirs. I had the happiness of accompanying her. In fine I went with her to Rome, where after having experienced with joy, unheard of sufferings for the glory of God, she happily attained the term of her terrestrial pilgrimage. I carried her body with my own hands to the church of the Minerva, where it is deposited in a coffin or chest of cypress-wood, and enclosed in a handsome monument.

In her last moments she told each one of us what we ought to do after her decease; then she turned towards me and pointing me out with her finger said: "As to you, I command you on the part of Almighty God, and in the name of holy Obedience, to enter the Order of the Carthusians, because God wills it, and calls you to it:" And as she beheld us in tears on all sides : "My beloved children," said she, "you should not be distressed, but rejoice in the Lord and regard this as a festival day; for I am about to leave my prison, to be united to the Spouse of my soul, and I promise you to be more useful to you after my death, than I could possibly have been during my life." That promise she kept, and never ceases to observe it daily.

As a proof I will declare, to my shame, a circumstance for the honor of God and praise of Catharine. When she commanded me to enter the Order of the Chartreux, I had never thought of that nor of any other Order, but as soon as she ascended to Heaven, I felt in my heart so strong a desire of obeying her, that had the whole world opposed it, I should have paid no kind of attention to it, and indeed I have proved it. This is not the time nor place to relate all that Catharine did and still does for her unworthy son. I merely declare, that after God and his holy Mother, I consider myself more indeb'ed to her than to all other beings.

It will be seen that, during several years, I had very intimate relations with Catharine, because I wrote her letters, she also informed me concerning her most secret transactions and dictated to me a portion of her book. She loved me with the tenderness of a mother; much more indeed than I deserved; consequently several of her children conceived a strong sentiment of envy. I studied with the greatest attention, her words, her conduct and all her actions, and I say, in my soul and on my conscience, before God and the church militant, sinner as I am, that I have frequented more than sixty years the company of several great servants of God, but never have I seen, never have I heard any one who had attained so high a degree of perfection or a virtue so exalted. Every one recognized in her the image of all the virtues, and the pure mirror of all true Christians. *I do not remember ever to have heard an idle word from her virginal mouth!* She instantly turned our most frivolous conversations to our spiritual good. Her heart could never be satisfied with speaking of God and sacred things, and I think she would never have slept or ate, had she had some one to listen to her. When persons spoke in her presence of affairs of the world, or on subjects having no reference to the salvation of souls, she took refuge in contemplation, and her body became insensible as when she was in prayer. Her ecstasies were continual, and we have witnessed them a thousand times. Her members then became motionless and stiff—and it would have been easier to have broken them, than to have changed their position. To prove that this state was not feigned, I will relate a fact of which I was a personal witness.

When we were at Avignon, the Pope, Gregory XI., caused us to have handsome lodgings with a chapel richly adorned. The sister of the Pope, who was a pious woman, after holding conversations with Catharine, conceived a great affection and deep veneration for her. She told Father Raymond, her confessor, that she had a great desire to be present when that devout person would have the happiness of receiving holy Communion. Father Raymond promised to notify her. The Sunday following, Catharine entered the chapel, having only sandals on her feet. She wished to receive Communion, and during her preparation, she was, as usual, ravished in ecstacy. Father Raymond called me and told me to go to the Palace and tell the Pope's sister, that Catharine intended receiving holy Communion this morning. That lady was then hearing Mass; when I entered, she perceived me, and as she recognized me as belonging to Catharine's suite, she came to me and said: "My son, what do you wish?" I communicated my message. She quickly repaired with a great many individuals of high rank to our residence. Among others she brought with her the wife of the Pope's Nephew, Raymond de Turenne; a young person full of vanity and an entire stranger to divine things. Whilst the Pope's sister was praying in a very recollected manner, this person imagined, I presume, that Catharine feigned an ecstasy, and after the Mass, she pretended to stoop down, from devotion, to the feet of the Saint, and pierced them several times with a great pin. Catharine remained motionless and would not have stirred even had they cut off her feet. When all the people had withdrawn, Catharine resumed the use of her senses and then experienced such acute pain in her feet that she could hardly walk. Her companions on discovering **where and how** she suffered, remarked the dried **blood** which oozed from her wounds, and thereby understood the malice of her who suspected her!*

In reference to Catharine's ecstasies, there is one thing which must not be passed over in silence. In the midst of difficulties, her soul applied with greater ardor to mental prayer, and made such reiterated efforts to raise itself towards Heaven, that her body quitted the earth without regard to the laws of gravity. Many persons have seen her suspended in air, and I have personally witnessed that fact, which filled me with the most profound amazement. The explanation of that phenomenon is to be found in the book which Catharine composed, and which I partially wrote under her dictation. God had granted his faithful Spouse so great power and such intimacy, that during her prayers, she would say; "*I will it!*" and when she thus spoke she was instantly obeyed. We could give many proofs of this. The following happened to myself on my return to Avignon: We remained at Gênes more than a month, at the house of a respectable lady named Orietta Scotta; we were nearly all sick. Our hostess took great care of us, and employed two skillful physicians to come to see us every day. I fatigued myself with them, because I was anxious to nurse the sick. They warned me that I would become ill myself, and indeed, in two or three days, I took to my bed with a violent fever accompanied with a strong headache and very painful vomiting. Catharine having been informed of it, came to pay me a visit with her confessors and companions, and inquired of me what I was suffering. I, quite delighted at her sweet presence, answered cheerfully: "They *say* that I suffer; I know not what."

---

*Dom Martene, p. 1327.

Then with maternal tenderness she placed her virginal hand on my forehead and said, shaking her head a little; "Do you hear that child answering me. 'They tell me that I suffer, and I know not what?' And he has a violent fever;" and she added; "I do not allow you to follow the example of the other patients, I command you, in virtue of holy obedience no longer to suffer this malady. I will that you be completely restored and serve the others as usual." She then began talking of God as was her custom, and while she conversed I was healed. I interrupted her to declare it to all the spectators who were in admiration, and I have since enjoyed long years of perfect health. Catharine spoke in the same tone of authority, when she cured the venerable Giovanni, a Monk who dwelt in the solitude of Vallombrosa, as he affirmed to me when he was in his last agony, at the Abbey of Passignano, near Sienna. I heard from the very lips of Catharine a similar order given in the absence of the same Monk, to two of his disciples whom he had sent to her. She commanded him by their intermediation to be sick no longer, and to come to her without delay, which he did immediately. The holy Religious wrote an admirable letter on this occasion, which I carefully preserve in our Convent.

Although the whole interior and exterior life of Catharine was, so to speak, miraculous, yet, several servants of God, of high integrity, have admired in it one circumstance very extraordinary in the pilgrimage of man on earth. Whatever she did, said, or heard, never hindered her holy soul from being intimately united to God and plunged, as it were in the Divinity. As out of the abundance of the heart the mouth speaketh, she never conversed except on God, and what referred to Him. She sought him, found him, possessed him in all things by an actual and sensible love. I recollect that when she saw flowers in a meadow, she said to us: "Do you not perceive how everything honors God and proclaims his praise to us? Do not those crimson flowers represent to us the bleeding wounds of Jesus?" On descrying an ant-hill, she said: "Those little creatures emanated from the sacred thought of God, and he used as much care in creating the insects and the flowers as in forming the holy Angels." We were so much consoled by her presence on every occasion, and in all things, that, in order to listen to her, we forgot to take our repasts; we thought no more of our pains and trials. Those who were condemned to death called for her; she visited them often, and they seemed no longer to reflect on the destiny that awaited them. In her presence, the temptations of Satan vanished; the sun in its highest splendor cannot more triumphantly dissipate darkness. I remember often going to her with my interior trouble, and afterwards acknowledging that I had forgotten it. I would inquire of her what it was, and she would explain it to me better than I could have exposed it myself.

There is in this no reason for astonishment, for it is generally known that that holy Virgin saw souls as we saw faces; we could hide nothing from her. And one day I said to her, "Indeed, Mother it is very dangerous to be near you, for you discover all our secrets." "Know, my dear Son," answered she, "that in souls especially in those confided to me, there does not appear a spot or even a shadow of a defect that I do not instantly perceive by the intermediation of our Divine Saviour."

Her holy exhortations brought back to the path of rectitude a multitude of persons whom she led to the determination of confessing their sins;—it was impossible to resist her. On account of the admirable results which she accomplished in souls, Pope Gregory XI. allowed her always to have three Confessors with very extended faculties. Sometimes sinners presented themselves who were so in bonds of sin that they would say to her: "Madame, were you to ask us to go to Rome or to St. James, we would do it directly; but to go to confession; do not mention it, it is impossible." When she had exhausted every other method, she would say to them: "If I tell you why you refuse to go to confession, would you then go?" The astonished sinners would accept this condition, and she would say to them: "My dear Brother, we may sometimes escape the eyes of men, but never those of God. You committed such a sin, in such a place, and in such a time, and that is the reason that Satan troubles your soul and hinders you from confessing." The sinner finding himself discovered would prostrate himself at her feet, and avow his fault and with a profusion of tears confess without delay. This I can certify occurred to many. One among others who held a high position and enjoyed a great reputation throughout all Italy, told me: "God and myself alone know what that saint revealed to me, I therefore cannot doubt that she is much greater before God than we think."

Catharine's exterior life also was miraculous. Her virginal body sustained itself a long time without taking any material nourishment, the Holy Eucharirt sufficed for it. I had it in my power to observe her during several years and the following was her mode of life. She held meat, wine, confectionary, and eggs in abhorrence; her companions prepared her a little salad, when they had it, and sometime vegetables dressed in oil. She would only take the head and tail of an eel; she never took cheese except it was spoiled; it was the same way with grapes fresh or dry; she did not eat of these articles, she merely masticated them, with or without bread, and rejected them as soon as she had extracted a portion of their juice. She often drank pure water, but by little mouthfuls. She waited to take this little nourishment until her companions had quitted the table, then she would rise, saying: "Let us go and do justice to this miserable sinner." She was obliged to aid herself in rejecting whatever she had taken, and sometimes she had so much difficulty that she vomited blood abundantly.

This circumstance is calculated to confound the incredulous who calumniated her by saying; she does not eat in public, but she deprives herself of nothing in secret. As soon as she had any substance in her stomach as large as a hazel-nut, her whole system was in a state of suffering, and if the visit of any person prevented her from relieving herself, she would faint away, and remain as though dead until she had vomited. We have been witness of this a thousand times.

I said to her one day in private: "My very dear Mother, the food that you take is so very little, and you retain such an insignificant portion even of that, that it is quite useless to you; and you reject it with such extreme difficulty that it appears to me preferable to deprive yourself wholly." She answered me with her wonted prudence; ' My beloved Son, I have several reasons for taking this food. First, I have asked of God that he would punish me in this life, for the sin of gluttony, and I therefore gladly accept this pain which he sends me. Next, I endeavour to content some persons, who appear to be scandalized when I do not eat; they say that the devil deceives me: then I exert myself to eat. There is also one more reason : by these sufferings, I am brought back to my natural faculties, without that, my mind would be too much absorbed, and my body would perhaps sink." After such explanations, I had no reply.

The Blessed Catharine had received the gift of wisdom in so high a degree, that all who heard her, were filled with admiration. She explained the Sacred Scriptures with such astonishing clearness, that her interpretations surprised the most able Doctors. Human science vanished before her, as snow dissolves before the mid-day sun : she delivered several most eloquent discourses as well as highly practical ones in presence of Gregory XI. and some cardinals, and all declared: "Never man spoke like this: it is not this woman that speaks—but the Holy Spirit himself." Pope Gregory XI. often gave audience to Catharine, and testified a great respect for her. Three Prelates of very high rank, came to see him on the subject: "Most Holy Father" said they to him, "is this Catharine of Sienna as saintly as is pretended?" The Pope replied: "I am persuaded that she is a *Saint.*" "We will pay her a visit with permission from your Holiness." "I think that you will be extremely edified." In effect they came to our residence, at the hour of NONE; it was in summer; they knocked, and I opened the door for them. "Give Catharine notice," said they to me, "that we would like to speak with her." Immediately the Blessed went down with her Confessor, and a few other monks. The Prelates bade her to be seated; then they commenced speaking to her in a haughty tone, endeavoring to irritate her by words calculated to wound. Among other things they said : "We come from the Sovereign Pontiff, and we wish to know whether the Florentines did actually send you to him, as is pretended. If they sent you, it must be that they have no man capable of transacting such important business; but if they did not send you, we are greatly surprised that a little insignificant woman like you, should presume to converse with the Holy Father on subjects so difficult." Catharine, always calm, answered them humbly, but clearly in a manner that excited their surprise. When she had satisfied them on this subject, they proposed her some very difficult questions, concerning her ecstasies, her extraordinary life, on the passages in which the Apostle says that Satan transforms himself into an Angel of light, and on the means which she adopted for avoiding the deceits of Satan. The Conference lasted until night, and I was witness to it. Occasionally, Father Jean, her Confessor attempted to reply for Catharine, and although he was Professor of Theology, the Prelates were so skilful they confounded him in a few words; they said to him: "You should blush to advance such things in our presence: let her reply, she satisfies us far better than you can." There was among those Prelates an Archbishop from the Friars Minor who did not appear to accept sometimes at least, what Catharine said: then the other two opposed him: saying "Why interrogate her any further it is evident that she has explained these subjects to us with more clearness and precision than any Doctor could have done." At length they withdrew edified and comforted, and told the Pope that they had never met a soul so humble and so enlightened.

When the Pope was informed what had transpired, he was extremely pained, and offered excuses to Catharine, assuring her that it was against his will that the Prelates had thus acted and recommending her not to receive them if they presented themselves again. On the following day, M. François of Sienna, who was then physician to his Holiness, said to me. "Are you acquainted with the Prelates who went to see you?" I answered, "No!" "Well," said he, "know that were the knowledge and learning of these three men on one scale of a balance; and that of the whole Roman Court on the other, the acquirements of these three would overbalance, and I can tell you that if they had not found Catharine so solid, she would have passed a severe trial."

Finally, who can worthily recount the interior virtues of the Blessed, and the works which she caused to be effected by her profound humility and the inalterable resignation? Never did a shadow of trouble overcast her face; never did she utter a single word which might indicate anger or impatience, and this last is a mark of high perfection. Who shall describe the ardent charity which inspired her to give not merely her temporal goods, when she was in the house of her father, but which induced her to sacrifice herself unrelentingly for the honor of God and the relief of her neighbor. One day as she was setting out with her Confessors and her companions, she met a poor person who begged an alms with a certain degree of importunity. She said to him: "I assure you my dear Brother, that I have no money." "But," said he, "you could give me that mantle:" "That is true," said Catharine, giving it to him. Those who accompanied her, had much difficulty in redeeming the mantle, because the poor man made her pay very dear for it, and when they asked her how she could resolve to walk out without the cloak of her Order, she replied; "*I prefer being destitute of clothing to being destitute of charity.*"

My health and pressing occupations oblige me to terminate these recitals without order; I might have written many books on this rich subject, but those persons who desire to become oetter acquainted with the admirable virtues of that Blessed woman, her visions and her intimacy with our Lord, may peruse her history written by the the Most Rev. Father Raymond of Capua, who was her Confessor for a long time, and after her death, became General of the Order of Preaching Friars, in which he did very remarkable things. Some difficult readers, who easily become weary of pious subjects, pretend that his book is too long. It should rather be said that her life is too much abridged, but whatever he wrote, was dictated by the Holy Ghost Himself. I was well acquainted with him, and am capable of appreciating the holiness of his life, the charm attendant on his virtues, the purity and nobility of his soul, the depth of his learning, and other merits with which God had enriched him. His devotion to the Blessed Virgin was very great, as may be proved by reading his admirable treatise on the *Magnificat*. He is now without doubt in Heaven, and I am at liberty to disclose a circumstance hitherto secret. Several years previous to holding any relation with her whose life he wrote, the Blessed Virgin Mary appeared to our Saint, and promised to give her a Confessor who would afford her more consolation than the others whom she had formerly consulted: which took place.

Here then is my testimony to the life of St. Catharine of Sienna; you have earnestly requested it, and I have written it without research and in the simplicity of my heart, though oppressed with sufferings and numerous occupations. You asked me to be *truthful* in all that I would advance, and I affirm, in the sincerity and peace of my conscience, that I have added nothing to the truth.

I know that a lying tongue slays the soul, and that God has no need of our falsehoods, and also that it is not allowable to do evil that good may come. Be persuaded therefore that I have told the truth, I am ready to affirm it by oath, and in the form that you wish, for the honor of God, and for the edification and consolation of the neighbor. If it be necessary I will put my hand into fire; I attest it in presence of the Omniscient; HIM to whom be all praise and glory forever and ever.

Two notaries wrote this declaration on the 26th of October, 1477, in the presence of numerous witnesses. We have appended to it the Great Seal of our Convent, in order to satisfy your request.

DOM BARTHOLOMEW OF RAVENNA

DOM BARTHOLOMEW OF RAVENNA SENT HIS DEPOSITION ON THE TWENTY-SEVENTH OF OCTOBER 1411; IT WAS PRESENTED WITH THE OTHERS TO THE VICAR GENERAL OF THE BISHOP. DOM BARTHOLOMEW WAS THE PRIOR OF THE CHARTREUSE THAT CATHARINE WENT TO VISIT IN GORGON ISLE, THIRTY MILES FROM THE PORT OF LIVOURNE (2. PART. CHAP. IX. P. 215.) HIS TESTIMONY HAS PARTICULAR REFERENCE TO THAT VISIT.

AFTER having told the good that the discourse of Catharine produced in the souls of his Monks, Dom Bartholomew adds: At the moment of leaving "the Blessed" said to me in private: "Father Prior, watch over your Flock, for I announce to you, that the enemy is seeking to produce scandal in the monastery." And to calm the trouble that these words excited, she added: "But do not fear, the enemy cannot prevail." In effect, a few days after, the master of a boat from Pisa which brought wood to our Island gave a young Monk bad news from his Mother. That Religious asked permission to return to Pisa with the sloop, and as this permission was refused him, he became sad and the devil tempted him violently. One day as I was in the cloister with the Religious, he came to me with a countenance indicating great interior disorder, and imperiously demanded permission to go to Pisa. I was unwilling to yield to a command so unsuitable and sent him away, recommending one of the senior Religious to follow him. He ran to his cell, took a sword and attempted to kill himself; his companion had merely time to arrest his hand and call for assistance. I arrived with all speed and endeavored to calm the poor insensate, by promising him to grant what he had requested. But he began at once to cry out: "No I do not wish to go: the devil tempts me and he also wished to induce me to throw myself from the top of the Convent." And as all the Religious were agitated and terrified, I ordered the cloak that the Saint had given me as a remembrance on quitting the Isle to be brought, and I placed it in the arms of the Religious who recovered his peace directly. I said, "My Son, recommend yourself to St. Catharine." He answered: "She is truly praying for me; I had been lost if she had not prayed."

Being at Pisa, after Catharine's departure, Dom Bartholomew interrogated a person obsessed. "Is that saint in Sienna as holy as persons think?" "More holy," answered the obsessed. Another Religious asked him whether Catharine could deliver him: "*She* could do what *you* could not do, because although you are a good Religious you have not arrived to the same degree of perfection."

When the saint quitted Gorgon Isle, the Monks accompanied her to Pisa and craved her Benediction before withdrawing. She said to them, "Should any accident occur to you on the route fear not, the Lord will be with you." When approaching the Island, a tempest arose, the helm was broken, and the barque dragged towards a dangerous spot, touched the ground on her side and filled with water. A Religious, who was desirous of bringing help, was drawn away by the force of the waves, but he was saved as well as the others, and the Barque was not damaged in the least.

When the Process was terminated, they also received the deposition of Brother Angelo Salvatti of Sienna, of the Order of Friars Minor, Professor of Sacred Scripture. This deposition, dated the 10th of March 1413, confirms the preceding depositions without giving any new details. Friar Ange speaks at length of the conversion of Friar Lazarini and of the exalted sanctity to which he attained under Catharine's direction. He describes a visit which he paid Etienne Maconi; and when he was telling him that a Monk had seen Catharine elevated from the ground in ecstasy, Etienne smiled, saying that he had seen her not only once but many and many a time.

BULL OF PIUS II.

FOR THE CANONIZATION OF SAINT CATHARINE OF SIENNA.

Pius, Bishop, Servant of the Servants of God, to all the Faithful of Christ, Health, and apostolical Benediction.

The mercies of the Lord, which we have so abundantly experienced in our days, cannot be described by mortal lips; the blessings of God surpass human language, and though man were capable of expressing himself by all his members, never could he worthily celebrate his great Creator; we were formed from nothing; we sprung from nothingness into existence; not only have we being as the stones, plants and animals, but we have been endowed with reason and have become capable of divine things: we have been created not merely similar to the Angels, but also in the image of the omnipotent and invisible God; we have been crowned with glory and honor, and have received power over all his works. And yet, if we set aside the pride of Lucifer and his followers, man alone, among all creatures, has proved ungrateful and rebellious towards God. All inanimate creation celebrates the divine Goodness in its being, and never transgresses his commandments; every thing irrational obeys the laws of nature and fulfills the end for which it was created. The earth opens to the plough, and receives the seed which it returns with usury: faithful to the orders of man either civilized or savage, it always renders service to him, the stone that is taken from it for building, yields without resistance to the iron or the fire that works it; the trees that protect the field with their shady foliage bear fruit and when withered, they afford fuel, or support houses and their roofy coverings. How useful are the plants by their leaves, roots, flowers, seed or the juice that is extracted from them? how serviceable the rivers, lakes and seas, which are furrowed by the track of myriads of vessels uniting by commercial intercourse the very "ends of the earth." God is praised by the inhabitants of the land, the water, the air, each order glorifying him by submissively obeying the instincts of its respective nature. The elements, the stars and the planets obey his high command! mark, how the sun performs his annual circuit without exceeding the boundaries of zodiac; the gentle moon shining with mild reflected light, never fails to perform her destined functions; while the orbs that revolve throughout the universal sky never wander, but undeviatingly pursue their established course. All things material in heaven and on earth bless the Lord, and praise him by steadily fulfilling the end of their creation. All follow their general laws and remain within their prescribed limits obedient to Deity their great first Cause.

Man alone, ungrateful, disobedient and rebellious man, has imitated the sin of the fallen Angel. Lucifer, who proud in the very height of Heaven, aimed at becoming like his Creator, and was precipitated into the infernal abyss for indulging his guilty thought: man formed from the dust of the Earth, on whose surface he was placed as lord, forgot his weakness and lowly origin, and also aimed at exaltation, by "eating the forbidden fruit;" he determined to become, by knowing good and evil, equal to God, and in consequence was driven away from the terrestrial Paradise and condemned to countless afflictions.

Heaven's Gate was closed against him; a subject of the tyrant death, the vengeance that ensued proved how deeply he had offended God, and how remote during the ages previous to the deluge were his sons from the fulfilment of God's holy will. All flesh was destroyed by the waters from heaven, except the virtuous Noah, and those who like him entered the Ark. Even children were not exempt from malice, they also became wicked, and fell into manifold crimes. The tower of Babel was an impious enterprise against the God of punishment, but the division of tongues arrested it, and from that moment arose wars, rapine, disorder, confusion, conflagration, carnage, adultery, incest, perjury, the worship of idols and all the ills that pride and luxury produce. Until the time of Abraham, the faithful observers of the divine law were very rare; but that holy patriarch gave singular exampl\` of the sincerity of his Faith, in obeying God, even so fa. as unhesitatingly to immolate his own dear son. All the nations of the earth were blessed in his race. Not only were the prophets of the divine law to descend from him, but Christ the Saviour deigned to be born from him according to the flesh, *when* to redeem mankind, he, the equal of his Father by his divine nature, determined to "annihilate himself," to be clothed with our infirmities, to endure the most cruel torments, and accept on the Cross a death, not ordinary, but violent, ignominious, horrible and above the endurance of mere human strength. By dying he destroyed our death and restored us to life; he conquered hell, delivered the just, and victorious over death and the demon, opened triumphantly the long closed portals of Heaven. When ascending to his Father, He showed us the way we are to follow, and left us in his

Gospel, in Baptism and the other Sacraments, the means rising from our falls, and obtaining salvation.

And yet, so many benefits have not captivated our hearts! Our malice and our evil inclinations have not been destroyed; the heart of man, while destitute of gratitude has not yet deserted vice. The more we have been favored with graces, the more we have shown ourselves ungrateful and inclined to evil. For how do we love and honor the great God? how observe his laws? Who obeys the Gospel? Where is there any dread of the decisions of the Church, submission towards superiors, charity in regard to inferiors? Where is equity, where are piety, justice, reverence and morality among men? How many say in their hearts, there is no God? Some draw up formulas of impious dogmas, and forge blasphemies; others, slaves of voluptuousness, think merely on the means of gratifying their passions; others ambition the riches which they do not possess; others again thirst for the blood of their fellows. Innocence is rare and almost always in danger. What avail the bonds of family, what *laws* human, or divine? force and fraud govern on all occasions and it is with good reason, that the devil is called the Prince of the world, for he actually governs the greater portion of the earth. Does not the false religion of Mahomet govern the East, with the great States of Africa? His followers blaspheme Christ in the kingdom of Granada, in Spain, and in many of the provinces of Greece. The Jewish Nation scattered throughout the wide world, is the enemy of the Gospel and of the laws of Christianity. Idolaters abound in the East as in the North, Christendom is reduced to a corner of Europe; for although we are assured that there are many christians spread throughout Asia and Lybia, yet their faith is not sincere, they live remote from the Holy See and in the midst of infidels and heretics; they commit evil deeds, and are infected with errors. And are not European Christians merely nominal? The religion of a vast number is uncertain and false; their conduct is the proof. How many of them perform works worthy of the Christian? *"By their fruits ye shall know them,"* said the Saviour. (St. Matt. vii. 16.) If we live as Christ ordains, we are genuine Christians. (St. John. iii. 10.) The Apostle Saint John says, *"men are the children of him whose works they perform."* (St. Jno. viii. 44.) If we keep the commandments of God, we are the sons of God; if we perform the works of the devil, we belong to him, for the Lord has said of such: *"you have the devil for your father;"*—terrible, but just saying. Every one is the son and subject of him whose commandments he keeps. How many are there among Christians that do not swerve from the divine law, and how numerous are they who follow the suggestions of Satan? Let each one interrogate his conscience and repass his life in spirit, and he will discern how remote he is from accomplishing the obligations of a real Christian. Ah! how great and incomparable are the bounty and mercy of God which bears with us, and does not cut us off from life, because he expects our conversion and return to him, that he may pardon our heavy guilt.

But in every age, there have been men agreeable to God by their sanctity. Though clothed with our common mortality, they have overcome the flesh and have led a heavenly life on earth. By their merits and intercession the world is preserved, the destroying fire which menaces it is arrested, God's anger and vengeance kindled against it are suspended. We doubt not that at this very hour, there are some souls who appease God, and render the King of heaven propitious and favorable. Among those who have calmed Almighty God and merited his clemency, the city of Sienna, one of the glories of Tuscany, reckoned Bernardin. Descended from a noble family, he renounced the world in his youth and entered the Order of St. Francis. He found there Religious who lived very far from their Rule and the examples of their holy Father; he rebuked them with energy, and as he was unable to bring them all back into the right path, he separated those who desired to practice the Rule in its primitive fervor, and with them, he visited the existing monasteries, constructed new ones and introduced into them the most sage reformation. He ran over Italy, destroying vice and inciting to virtue. He was admired for his abstinence, his angelical purity, his winning gravity the charms of his discourse, and the depth of his teachings; and being a sincere lover of poverty, and an enemy of riches and pleasures, the liveliest joy ever shone on his countenance, and the most profound peace reigned within his soul. Innocence rendered him happy and no stain sullied or troubled his conscience. He abolished a great many scandals in Italy and performed many miracles, so that during his life-time he was regarded as a Saint, was venerated everywhere, and the people collected in crowds to pay him honor. He terminated his career at Aquilea, and in the very year of the jubilee in which the whole Christian world visits Rome to be purified from defects, Nicholas V. our predecessor, placed him in the number of the Holy Confessors of Christ.

Before Bernardin, our Fathers had seen in the same

city of Sierna, the virgin Catharine, not less exalted in merit and not less agreeable to God. Her prayers offered to the divine Majesty have been, are still, and always will be useful to mankind; for if the crimes of the wicked and their blasphemies draw down upon us the wrath of God, the works and supplications of the Saints preserve us from them. Catharine led an angelic life on earth; she has been in heaven twenty-four years; unnumbered miracles have manifested her glory and nevertheless the Church militant has not yet inscribed her among the faithful Virgins of Christ. The Roman Pontiffs, our predecessors have not decreed it. Urban VI. and after him Innocent VII. and Gregory XII., who had a particular knowledge of her deserts, designed rendering her this honor, but they were prevented by schism, troubles and the wars which agitated their pontificates. God without doubt permitted it, because in the midst of those tempests, what was proclaimed in one obedience would have been despised in the other. This affair was consequently deferred until our time, and the Canonization of that Virgin, our countrywoman, has been reserved to us. The sanctity of the virgin of Sienna shall be proclaimed by a native of Sienna, occupying the throne of Peter; and we admit that in this we experience a sensible consolation. Who does not like, when he may do so with justice, to celebrate his own country, his own city, or his own family? We take pleasure in lauding the illustrious of all nations, but with how much greater eagerness do we sound the trumpet of fame when there is question of our fellow citizens! We should have contemplated with joy, the sublime virtues, the genius, the greatness of soul, the all-powerful strength and fortitude of the blessed Catharine: but we admire them more because she like ourselves first saw the light in the city of Sienna. We anticipate more favors through her intercession and in her merits than if she had been born in Africa, or in the Indies. Why should not the bonds that link us to the Saints, procure us some advantage?

However this consideration shall never prompt us to deviate from truth. The love of family or of country does not dispense with the proofs, informations and formalities customary on such occasions, and notwithstanding our pleasure at the circumstance that Catharine is a native of Sienna, we have neglected nothing. Petitions have been addressed to us not only from Sienna, but from many other lands. Our dear Son in the Lord, Frederic, Emperor of the Romans, and our own beloved Son, Paschal, Doge of Venice, have entreated us to permit the homage of this virgin in their respective States, because the people entertain a great devotion to her, and relate numerous wonders concerning her. When we ourselves were repairing to Mantua, we sojourned a long time at Sienna and there, in public Consistory her virtues and her miracles were laid before us, and we were supplicated to decree to her the honors of the Saints of Jesus Christ. We did not grant it immediately, but in conformity with ancient usage, we designated three of our Brethren, Cardinals of the Holy Roman Church, a Bishop, a Priest and a Deacon, to examine regularly the life, and actions of Catharine, with the miracles that she performed during her life and after her death, and to pursue the whole process necessary to her Canonization and then lay before us a faithful narration in secret Consistory. More than a year after, when we came back from Mantua to Rome, the commissaries whom We had designated after having discussed the business, studied the ancient procedures made at Venice and elsewhere, examined the witnesses anew, and noting every particular with great care, presented an authentic relation of them to the Cardinals and to Us alone. They were afterwards repeated by an Advocate, in public Consistory. Finally, in the presence of all the Bishops whom we had convoked at the Court of Rome, and the Cardinals who assist us, the appointed Commissaries, by the organ of our venerable Brother, William, Bishop of Porto, (a Frenchman by birth,) who presided over them, exposed anew all that they had learned and all that appeared to them to be authentic. WE have summed up, from their very extensive and well-made depositions the following facts, all perfectly valid, clearly proved and certified.

Catharine was born in Sienna of persons in a middling condition. She consecrated herself to God at an age when she could scarcely have had any knowledge of him. At six years of age, so as to serve him better, she sought solitude and went with the intention of concealing herself in a wild cavern, but she did not remain there, for the Holy Spirit brought her home to her parents. At seven years of age, she consecrated her Virginity to our Lord who appeared to her on his throne of Majesty, and she saw the secrets of the heavenly court, which human tongue can never utter. She renounced from that moment all worldly pleasures, gave herself entirely to meditation and afflicted her delicate frame with vigils, fasts and disciplines. Her companions attracted by her discourse and example, imitated her conduct. When she was of suitable age to select a state of life, she refused to marry, though urged by her parents, but cut off her hair, and despised the consequent injuries and persecutions. Many petitions and endeavors were requisite before she could obtain the habit of St. Dominic, worn by the Sisters of Penance. She fulfilled the office of servant in the house of her parents and desired nothing so much as to appear little and contemptible in the eyes of all. With her father's permission she gave abundant alms: she carefully nursed the sick, and surmounted the temptations of Satan and the continual combats of hell with the buckler of patience and the arms of faith; she comforted, by all possible methods, prisoners and the oppressed. She was never heard to utter a word that was not pious and holy; all her conversations had for their objects morality, religion, piety, contempt of the world, love of God and of the neighbor, with the desire of the better country. No one approached her, without leaving her with their minds and hearts more informed and better. Her knowledge came down to her from Heaven; hence she could teach without having had masters. When Professors of the Sacred Writings, and illustrious Bishops, proposed to her the most difficult questions in Theology, she answered them with so much wisdom and satisfied them so fully that they became gentle as lambs, after having shown themselves to her at first as menacing wolves and lions. Some of them, captivated by the all divine wisdom of that youthful maiden, distributed their possessions to the poor of Jesus Christ, and embraced the Cross by leading a perfect life.

Catharine's abstinence was surprising, and her austerity prodigious. She rejected the use of wine, of meat, and every kind of seasoning. She finished by depriving herself of vegetables, and took no other bread, than that heavenly BREAD with which the true Christian is nourished at the Sacrament of the Altar. It sometimes happened that she fasted from Ash-Wednesday till the Ascension, having taken no other food than the Blessed Eucharist. During eight years, she sustained life with a little juice of herbs which she could not even retain on her stomach; she went to her repasts as to a punishment, but she flew on the wings of love to the Holy Communion, receiving it almost daily, as a celestial banquet.

She wore a hair-cloth under her garments; and used neither matress nor pillow. Her bed was composed of boards, and on them she took but a few moments of repose. She rarely slept more than two hours during the day or night; the remainder of the time was consecrated to pious vigils, prayer, and to works of mercy; she tore her body with rude disciplines; she suffered a constant and violent head-ache, and was tried by fever and by various other maladies. She was often obliged to contend against the demons, who persecuted her in every way; she said with the Apostle: *cum infirmor, tune potens sum.* (II. Corinth. xii. 10.) In all her trials, she never became dejected and never neglected her ordinary works of charity. She assisted the unfortunate and the oppressed, converted sinners, and attracted them to penance by the mildness of her discourse; she gave counsel with joy, and indicated to each one what he should do and what he should avoid · she calmed disputants, appeased a great number of violent hatreds and terminated many bloody enmities; to reconcile the Florentines and the Church, she did not hesitate to pass the Appenines and the Alps, to be near to Gregory XI., our predecessor, at Avignon, and she told him of the Vow that he had taken of returning to Rome; that vow having been taken secretly, God alone could have made her acquainted with it.

She was also endowed with the spirit of prophecy,

announcing future events, and revealing the most hidden things; she was ravished in ecstacy, and remained suspended in air. When she enjoyed these heavenly contemplations, she became so absorbed that she was insensible to blows and wounds; and she fell into this state, almost always after receiving holy Communion.

Catharine's name was held in great veneration among the people; from every side they brought the sick and those possessed by the devil, and many were healed. She commanded sickness and fever in the name of Jesus Christ, and drove Satan from the obsessed. In consequence, two Roman Pontiffs, Gregory XI. and Urban VI., esteemed her so highly that they charged her with several negotiations, and granted her a great number of spiritual favors. She terminated her career at the age of thirty-three, and slept at Rome, in the peace of God. Her happiness and her triumph in Heaven were revealed by marvelous visions to persons who had been particularly attached to her, especially her Confessor, Raymond of Capua, Doctor in Theology, and General of the Order of Preaching Friars. He was at Gênes, the night in which Catharine died, and whilst at the Matin hour, he was praying before an image of the Blessed Virgin Mary, she appeared to him all resplendent with light, and addressed him with consoling words. Her body, exposed a certain time, was buried at Rome, in the Church of the Minerve, amid the testimonies of respect and devotion of an enthusiastic multitude. Many sick persons, by touching her, obtained their cure from God; others recovered their health by means of the objects which had been in contact with her precious remains. When Catharine had ascended to heaven, she listened graciously to the prayers that were addressed to her, and she caused them to be heard by her Spouse and **Saviour Jesus Christ.** Many, on hearing of her powerful influence in heaven, had recourse to her intercession, and experienced its salutary effects. Therefore at Venice, where St. Catharine had never been, and in other places, great honors were tendered to her.

When our Venerable Brother, the Bishop of Porto, had exposed those things and many others, in the assembly of Cardinals and Prelates, and we had affirmed that they were certain and evident, the Cardinals and Prelates present, were invited to give their decision. All unanimously declared the holy virgin worthy of *Heaven* and of the *honors of earth*, and there was not a person present who did not give his opinion that the Canonization should be proceeded with directly.

Having attentively listened to all these things, we commanded that in the Basilica of the Prince of the Apostles, a lofty and decorated tribune should be erected, from which to-day, in presence of the people and the clergy, after having pronounced a discourse on the life and miracles of Catharine, after having celebrated Mass and fulfilled all the accustomed ceremonies, we would proceed in these terms to the canonization of the "Blessed" Catharine: "To the honor of the omnipotent and eternal God, Father, Son and Holy Ghost, for the exaltation of the Catholic Faith, and the extension of the Christian Religion, and in virtue of the authority of Jesus Christ, of the Blessed Apostles St. Peter and St. Paul, and of that which has been conferred on us, we declare, on the opinion of our Brethren, that Catharine of Sienna, virgin of illustrious and ineffaceable memory, whose body reposes at Rome in the Church of the Preaching Friars, called la Minerve, has been already received and crowned with glory in the heavenly Jerusalem, amid the choirs of Virgins, in the rank which her virtue merited, aided by divine grace. We determine and decree that she be honored as a Saint, in public and private, and we ordain that her name be inscribed in the catalogue of the Virgins who are venerated by the Roman Church; we wish that her festival be celebrated annually by the whole Church, on the first Sunday of May, and that the honors be paid to her which it is customary to render to other Virgins. To all such as may visit her tomb, on the day of her feast, we grant in perpetuity, an Indulgence of seven years and seven times forty days, on conforming to the obligations and usages of the Church.

" Let no one allow himself to change anything in this declaration, nor in whatever it contains, relates, ordains and settles ; let no one attack it with temerity; should any one thus render himself guilty, let him know that he exposes himself to the indignation of Almighty God, and of the Holy Apostles Peter and Paul.

"Given at Rome, at St. Peter's, in the year of the Incarnation, 1641, the 19th of June, and the third year of our Pontificate."

A Brief of Urban VIII., dated the 16th of February, 1630, changed the day of St. Catharine's feast : it is now fixed on the 30th April: it was not put on the 29th, which is the anniversary of her death, because the Church celebrates the Feast of St. Peter, Martyr, on that day.

RECOLLECTIONS
OF
St. Catharine in Italy.

In one of the most painful moments of my life, I implored the intercession of St. Catharine, and promised to endeavor to spread her fame in France, if God would deliver me from the malady which affected me mentally and corporeally. I was heard immediately and this book is the *ex-voto* of my gratitude. Before giving it to the public, I desired to present it personally at the tomb of our dear Saint; the Reader will kindly accompany me in this pious pilgrimage, and visit with me the localities consecrated by her memory.

It was in Rome that St. Catharine terminated her life, offering herself a victim for the Church. When the Sovereign Pontiff, Urban VI. implored her counsels, amid the tempest of the rising Schism, she resided, (as it is said in this biography III part. chap. 2.) between the Minerva and the Campo di Fiore The house which she occupied with her disciples in now found Via Santa Chsra No. 14 opposite the little church which has given a name to the street. Her companions continued living there, after her death under the direction of Alessia whom she had given them for their Superior, and that little community was long perpetuated. The Blessed Lucia de Narni, sojourned in that Convent, when she was summoned to Rome, in 1502, under Alexander VI. to certify to the reality of her stigmata. The room in which St. Catharine died is on the ground floor; it has been converted into a chapel, but the ceiling alone is of her time; the walls have been transported to the Minerva and reconstructed behind the Altar of the Sacristy. Such changes are to be regretted as it is especially to form that recollections are attached.

The obsequies of St. Catharine were celebrated in the Church of the Minerva in St. Dominic's Chapel, and her monument is at the right of the grand Altar, in the Chapel of the Rosary; the Blessed Virgin deigned to shelter her beneath the shadow of her sanctuary, that her relics might be gladdened by that angelical salutation she so loved to repeat.

Etienne Maconi, at the moment of quitting home, to go and assume the habit of the Carthusians, in obedience to her command, desired to possess a relic of his venerated Mother; he obtained from the other disciples of St. Catharine leave to open her coffin, and he took one of her teeth, which he carried away with him as a precious treasure. The pious mutilation of her body took place at the time of its translation by Blessed Raymond of Capua. The head was borne to Sienna, and considerable portions of her members went to enrich the Convents and churches in which her memory is honored, as we perceive in the process of Venice. In 1486, St. Antonius made a new opening in the tomb, and it is from this period without doubt that dates the monument which we discover beneath the Altar of the Chapel of the Rosary. St. Catharine is there represented with her religious drapery, reposing in the sweet slumber which precedes the glorious resurrection.

In Rome two Convents of Dominican Nuns, honor the memory of St. Catharine. The Religious that St. Dominic established at St. Sixtus, were forced, on account of the fever which ravaged that portion of the city, to abandon the places consecrated by such important recollections, they therefore settled on the Quirinal. The handsome Convent of St Dominic and of St. Sixtus, is in possession of St. Catharine's left hand, and that precious relic is extremely well preserved. The dried up flesh is of a brown hue, its fingers very small and slightly bent. In its centre the cicatrice of the stigmata with which our Lord honored his Spouse, are distinctly perceptible. The right hand is divided ; the Chartreuse of Pontiniano, near Florence have the finger which received the ring denoting her heavenly espousals, and that also restored sight to Blessed Etienne Maconi miraculously. The left foot is at Venice, the traces of the stigmata are visible in it ; Gregory Lombardelli affirms, that it was authentically recognized in 1597.

Beside the Convent of St. Dominic, rises that of St. Catharine, with its devotional church and old tower of the middle ages. They who dwell in it claim for ancestors, the companions that our Saint brought from Sienna to Rome, and who continued living in community until her death. Hence they have a tender and invincible confidence in their patroness. During the terrors of the siege of Rome, they secured themselves against danger, by additional ornaments placed on her Altar, and decorating her statue. A quite particular circumstance obtained for me leave of entrance into this "enclosed garden " of the Church, where so many virtues bloom for heaven. I knelt in an interior Chapel, where the Nuns showed me a crucifix said to have belonged to St. Catharine, and yet having traces of her devout embraces. The convent possesses an entire shoulder-blade of the Saint, one of her sandals, and a few bricks of the apartment in which she departed this life.

During my sojourn in Rome, the thought of Catharine incessantly accompanied me, and when visiting those sanctuaries in which ages have accumulated so many mementos, I implored her to warm my heart with a spark of that fire which consumed hers, when she made those pious pilgrimages with her disciples. I delighted in tracing out the paths she took, and following above all the way which leads from her humble abode, to the tomb of the Apostles : it was through those streets which in Rome, never change, that she went to pray for the church and consolidate on the immoveable Rock, the Sovereign Pontiff, Urban VI. In the last days of her martyrdom, she daily traversed this way, as did our Lord the road to Calvary; but the hour of sacrifice eluded her desires, and it was necessary to carry her back to her house in a dying condition.

How many times did she climb the silent declivity of the Aventine, and kneel in the Basilica of St. Sabinus, so dear to the Order of Preaching Friars. Her virginal lips have pressed that stone on which St. Dominic extended himself during the solitude of night, to pour forth in God's presence his tears and supplications. She saluted with pious affection, those recollected halls in which the holy Founder assembled his pacific conquests: she contemplated in the vigor of its prime, the blessed tree that his hands planted, and her prophetic eye undoubtedly perceived in the future, the new generations which were to renovate his work, like vigorous shoots emerging from an aged trunk, with the very year that was to witness the re-establishment of the Dominicans in France. May Heaven continue to multiply its branches and its fruit!

St. Catharine also visited frequently the Convent of St. Sixtus on the Appian Way. It was there that St. Dominic established his Order in Rome; there he assembled his nuns whom he refreshed with his discourse and with a miraculous wine; there too was divine power manifested in him, and vanquished death thrice restored to him its victims. At the period in which Catharine lived, the family of St. Sixtus was flourishing, and a proof that our Saint had gladdened it with her presence and illuminated it by her virtues, is that, a short time after her death, and considerably before her canonization, the Nuns caused her portrait to be painted in the choir of their church, and it may yet be seen behind more recent constructions. The Convent of St. Sixtus has long been a solitude, seldom visited by the piety of the faithful; let us hope that this sanctuary so rich in mementos, will share in the blessings which God pours with new effusion on the Order of St. Dominic and that the Religious life may ere long flourish in its now deserted Cloisters.

When going from Rome to Sienna, as one descends the rough upturned declivities of the Radicofani, the lines gradually soften on the horizon; plantations of Olive-trees in graceful rows adorn the hill-sides, the valleys present a high state of cultivation, and broad streamlets murmur beneath delicious shadowy foliage. Chateaux of the middle ages, with farm-houses of elegant architecture animate the landscape and as one advances on this road festooned by its luxuriant vines, nature appears milder and more gay: one would fancy he heard the distant hum of a concert, whose dulcet accords approached near and more near.

Sienna is a poetic city in which every thing harmonizes with the remembrance of St. Catharine; its ramparts and its monuments are contemporaries which speak of her, and the imagination easily retraces in them all the scenes of her blessed life. Its enclosure, devastated by the Pest, of which she was the consoling Angel, presents not the agitation of our modern cities. Instead of that febrile movement of luxury and of commerce, we meet therein a living reigning *peace*, that one would never, never quit. The Italian language is more melodious there than elsewhere, and the population, quite distinct from that of Gênes and of Florence, offers types of virginal beauty. One easily comprehends that here human genius must expand its blossoms beneath a beautiful and cheerful sky, and that human art must produce its almost breathing wonders. But I hastily traversed, its undulating streets its public squares, its Churches, and its palaces of rich and chivalrous architecture; my heart craved other delights: could the magnificent features of a city arrest the attention of a Son, who seeks the house of his *Mother*?

On descending from the Cathedral, at the turn of a little street, I suddenly found myself in presence of the localities consecrated by the life of St. Catharine. An inscription and a painting nearly effaced informed me that I was on the very spot in which she beheld her first vision. Opposite to me on the other side of the valley, where Jacomo's workmen washed their various colored wool, was delineated that beautiful church of St. Dominic which served as a pedestal to the throne of our Lord, when he appeared to her assisted by SS. Peter and Paul and St. John the Evangelist. I pursued the same road that Catharine and her little brother Etienne (Stephen) followed on that day, and arrived at length at the much desired residence.

The abode of the Blessed Catharine is situated at the entrance of the valley, on the left hand, ascending l'Oca street. The piety of her fellow-citizens has filled it with chapels. On the ground-floor, was the workshop of Jacomo, the shop and the back-shop in which is founa the cellar where God rendered to her family a hundred-fold of good wine that she distributed to the poor. By the stair-way which the holy child mounted, reciting the angelical salutation at every step, we arrive at an apartment, where, during her life-time Mass was celebrated: this was a privilege that she had obtained from the Sovereign Pontiff, at the period of her journey to Avignon. The back of the Altar is against the wall towards the street; *there*, are to be seen, enclosed in Reliquaries, the extremity of the cane that supported her, when notwithstanding her sufferings, she went whither the love of God and of her neighbor called her, the little lantern which enlightened her in her charitable vigils, a small flagon of scent that friendship perchance would fain oblige her to wear during the Plague, but of which without doubt she used very little, *she*, who had so courageously overcome nature, in the service of the sick. Among the garments that had belonged to her, we remarked a rich silk stuff which served a long time to envelope her head, brought from Rome to Sienna by the Blessed Raymond.

Opposite the Altar at the right hand of the entrance is found the spot richest in her memory; it is in that

little cell that God was pleased to adorn Catharine with
so many virtues; those walls have witnessed her prayers,
her penances, and her ecstasies; there, our Lord, the
Blessed Virgin, and the Saints, came and conversed with
her; in that place were celebrated her glorious nuptials,
and she enjoyed the familiar embraces of her Spouse;
there her heart broken with love, and her soul inebriated
with celestial lights, was again united to her body in
order to commence the greater miracle of her public life.
O! sanctuary, in which the presence of Catharine is
sensible, how shall I describe thy mysterious peace and
thy delicious inspirations?

The cell of Catharine, which is only five meters long
by three in width, was enlightened by a little window, at
the bottom of which there still exists some remnant of
mason-work.* There, it is said, her head rested during
sleep; but her bed which was of planks, must have been
placed in the bottom against the wall, and the Blessed
Raymond says positively, that she had a piece of wood
for a pillow. (1 p. chap. 9.) Those bricks are without
doubt, the ruins of the steps which served her to go up to
the window. In the corner is the door of a small closet
which opened into her room. Happily marble has not
new covered the walls of this sanctuary; the same soil is
there which was pressed by her feet, and the lips of the
pilgrim may venerate its dust.

In the upper part of the house were the rooms occupied
by her family, among others that of her brother Etienne,

---

* Morantem in quadam cellula parva, infra domum paternam, eugus ostium et fenestra semper clausa erant, sed joram imagines Christi, beatæ Mariæ et aliorum Sanctorum quæ ibi depictæ erant, in cessanter, die noctuque lampas ardebat. (Dom Martene, p. 1312.)

in which her father saw a white dove reposing on her head
Behind the Altar of a chapel is shown the chimney in
which the Blessed prepared the repasts of her parents, at
the time she suffered their persecutions. Opposite the
house, on the other side of the narrow street on which St.
Catharine's window opened, was a garden where a church
is built, which serves for the meetings of the confraternity
of Fontebrands. Above the Altar, the Crucifix is preserved before which St. Catharine received the stigmata,
in the church of St. Christina at Pisa. On all the walls
of these sanctuaries are painted and sculptured different
circumstances of the Life of St. Catharine, but *the eye
hardly rests upon them,—the heart* has apparitions which
are more real than are all these images!

Catharine could descry from the top of her Father's
house, the Palace of her Spouse, the church of St. Dominic, and tradition asserts that she passed hours there in
holy contemplation. That monument which bespeaks
majestic simplicity, stands near the fortified enclosure on
one of the most elevated points of the village. At the
entrance of its vast enclosure, is the Chapel where the
Sisters of the Third Order of St. Dominic assembled.
The pavement is ornamented with inscriptions commemorative of the miraculous facts which transpired in that
sanctuary. Here, Christ changed the Heart of Catharine—there, he recited the psalms with her—in that spot
Catharine gave her silver Cross to the Saviour,—farther
on, she disrobed herself to bestow on him a garment.*
On the Altar is placed the portrait of the Blessed, drawn

---

* CAT. COR MUTAT XPVS—CATA. CRVCEM EROGAT XPO—CATA. VESTE
INDVIT XPVM—EX LATERIBVS QVO HIC PATENTI CVM CHRISTO. DIVINA
ALTERNATIM PERSOLVENDO VNA CREBERRIME SPATIABANTVR.

during her life-time by her disciple, Andrew Vanni. Catharine is represented standing, holding a lily in her left hand, and touching a young maiden who is kneeling before her with her right.

In the Church on the right side, is the Chapel of St. Catharine; it is adorned with pictures, representing some circumstances in her life: there are also the portraits of Father Thomas de Fonte and of Blessed Raymond of Capua, who were her Confessors and biographers. On the Altar, in the wall that divides the Church from the Sacristy, is placed the relic that Sienna rightly considers, her most precious treasure, *the head of St. Catharine* is enclosed in a reliquary, the keys of which are in the hands of the Gonfalonier of the city, and of the Prior of the Convent. It is exposed only twice annually, on St. Catharine's festival, and on the Wednesday of Septuagesima, in remembrance of her mystical marriage with our Lord.

The Religious costume with which the bust of the Saint is clothed, merely permits a view of her countenance, which beams with a mysterious majesty. It is impossible to depict the emotions one experiences in presence of that august Relic; the obscurities of death vanish, and the heart contemplates with love, that brow ever calm and joyous, those eyes that ecstacy enlightened, those features that charity animated, those lips whence escaped, as from an inexhaustible fountain, words endued with power for converting souls. O sacred remains which Earth preserves for Eternity, consecrated *head*, which the Divinity deigned to use as a sanctuary, *brow*, that, heavenly glory shall wreathe on the day of the Resurection, lovely, benignant, *countenance* which shall gladden the heavenly Jerusalem, O Catharine, the Saviour shall take complacency in his Spouse, and will crown you with that precious diadem he promised, when you chose his crown of *Thorns* on Earth. Now you conceal from us your splendor, you only exhibit yourself to our view, in the infirmity of our nature, so that the traces of your sufferings and your death may teach us the true path to happiness and glory.

The Church of St. Dominic is in possession of another relic of St. Catharine: at the base of the silver bust that is borne through the city on her festival, is, I believe, the thumb of the right hand. Another Reliquary contains two disciplines which belonged to her, one of iron, the other of cords. The Dominican Convent San Spirito has a considerable portion of a hair-shirt that was worn by Catharine.

One of the finest establishments of Sienna, the hospital of the Scala, also preserves the recollection of St. Catharine; it was there she exercised charity towards the sick, there she combated against nature, by embracing infected wounds and drinking the water which had been employed in washing an ulcer; there she supported the calumnies of Andrèa, and also appeared to that patient enveloped in resplendent light. In the inferior part of the hospital is shown an obscure shed, whither she retired to take a few brief moments of repose. Above the stone on which she extended herself, may be read the following inscription: *Here reposed the Spouse of Jesus Christ, the seraphic mother, St. Catharine of Sienna. Praise be to God.** This place is entrusted to the guard of the Confraternity Brothers for the night, who assemble in pious vigils at the season of her festival.

---

* Ovi Giaceva la Sposa di Giesu-Christo, la Serafica madre Santa Caterina da Siena.—LAVS DEO

Pisa had not forgotton the sojourn of Catharine. On the right shore of the Arno, is the little Church of St Catharine, in which she received the stigmata. Near a side Altar a little column indicates the place where she sunk down insensible under the divine impression, on it is seen this inscription. *The Lord here marked his servant Catharine, with the signs of our Redemption.**

On the two side Altars, these two inscription are found.

Catharine, who pierced your hands, who marked your feet, with the bloody impress of the Cross?

Christ my beloved, shared with me his honors, and deigned to adorn me with his wounds.

The wounds of Christ are *bloody;* why Catharine are yours *radiant?*

The wounds of Christ are red, they were made by the enemy in expiation of our faults; mine are shining, because they were the gift of love.†

On the Altar is the copy of the crucifix before which St. Cathariue received the Stigmata; the original was a pledge of peace between the Republics of Pisa and Sienna. Near St. Christina at No. 8 of the Street that passes near the Church, is found the house of Buonconti in which St. Catharine received hospitality. There is also

---

* Signavit Dominus servam suam Catharinam hie signis redemptionis nostræ.

† Hæc Catharina tuis manibus quis Stigmata fixit?
  Quis pedibus duræ signa cruenta Crucis?
 Me meus hic Christus proprio signavit honore
  Ornavitque suis quam bene vulneribus.
 Vulnera cum rubeant Christi fœdata cruore.
  Vulnera sic rutilant qui, Catharina tua?
 Illa rubent merito cedens inflixerat hostis
  Istaque pellucent, aurea pinxit amor.
Sacra accepit Stigmata hoc in Sacello. A. D. MCCCLXXV, Mortem obiit A. D. MCCCLXXX.

shown the room that she occupied and the Madonna before which it is said that she prayed, but the basso relievo is less ancient.

Hearts have preserved as faithfully as monuments, the souvenir of St. Catharine. Her devotion is widely spread throughout Italy. A great number of convents and of churches are erected under her invocation, and the festivals that are mentioned in the Process of Venice are perpetuated to our own day; the people always have *for her* prayers, canticles and choicest flowers.

At Sienna hers is a national festival: it is celebrated on the 29th of April, but the public ceremony does not take place until the following Sunday. Then the house on Oca Street is adorned with all its riches, the Altars are decorated with their gayest ornaments; Catharine's little cell is glittering with garlands and lights; emblems and verses that recal her life, speak from the walls, as, "**Because she preferred the crown of thorns to those of kings**, had she merited a heavenly diadem."—"**God** filled with precious jewels the garment which she gave to the poor."—Her thoughts were pure as lilies. "**Eternal Wisdom was her book.**"—"**She** attained peace by suffering."—"On the cross she found the object of her desires, and her heart was transformed into God's."

The Confraternity of Fonte-Branda do the honors of the devout sanctuary; it offers to the poor and to the rich, little loaves of Blessed Bread in remembrance of those that Catharine formerly multiplied and distributed. The neighboring streets are strewn with foliage, and dressed with Flags and pendants; all the windows are adorned with rich suits of hangings. At nine o'clock, the procession moves from the Church of St. Dominic. The clergy **and the two confraternities of Fonte-Branda, and Friars** of the Night, accompany the silver statue of St. Catharine,—it passes in triumph through the city, and the bells of every parish hail its passage. On the public square, the authorities, the Gonfalonier, and the magistracy, come forth from the palace and join the cortêge. They visit the house of the Blessed; then ascend to the Church of St. Dominic, where a young nobleman of the college of the Tholomèi pronounces the eulogium of the *illustrious countrywoman*. That discourse is sometimes the début of great talent; it is always a useful and beautiful remembrance for the remainder o˘ life.

The head of St. Catharine is exposed from morning until evening, and the multitude never discontinue pouring out before her, tender and fervent prayers. When night comes on, the entire hill of Fonte-Branda is illuminated, the Rosary is recited at the feet of the Madonna, and hymns are sung in honor of the Saint; the crowd walk amid a blaze of light and in fine, taste all the happiness of the Christian festivals, which alone have evenings without weariness, and morrows without sadness.

This feast will be one of my most delicious recollections. Sienna received me as one of her own children; the Religious of St. Dominic offered me the hospitality of other days, and all welcomed me like a brother come from a distant land. I had the place of choice in the house of St. Catharine and in the ranks of those who accompanied her image; I received the hallowed bread of her charity: and could contemplate her holy relics and even approach them with my lips. O Catharine, the prayer I then made you, I repeat anew, Be my mother and my patroness! watch over all that my heart loves, *Protect France*, tried by so many misfortunes, and let her **henceforth consecrate to the** cause of truth all the energy and activity of her devotedness. Defend Italy from the dangers that manace her faith; Bless the city of Sienna the sweet land of thy nativity; but above all pray for the Church by which all nations are to be saved. When still on earth, you predicted that after many calamities she would enjoy sunny days of prosperity. Since you were in heaven, has the Church experienced one day without trials and tempests? Schism has rent it, scandals have outraged it, heresy has ravished her children; the blood of martyrs has inundated Europe; the policy of Princes has given her chains, knowledge, and denial; genius has insulted her, the French Revolution levelled her Crosses, destroyed her Altars, and the **Papacy has been** captive and exiled: the Church would have perished but for the eternal promise of her invisible Head. But after the miracles of her combats, shall be seen the spectacle of her triumphs and of her glory!

O Catharine! thy soul bounded with a holy joy, when perceiving in the future, prodigies of divine Mercy and the renovation of the Church by novel means. Thou didst lovingly salute those times in which the Church of Jesus Christ will appear in the world, in all the brilliancy of its virtues and its beauty. The nations shall rejoice at the sanctity of their pastors and strayed sheep return in crowds to the sheep-fold. O Catharine! hasten by your prayers those better days and render us worthy by our faith, in the trials which we have yet to suffer.

Iconography of St. Catharine.

ON reading the lives of the Saints, the heart demands their *portraits*, and the most beautiful mission of ART is to satisfy this desire. The picture of a Saint is the representation of his soul: the Artist should therefore seek his inspirations in the meditation of their virtues, but he should also consult tradition, to discover, whether time has not respected the features which he intends to render, and whether there does not already exist some type consecrated by the piety of the faithful. Truth can never be opposed to beauty; sanctity transfigures the body, and the triumph of Christian art is to do what God himself will do on the day of the Resurrection: the bodies of the Just shall be glorified, deformities will disappear without annihilating resemblance, even faults will be resplendent with the tears of repentance, and with the tender mercies of the Saviour.

It is generally believed that the beauty of St. Catharine was wholly interior, and this opinion is based upon the account given of her admission into the Third Order of St. Dominic. The Sisters of Penance only received aged persons, and they said they would by a sort of dispensation admit Catharine if she were not too beautiful. But the Blessed Raymond also observes, that they could not form a correct judgment concerning her, because sickness had rendered her not easily recognized; he says also, that her beauty had naught that was excessive. All her other disciples mention the radiance of her soul beaming on her countenance—the most cruel sufferings could never disturb its joy and serenity. Every one was captivated with the winning sweetness of her smile. Friar Bartholomew in his deposition, observes that the graces of her youth gave no trouble to her visitors, because they perceived in her the purity of the Angels. When describing her last illness, the same witness says, that Catharine's body seemed to have been sun-dried, whilst it had always hitherto been really handsome. *Cum consuevisset esse competenter formosum.*

The head of St. Catharine preserved at Sienna, furnishes but little indication; it is of middling size, and of an oval form; the eyes are closed, the mouth partially open; the shrinking of the lips, discover teeth of pearly whiteness; the general expression is full of calm and resigned majesty, and on it may be read the marks of the cruel sufferings which terminated her life. The almost natural color of her countenance accorded ill with the testimony of the Dominicans who wrote to the Bollandists in 1673 that the head of St. Catharine was withered and dried, and of a color obscure and almost black. I had it in my power to examine this very precious relic, and I remarked that the whole face was plastered over with a sort of pale rose color. This observation was confirmed by the testimony of the Chevalier Grotanelli, a distinguished physician of Sienna. He was one of a scientific committee appointed a few years ago, to certify to the state of the relic, and he thinks that this species of paste was put on to repair the damages caused by the conflagration that ravaged the Church of St. Dominic in 1531, and reduced to ashes the body of the Blessed Ambrose Sansedoni, protector of the city.

The most valuable monument of the iconography of St. Catharine, is the portrait said to have been drawn during her life-time by Andrew Vanni, her disciple. It is placed over the Chapel of the Third Order, in the Church of St. Dominic. The Saint in that picture is represented standing, holding a lily in her left hand, and touching with her right hand the lips of a young person kneeling before her. The face is thin and long, its expression sweet and virginal. I am not informed of the proofs of the authenticity of this portrait; the branch of lilies that is seen in it, would seem to indicate a work accomplished after her death, it is evident at least, that this picture has been denaturalized by successive restorations some of which are very modern.

The tradition of St. Catharine's features ought to have been easily preserved in Italy, on account of the public reverence of which she was the subject immediately after her death; they painted her picture and her history in a great number of churches, under the eyes of her relatives and of her own mother: they could not, by departing from the resemblance contradict those numerous and faithful recollections. Friar Thomas, who had known Catharine from her infancy, had her frequently painted with such luminous rays as usually surround the heads of the Beatified but not canonized, although he had seen several represented with the aureola of the Saints. Friar Thomas says that her image was spread throughout the whole christian world, that it was painted in every variety of style, in Poland, Hungary, Dalmatia, in Tuscan? Lombardy, Venice, and especially at Rome;

whilst he was writing his deposition, they were forwarding pictures of the venerable Catharine even to Alexandria. " When they commenced, " says he, " to honor Catharine's memory in Venice, a person who entertained a particular devotion towards her, had her likeness represented on cards, so as to spread it abroad with greater facility on the day of her feast. Many of the Pictures were placed in churches and surrounded with flowers. Thus all could enjoy and pay homage to the Saint, not only in public, but in their own houses. I am certain that since these portraits of the Blessed have been drawn, thousands have been made and are daily making; there are vast numbers of them at Venice, and in every portion of the (known) world. These pictures of Catharine suggested the idea of making on similar cards, images of other Saints for the churches of Venice, the faithful could thereby procure them on their festivals and augment their piety by honoring them."* This text is a precious historical document; it connects we may say, with the worship of Catharine, the origin of engraving on wood, and consequently that of printing. This method of multiplying the images or pictures spoken of by the witness, is evidently a novel invention; there is not question of painting them by hand on the paper, but of reproducing them *ad infinitum.* Playing cards preceded engraving on wood; Venice fabricated many of them and carried on a considerable trade in them. The process that was employed for making those cards served to stamp the pictures of St. Catharine. The most ancient wood engraving, bearing a certain date, is the St. Christopher of the

---

* Notabile circa materiam istam, etc. (Dom Martene, Proc. Ven. p, 1292.

Library of Prints of Paris, it is dated 1423.* The deposition of Friar Thomas is of 1411, and in it is said that the pictures of Catharine were made at Venice, directly they began to celebrate her feast, that is to say in 1394 or 1395, since we read a few lines below, that it had been made during sixteen years in the Convent of St. John and St Paul. These pictures would therefore be the first engravings on wood. Perchance, some of them have been spared by time, and are preserved in some collections of engravings or in some ancient manuscripts of the life or of the deeds of St. Catharine.

A cotemporaneous painting of these prints exists at Rome. In the month of July, 1852, the Rev. P. Assaut, Prior of the Convent of the Dominicans at Paris, when visiting the ruins of the Church of St. Sixtus, discovered, behind the walls of the actual choir, the remnants of the Pictures which decorated the ancient vault. These paintings, unhappily injured by the scaffolding of more recent constructions, certainly belonged to the XIV. Century. Different scenes from the Gospel and from the lives of the Saints are there represented. On the right are extremely well preserved pictures of St. Paul, St. John the Baptist, of St. Dominic and of St. Peter, martyr. On the left, is seen our Blessed Lord, drawing from the wound in his side, a garment which he presents to St. Catharine who is in adoration before him. At her feet is painted, in smaller proportions, according to the custom of that date, the Nun who caused the picture to be exe-

---

* Leber: Essai sur les cartes à jouer.—Emeric David: Histoire de la gravure.—Heinecken : Idee générale d'une collection d'estampes.—Duchesne aîné ; Notice sur les estampes de la Bibliotheque.

cuted, without doubt the Prioress of St. Sixtus. The head of the Saviour is very fine, that of St. Catharine breathes ecstatic sweetness, its features are delicate, the eyes small, the nose slender, and the mouth exquisitely traced. Her veil is white, and her mantle black. She has not the aureola of the Saints, but simply the rays of the Beatified, as remark the witnesses of the Process at Venice. This painting was evidently taken a short time after her death: there must be pictures of Catharine similar to it in Rome. The Blessed Etienne Maconi informs us that the same vision was represented near her tomb.

The Artist most worthy and most capable of painting St. Catharine of Sienna, was assuredly Fra Angelico de Fiesole. Born seven years after her death, he found her memory living in Tuscany. The Blessed John de Dominici, his Prior, and the Blessed Lorenzo de Ripa Fratta, his master of Novices, were cotemporaries of Catharine, and must have seen her at Pisa and at Florence, Fra Angelico lived with many Religious who had been her disciples, and he assisted at the annual festival in her honor.

In the coronation of the Blessed Virgin Mary, the only painting of Fra Angelico, possessed by the museum of the Louvre, I had remarked amid the group of Saints at the base of the throne, a countenance indicative of charming purity; it is in profile, the hands spread in the attitude of ecstasy, I could not refrain from attaching to it the name of St. Catharine.

In the public gallery of the Offices of Florence (Tuscan School, Hall No. 1.) there is another master-piece of Fra Angelico The composition has considerable reference to the one in the Louvre, only the scene breathes more of heaven ; all the personages are placed in clouds and amid waves of light. Our Lord, instead of crowning his Mother, simply adds a magnificent diamond to her radiant diadem. These two pictures must have been made at the same time, for the same Saints are found in them, with the same types and attributes. The face, which appeared to me to denote St. Catharine is found exactly re-produced in the picture at Florence.

The figure most in relation with those paintings, is the statue of St Catharine, which was found before the revolution, in the Dominican Convent of Poissy, and which is now in the Church of the Dominicans of Chalais. This statue is very ancient, and if it were not made before the canonization of the Saint, it must have directly succeeded it ; for it is anterior to the defence made by Sixtus IV for representing St. Catharine with the stigmata ; the stigmata are marked on her feet and on her hands : her head is crowned with thorns, and her arms opened like those of the *orantes* in the catacombs. The head is very handsome, and resembles those of Fra Angelico and that of St. Sixtus.

The attributes or characteristic signs of St. Catharine are the stigmata, the crown of thorns, the heart, a book, and a branch of lilies.

The crown of thorns that is placed on the head of the Beatified Catharine recals the vision, in which our Lord offers her two crowns, one of gold enriched with precious gems, the other of woven thorns. St. Catharine chose the one that would render her most like to our Saviour on Earth. In the celebrated picture of Sassoferado, which decorated the Chapel of the Rosary at St. Sabines, the Infant Jesus is placing the crown of thorns on the head of St. Catharine.

The heart which St. Catharine holds, not only recals her burning charity, but also the vision in which our Lord granted her prayer, by renewing her heart. The lily is her sceptre of virginity. As to the book, it may signify, as in the case of other Saints, her fidelity in accomplishing, and her zeal in teaching the Divine Law. It also reminds us of the miraculous manner in which St. Catharine learned to read.

I might terminate these iconographical researches, by indicating the paintings and sculptures of St. Catharine, which I have remarked in the churches, and in the museums of France and of Italy, but this nomenclature would be of no utility. From the sixteenth century, tradition is interrupted, and the Artist is but an individual destitute of high pursuits in religious Art, and seeking without the bounds of pious inspiration the mere glorification of his talent.

Facility in the use of the pencil, breadth of model, and richness of coloring can never suffice to express purity of soul, and the ardors, of heavenly ecstasy; when an Artist desires to depict the beauty of the SAINTS, he must first of all have recourse to Meditation and devout prayer.

THE END.